AF612582

MORE THAN A DEAN

Quiester Craig's

Journey from Humble Roots to Reshaping Business School Education and Advancing Equity at HBCUs and Beyond

TANYA Y. MITCHELL

MINOAFB PUBLISHING, MARCH, 2026

Published by: MINOAFB Publishing

Photograph credits are included on page 399.

For information, permissions, or bulk orders, contact:
info@morethanadean.com

Library of Congress Control Number: 2025923313
Paperback ISBN: 979-8-218-79558-0
eBook ISBN: 979-8-218-92881-0

Printed in the United States of America
First Edition

Cover Photographs courtesy of the Willie A. Deese College of Business and Economics at North Carolina Agricultural and Technical State University

This work is dedicated to my son, Omar Mitchell, who, even in his absence, inspired this project.

CONTENTS

Part V: Mama, Look at Your Baby Son Now

FOREWORD

The history of black education in America is one of determination in the face of seemingly insurmountable odds. From the earliest years of Reconstruction, when determined whites from the North and newly freed men and women began schools in church basements, understanding that education was the key to freedom, African Americans have invested in learning as both a means of survival and a pathway to dignity. Out of those roots grew Historically Black Colleges and Universities (HBCUs), institutions that carried forward this belief that knowledge was power and that opportunity could be created where none existed before.

Within that broader history, business education emerged to support the growth of the post-Civil War economy. For decades, African American students were systematically challenged in pursuing business school education and shut out of the very professions that shaped corporate America and defined economic mobility. With the enactment of Title VII of the Civil Rights Act of 1964, HBCUs stepped into that void, creating business programs to equip their students with the skills, credentials, and confidence to claim their rightful place in boardrooms, accounting firms, faculty ranks, and as entrepreneurs. The stakes were never small—business education at HBCUs was not simply about jobs; it was about access, equity, and rewriting the terms of participation in the American economy.

It is within this sweeping history that author Tanya Y. Mitchell introduces us to the life and career of Dean Quiester Craig in *More Than a Dean: Quiester Craig's Journey from Humble Roots to Reshaping*

Business School Education and Advancing Equity at HBCUs and Beyond. She studied accounting under him from 1975 to 1979 at North Carolina Agricultural and Technical State University (A&T), an HBCU in Greensboro, North Carolina. It was there that he mentored her and provided an education that changed the trajectory of her life, a service he offered to thousands of students over his forty-one years as dean. To call him simply a dean is to diminish the scope of his vision, the depth of his character, and the enduring impact of his life's work.

He was a builder—not only of programs and institutions, but of people, opportunities, and pathways where none had existed before. One enduring example of that vision was the Financial Trading Room he established at the business school—a hands-on learning environment designed to mirror the realities of global financial markets. In keeping with experiential learning as a higher-education imperative, Dean Craig ensured that A&T students had access to professional-grade tools, real-time market exposure, and the confidence that comes from being fully prepared to compete. Where resources were scarce, he created opportunity. Where recognition was denied, he insisted on excellence that could not be ignored.

In every generation, there are leaders whose work transcends the boundaries of their titles. Dean Quiester Craig was one such leader. His persistent efforts to secure accreditation of A&T's business and accounting programs were not only about prestige; it was a mandate that African American students receive the same quality of education and professional preparation afforded to others. His advocacy for expanding the pipeline of minority PhDs in the business disciplines, along with his historic leadership of international business school organizations, broke open doors that had long been closed—doors that still influence higher education today.

But this book is not only about Dean Craig's leadership—it is about legacy and relevance. At a time when the role of HBCUs is once again under scrutiny, and when Diversity, Equity, and Inclusion face resistance, his story proves why these institutions and ideals matter. He believed that preparation builds confidence, and he devoted his career to ensuring that his students, many of whom were the first in their families to enter corporate America, were fully prepared to lead.

Reading *More Than a Dean* offers both education and inspiration. It challenges us to recognize the enduring importance of HBCUs. It also reminds us that success is never automatic. Growing up in North Carolina during the Jim Crow era, attending A&T, and earning a few firsts of my own, his story resonates deeply with me. As the first African American woman to found, build, and own a multibillion (USD) global workforce solutions company addressing the delivery of methodologies and technologies that support the process of acquiring services of human and agentic workers, and a member of the first-ever woman-led Special Purpose Acquisition Company, I know firsthand that success is never handed down. It is earned, inch by inch, by those who refuse to settle for less. Dean Craig's legacy teaches us that excellence is not negotiable, that preparation is power, and that authentic leadership is measured by the lives we elevate and the legacies we leave. By honoring his journey, we are also called to reflect on our own duty to open doors for others, to pursue excellence, and to make meaningful contributions wherever we stand.

This is more than the story of a dean. It is the story of a man who understood, as I do, that the true measure of leadership is not the title you hold—it is about purpose, the lives you touch, and the legacies you create. It is about building a future others can inherit, with pride and hope. Dean Craig was a man I knew and loved, having worked with him while serving on both A&T's Board of Trustees and the business school's Board of Advisors. *More Than a Dean* captures his essence in a way he would celebrate!

Janice Bryant Howroyd
Chief Executive Officer
The ActOne Group

Left to right, Dean Quiester Craig, presenting diploma to author, Tanya Y. Mitchell at the 88th Annual Commencement of North Carolina Agricultural and Technical State University on May 6, 1979.

HOW I CAME TO TELL THIS STORY

It's amazing how a seemingly simple thought can steer your life in a profoundly unexpected direction. This is how I found myself compelled to tell this story.

In the spring of 2010, a wave of nostalgia enveloped me as I anticipated the retirement of my beloved business school dean, Dr. Quiester Craig, from the School of Business and Economics at North Carolina Agricultural & Technical State University (A&T), a historically black college in Greensboro, North Carolina. My heart swelled with gratitude, recalling the countless acts of kindness he had shown me during my time as a student from 1975 to 1979. He didn't just see a student in me; he recognized my potential and, in doing so, changed the course of my life forever. His decision to award me a full accounting scholarship lifted a tremendous financial burden from my family, allowing me to focus entirely on my studies.

But Dean Craig's impact was not limited to that single generous act. He opened doors I never dreamed I could walk through, arranging a summer internship at Arthur Andersen & Co., one of the most prestigious Big Eight accounting firms of that time. He introduced me to the world of Certified Public Accountants and ignited my ambition to pursue the highest credential in the field. These acts led to the start of my corporate career—the first in my family to pursue this path. After graduating, I felt a mix of excitement and nervousness, knowing I was about to embark on my career. Before leaving campus, I visited Dean Craig to express my heartfelt appreciation for all he had done for me.

During that visit, he imparted three invaluable pieces of advice that have echoed through the years: "Buy yourself a watch and always be on time," "Remember, we all go to the bathroom the same way," and "Andersen is spelled with an E, not an O," something he told all his students who joined that firm. These lessons weren't just casual remarks; they reflected his wisdom and how he observed me, encouraging me to cultivate punctuality, self-confidence, and attention to detail—traits I greatly needed to improve as I stepped into my corporate career.

Having kept my ear to the ground for three years, I learned of the announcement of Dean Craig's retirement, and I was enthusiastic to celebrate his incredible career at his retirement dinner on April 19, 2013. As fate would have it, I never made it. Just two days before the event, my world shattered. My son, Omar, also a graduate of A&T's business school, called with heartbreaking news: He was diagnosed with kidney disease and required immediate care. In that moment, my priority shifted entirely. While attending the dinner was no longer an option, a thought occurred to me to write a letter to Dean Craig to convey my gratitude, but life swept me away. That thought faded into the background over the following eighteen months as I devoted myself to supporting my son in a fight that ultimately took his life.

Fast forward to October 2015: In my attempt to return to normalcy in my life, I attended A&T's homecoming weekend. I ran into Kevin Buncum, a fellow Aggie (our school mascot), who mentioned he did not see me at Dean Craig's retirement dinner. It was kind of strange that he brought that up more than two years later, especially since he was an engineering major and not someone I knew very well. As I shared the gut-wrenching challenges that kept me away, my emotions surfaced, and the idea of writing a letter to Dean Craig expressing my gratitude for everything he did for me seeped back into my consciousness. Connecting to my feelings, Kevin looked me straight in the eyes and said with authority, "Tanya, you should write that letter." He propelled me into action, and the idea later evolved, transforming from a solitary letter into something even more meaningful: a book of letters from Dean Craig's former students honoring his profound impact on our lives.

Over the next year, I gathered 113 heartfelt letters from former students, faculty, administrators, and special friends—all focused on the theme of gratitude and each reflecting a unique experience with Dean Craig. The project was a labor of love, and as I pieced it together, I discovered layers of his legacy that he had never shared during our annual visits, too humble to boast about his accomplishments even as he inspired generations of students. As I became acquainted with his life's work, what started as a simple intention to express my gratitude evolved into a testament of affection and admiration from 113 individuals, and then, a thought to document the life's work and legacy of a remarkable man.

When I approached Dean Craig with the idea of documenting his life's work, he responded with humility, saying, "I never thought about documenting my life's work, but I am proud of what I accomplished. I'll give you the sketch, and you can fill in the blanks."

Over the next seven years, we collaborated to paint a vivid portrait of his early home life growing up in Jim Crow Montgomery, Alabama, and being educated in segregated black schools, colleges, and universities where he learned of the promises of American democracy and, in spite of his environment, was challenged to go out into the world and make a difference. These invaluable life lessons shaped his character, ultimately guiding him to his life's work and allowing him to leave a lasting impact on both people and organizations. He played a key role in driving change and helped to diversify the accounting profession, corporate America, and business school education in the United States.

A central aspect of Dean Craig's life's work was expanding access to business school education for students at Historically Black Colleges and Universities (HBCUs) and creating pathways into management positions in the corporate sector. His efforts were influenced by the landmark Supreme Court decision, *Brown v. Board of Education of Topeka,* and Title VII of the Civil Rights Act of 1964.

As I delved deeper into his life's work, I became aware of the challenges faced by pioneering African Americans who earned business degrees at a time when corporate America offered them few opportunities. Dean Craig was one of these individuals. When he graduated from Morehouse College in 1957, segregation prevented him from realizing his dream of a professional career in corporate America. This motivated him, as a dean, to work tirelessly to prepare his students for the opportunities he had been denied. To do this effectively, he recognized the need for change in American business school education, advocated for reform, and ultimately helped implement needed improvements.

Through his dedication and impact, Dean Craig reached a time of well-earned recognition, ultimately ascending to a pinnacle of success in American business school education, making history as an African American and HBCU representative. The impact he had on his students, me included, fostered lasting gratitude for the kindness and support he provided during our time at the business school and beyond.

Writing this book has been a journey—one that began in grief, however, concludes in gratitude—documenting the story of a man who gave so much to so many. I am still amazed at how the simple thought of writing Dean Craig a letter evolved into seven years of research, conversations, and storytelling. Given how everything unfolded, I believe it was a spiritual calling that led to the completion of *More Than a Dean: Quiester Craig's Journey from Humble Roots to Reshaping Business School Education and Advancing Equity at HBCUs and Beyond.*

In this book, I have incorporated insights from countless hours of personal interviews with Dean Craig and others, extensive scholarly research, and selected personal stories from his former students, faculty, staff, colleagues, university administrators, and special friends who contributed to the letter writing campaign entitled *Letters of Gratitude to Dr. Q: An Anthology from the Heart.*

I hope you enjoy this story, which seeks to illuminate Dean Craig's undeniable legacy. The book is divided into five parts.

Part I: Farewell, Dean Craig announces Dean Craig's retirement and provides a brief overview of his retirement celebration, culminating in a farewell dinner attended by over one thousand guests from all aspects of his life.

Part II: Growing Up Baby Bro explores Quiester Craig's upbringing in segregated Montgomery, Alabama. This section examines how segregation influenced his home life, his primary and secondary education at a laboratory school, his enrollment at both Morehouse College and Atlanta University (now Clark Atlanta University), and his career choice. It also highlights the early influences that shaped his character—lessons he learned and credited with his later success.

Much of this section is informed by Dr. Sharon Gay Pierson, Dean Craig's personal friend and author of *Laboratory of Learning: HBCU Laboratory Schools and Alabama State College Lab High in the Era of Jim Crow*—the first book of its kind to illuminate the history of laboratory schools within Historically Black Colleges and Universities. The school Dean Craig attended for his primary and secondary education is the subject of her book. In the acknowledgments of her book, Dr. Pierson stated, "*My deepest gratitude to the 'Godfather' of this project, Dean Quiester Craig, a cherished friend and brilliant scholar whose personal journey*" inspired her book.

Part III: Becoming Quiester explores his transition from college to the workforce, highlighting his journey to earning his professional credentials—the Certified Public Accountant (CPA) license—and beginning the process of obtaining his PhD in accounting.

Although he initially lacked a clear career plan, one emerged through his teaching assignments at the HBCUs—South Carolina State College (now South Carolina State University), Lincoln University in Missouri, and Florida Agricultural and Mechanical University (FAMU)—where he found employment. Obtaining his CPA marked a significant milestone in Quiester's professional development, solidifying his path as an accounting business school professor and launching a long, highly productive career as an HBCU business school educator and dean.

To provide context on the significance of Quiester's achievement in obtaining his CPA, this section examines the history of the accounting profession and the challenges faced by the first African American CPAs in securing their credentials. Much of this discussion is informed by *A White-Collar Profession: African American Certified Public Accountants Since 1921*, authored by Dean Craig's colleague and friend, Dr. Theresa Hammond, which features him prominently.

Part IV: Making the Move to Leadership details Dean Craig's transition from the classroom to leadership as dean of the School of Business and Economics at North Carolina Agricultural and Technical State University (A&T), a land-grant HBCU in Greensboro, North Carolina.

The social changes brought about by Title VII of the Civil Rights Act of 1964, which prohibits employment discrimination based on race, color, religion, sex, and national origin, had a profound impact on higher education. Almost overnight, corporations began recruiting at HBCUs, prompting college presidents to enhance the quality of their business programs to better prepare students for the long-awaited opportunity to pursue professional careers in corporate America.

By 1972, Quiester had become highly sought after in academia as the tenth African American to earn an MBA, CPA, and PhD in accounting. That year, he was appointed dean of A&T's business school with a mandate to establish a business school accredited by the prestigious American Association of Collegiate Schools of Business (now Association to Advance Collegiate Schools of Business ([International] or [AACSB]), an organization founded in 1916 to set quality standards for business school education.

Part V: Mama, Look at Your Baby Son Now examines Dean Craig's challenges and achievements in his leadership role, from working with faculty and students to managing budgets, external relationships, and institutional growth. This section examines how he overcame obstacles, implemented meaningful change, and attained a pinnacle of achievement in American business school education. His contributions earned him numerous distinctions as the first African American and HBCU representative in century-old organizations within the American business school ecosystem.

At the heart of Dean Craig's ability to address challenges and drive change were his humanitarian spirit, determination, and unwavering belief in the power of education—traits he cultivated early in life. This section also highlights the accomplishments of his students, whose success has created opportunities that will benefit African Americans for generations to come.

PART I

FAREWELL, DEAN CRAIG

Dean Craig in his academic regalia, 2012.

CHAPTER 1

Aggies Celebrate Dean Craig's Legacy

In the fall of 2012, Dean Quiester Craig announced that he would retire at the end of the school year in May 2013. At the time, he was seventy-six years old, feeling great, and still enjoying his work. However, after forty-one years at the School of Business and Economics at North Carolina Agricultural and Technical State University (A&T), he had given his all and understood that there was a "time and season for everything." It was now the season for him to spend more time with his family and explore other interests. He would also no longer have to field questions about when he would retire—or whether he had already retired. While he was clear on his decision, it was undeniably bittersweet. Stepping down meant leaving behind the passion that had fueled him for so many years: developing students and working with his dedicated team of faculty and staff.[1]

The announcement sent shockwaves throughout the A&T community, even though everyone had anticipated this day. Many students, both past and present, reflected on the profound impact Dean Craig had on their personal and professional growth. Faculty members also expressed appreciation for his visionary leadership and the collaborative environment he had cultivated over the years. A shared sense of gratitude emerged for the legacy of excellence and innovation that he would leave behind, along with an undeniable sense of loss at moving forward without his steady guidance.

Ultimately, the community came together to plan a grand farewell celebration. Amid these discussions, curiosity grew about the business school's future direction and how the administration would fill such big shoes.

Chancellor Harold Martin reflected on Dean Craig's long service to the university during the four years they worked together, calling him "one of the finest examples of leadership, service, and educational success our institution has ever been privileged to behold." He also acknowledged the honor of partnering with him on numerous outstanding endeavors, particularly in advancing the university's educational vision.[2]

Chancellor Martin praised Dean Craig's dedication to excellence, innovative wisdom, extensive experience, noted independence, and "no-nonsense" persona, which was evident in his daily interactions with faculty, staff, students, and other university stakeholders. He also commended him for establishing several "firsts" for A&T, both educationally and in his role as dean of the business school.[3]

As his retirement date approached, Dean Craig received even more recognition, adding to the accolades he earned throughout his tenure. He retired as one of the longest-serving AACSB deans at an AACSB-accredited business school and was honored with the AACSB International Distinguished Leadership Award. He also received the Outstanding Dean Award from Beta Alpha Psi.

Dean Craig left such a lasting impression on the organizations he served that The PhD Project granted him a lifetime, all-expenses-paid pass to their events. The state of North Carolina bestowed its highest honor upon him: The Order of the Long Leaf Pine, awarded by the governor to individuals who make significant contributions to the state and their communities through exemplary service and exceptional achievements. Additionally, the Greensboro City Council passed a resolution recognizing and emphasizing the impact of his tenure as dean of A&T's business school.

Dean Craig retired in grand style, befitting one of A&T's longest-serving deans, who had brought about transformative change in countless ways. On the evening of April 19, 2013, more than one thousand people gathered at the Sheraton Greensboro at Four Seasons hotel in North Carolina to celebrate his forty-one years of service at what is now the Willie A. Deese College of Business and Economics. The retirement dinner marked the culmination of a weeklong series of festivities, drawing family, students, alumni, colleagues, faculty, administrators, former classmates, and friends—both young and old—from near and far. For those who knew Dean Craig, this was an event they simply could not miss.[4]

The evening began with an elegant cocktail party, where the guests mingled and exchanged pleasantries. The venue buzzed with excitement as attendees arrived in their finest attire, creating an atmosphere of sophistication. Laughter and reminiscences filled the air as guests reflected on the past, caught up on the present, and shared heartfelt wishes for Dean Craig's future.

The celebration dinner was held in the hotel's grand ballroom, where the university's colors radiated throughout. Tables, each seating ten guests, were draped in blue and gold linens, complementing the room's luxurious decor. Elegant floral arrangements, soft ambient lighting, and tasteful drapery enhanced the sophisticated and celebratory atmosphere. Every detail was thoughtfully coordinated, ensuring a night to remember.

Dean Craig sat on the beautifully decorated podium alongside Patricia Miller Zollar, class of 1984, who served as the mistress of ceremonies. She welcomed the crowd and acknowledged that the evening was a true celebration of a legacy of excellence and the culmination of a journey in business school education. Though that chapter had come to an end, she said, the standard of excellence Dean Craig had established at A&T's business school and instilled in his students would endure forever.[5]

Throughout the evening, guests enjoyed a sumptuous dinner, piano music, and singing, including Dean Craig's favorite song, "If I Can Help Somebody," made famous by Mahalia Jackson and performed by his Lab High classmate, Fanny B. Deloatch. Speeches were given, toasts were raised, and warm memories were shared. The entire evening was lighthearted and filled with laughter.

Another Lab High classmate, Jessica Pettus Rankin, presented an image of Dean Craig as a youth before his degrees and authority, eliciting roaring laughter from the crowd. Chancellor Harold Martin described him in one word: "intimidating," acknowledging that he could not think of anyone else with the capacity or stamina to sustain forty-one years in the role as Dean Craig had. Chancellor Emeritus Edward Fort praised Dean Craig and his faculty for their networking and marketing efforts, which had raised over $10 million for scholarships over the years. Chancellor Fort stated, "This man is not only the very epitome of what A&T stands for, but he represents the reality that this is the place where dreamers become achievers."[6]

In her keynote speech, Miller Zollar compared Dean Craig to biblical figures such as Moses and King Solomon, while Dean Emeritus James "Jim" Weeks from the Bryan School of Business at the University of North Carolina at Greensboro likened him to God. Another speaker referred to him as the Michael Jordan of business education. His colleague and retired dean from A&T's College of Engineering, Dr. Joseph Monroe, stated that Dean Craig always delivered on his promises. Dean Craig's three children, Derrick, Patrice, and Angie were present. Derrick and Patrice emphasized the consistency between his professional and personal life, confirming that his work ethic and leadership reflected the kind of father he was at home.[7]

When it was time for Dean Craig to speak, he expressed that he was overwhelmed and could hardly believe the turnout, especially given the inclement weather. His only explanation for his career and the number of people who came to wish him farewell was that he had been abundantly blessed. Dean Craig acknowledged that the greatest joy of his tenure as dean came from witnessing the impact he and his team had on students, particularly those who entered the business school with questionable academic records and went on to graduate. He emphasized that the success and achievements of the business school were the results of a collective effort, and he took the opportunity to recognize key individuals for their contributions. In fact, he dedicated most of his remarks to thanking his staff and honoring them with plaques. Overall, he was very pleased with the evening.[8]

As he retired, the memories of his students and the successes of his alumni accompanied him, reaffirming his belief that his greatest achievement was witnessing his students excel in their chosen fields. Dean Craig was enveloped in love and support as he bid farewell to his career and welcomed the next chapter in his life. His final act was to increase the Quiester Craig Endowed Scholarship with the $1.1 million raised during the weeklong retirement celebration.[9]

As the night drew to a close, guests lined up at the podium to say their goodbyes and take pictures with Dean Craig. Everyone departed with fond memories of a truly unforgettable retirement celebration.

PART II

GROWING UP BABY BRO

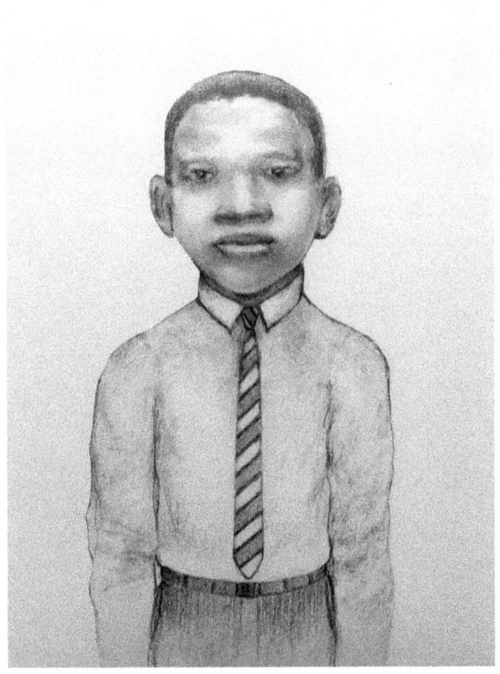

Quiester in the second grade while attending the laboratory school on the campus of Alabama State College, 1943.

CHAPTER 2

Montgomery, Alabama

Quiester Craig was born on July 15, 1936, in Montgomery, Alabama, when Jim Crow state, local, and county laws ruled throughout the Southern States. By 1936, these laws had been in force for almost fifty years, segregating blacks and whites in almost every aspect of life, including in the workplace, schools, hospitals, transportation, neighborhoods, public restrooms, building entrances, elevators, public parks, water fountains, theaters, restaurants, the military, and cemeteries. Even the local newspaper, *The Montgomery Advertiser*, was segregated. One page was devoted to the "Negro" news, and three stars were placed on the front page so whites could avoid buying those editions.[1]

During this period, violence was used to intimidate blacks, intending to keep them bound by the white supremacy system of separation. Hostility against black people was commonplace, and few laws favored or protected them. They functioned in a system where their race placed them at the bottom of the priority list for public funding. Many rejected this subordinate position and focused on education as a means of social uplift from their oppressive conditions. This was the environment in which Quiester Craig grew up.

Quiester lived with his family in a modest house with a large front porch. His house had running water, electricity provided by his papa, and an icebox. His parents purchased a television when he was about thirteen years old. Many of their neighbors did not have all those necessities because of the cost of utilities. "Papa supplemented his income as an entrepreneur," Dean Craig recalled. "He built two houses and rented them. Mr. Marcus and Mrs. Mary were tenants in one house and they had a son who was older and stronger than I was. I admired him because he could hit the baseball harder than anyone on the playground. Before I was born, Papa also operated Craig's barbeque across from the Loveless school, selling food to the community." Also, during that time, the natural gas line that supplied heating was extended to the edge of the black community, but not into the black community. It dropped off right at the start of the Craig family's neighborhood on Cleveland Avenue. During the Jim Crow era, this was common in the Southern States. Although black citizens paid taxes, the conveniences of everyday life were not always provided in their communities.

Quiester, nicknamed "Baby Bro," was the youngest of seven children. His siblings were Magnolia; Sam Jr., called "Bro," for brother; Betty, nicknamed "Doll"; Ralph; Iona; and Cary, called "Su," for sister.

In the Craig household, there were plenty of rules, and they were not to be broken. Mr. Samuel Craig, Quiester's father, stood at six-foot-four and 240 pounds and had what might have been the world's longest finger when he pointed it your way. He worked as a fireman on the old Atlantic Coast Line Railroad, which made most of his poundage muscular. Mr. Craig liked the house quiet when he was home and relied on his wife, Betty, to ensure it was that way. Quiester's older siblings warned him to watch out for their mother's right hand, especially when she held a switch.[2,3]

"In our home, Papa played the role of Chief Justice, and Bet, as Papa called her, was the Commander-in-Chief. I was always scheming how to get around the rules to get the things I wanted," Dean Craig shared, laughing.

Besides keeping the kids in line, education was also a top priority for Mr. and Mrs. Craig. They did not have the good fortune of being educated themselves, but "they both had CSE degrees—common sense education," as Mr. Craig called it. They wanted to make sure their kids understood their opportunities were limited and that getting an education was one way to create possibilities that could improve their lives.[4] By the time Quiester reached eleven years old, all of his siblings had left home. His niece, Gwendolyn, grew up alongside him, while his two brothers, Sam Jr. and Ralph, joined the military, and his four sisters attended Alabama State College for Negroes (now Alabama State University) and became teachers. After completing his military service, Sam Jr. returned to Montgomery, studied at Alabama State, and became a teacher before entering the ministry. Ralph and Doll moved to Cleveland, Ohio.

Along with education, attending church was a very important aspect of the Craig household. Quiester's parents raised him with a strict Baptist upbringing, which helped him develop characteristics such as faith and belief. Every Sunday, the family spent all day at Lilly Baptist Church for Sunday school, day service, and night service. Going to church was an expectation, an obligation, and a requirement in the Craig household. If you were too sick to go to church, you were too sick to go to the movies, watch television, or take part in any fun activities. That was the rule in the Craig household, and the Commander-in-Chief enforced it.

"When I was growing up, the drug problem of my generation was being 'drug' to church," Dean Craig recalled.

Dean Craig confided that he was not too eager to go to church at first, but it didn't take long for him to get the message that he had to go if he wanted to do anything else. Even more so, he witnessed an interesting experience with his papa—one that made him a believer and helped him understand the true purpose of the church. The experience, he said, "can only be explained as spiritual."

His papa had long struggled with accepting the call to become a minister. For the family, being a minister seemed normal, as they were most familiar with the careers of preaching and teaching. For reasons Dean Craig couldn't explain, his papa could not come to terms with the calling.

One evening, twelve-year-old Quiester came home from school and found his papa wearing his pajamas and robe. Though it struck him as odd for that time of day, he didn't give it much thought. After he had been home a while, he saw his papa fall to the floor. He was suddenly in a peculiar physical state, panting and looking very sick, with something coming out of his mouth that Quiester couldn't recognize. What he witnessed was alarming. His mother and Gwendolyn were out running an errand, so he was home alone with his papa and had to handle the situation. So, he walked his papa down to the community hospital, just a few blocks from their house.

When they got to the hospital, the doctors started working on his papa. They poked and prodded him, hooking him up to various instruments, but he didn't seem to get any better. After a while, Quiester returned home to let his mother know what was going on. Hearing the news, she was terribly upset, and they both rushed back to the hospital. As time passed, the doctor still could not determine what was wrong with his papa. The doctor worked on him all night, but his condition did not improve. Fortunately, by the next morning, his papa was back to normal. "The first thing Papa said," Dean Craig said, "was, 'Bet, I have got to preach.'"

Once his papa accepted the call to preach, he was no longer sick. He was perfectly normal, so he got up out of the hospital bed, got dressed, and they all went home. His papa forced him to go to school that day. When he came home that afternoon, he was happy to see his papa sitting on the front porch, rocking in the rocking chair, reading the newspaper. He was perfectly fine. Quiester asked, "Papa, what happened?"

His father replied, "I will tell you one day."

Well, his papa never got around to explaining, so Quiester reached his own conclusion. He believed he saw the power of God at work, which helped his papa decide to accept the calling to preach. After witnessing what he called a "spiritual experience," he became a staunch believer in God and better understood the purpose of the church.

From that point on, Quiester willingly spent all day in church on Sundays and any other day or night that his parents felt he should be there. He saw it as a good use of his time. Listening to the sermons and studying the Bible taught him about faith, kindness, respect, and compassion. "Papa loved the last verse of the 27th Psalm as his favorite: Wait on the Lord. Be of good courage, and he will strengthen your heart. I have followed that verse all these years," Dean Craig confessed.

Because of his parents' strong educational and religious beliefs and their desire to raise productive children, Quiester's home life was full of structure. Mrs. Craig, who ran the household, seemed to deliberate every decision regarding his life, which is why he nicknamed her the Commander-in-Chief.

All of his siblings attended the Loveless School, which was just three blocks from their house on West Jeff Davis Street, but Quiester attended a different school. In 1942, he started first grade at The Alabama State College Laboratory School—commonly known as Lab High—which served elementary through high school students. The laboratory school was part of the normal school on the campus of Alabama State College for Negroes (now Alabama State University) and functioned as a training ground for future teachers. He attended both primary and secondary school there in a rather serendipitous way.

The year before he was to enter first grade, Mrs. Craig observed two of his neighborhood playmates—Jean Carter and Richatta Quarles—as they walked past her house each morning to take the city bus to school. She admired how well they dressed and asked their parents what school they attended. Liking what she heard, Mrs. Craig went over to the school and enrolled Quiester, and the next year, he was taking the bus across town to school as well.

"Mama chose a different school for me. In our household, we did not question Mama, so I just went. She took the bus with me the first week, but I ended that. I didn't want anyone to think I was a mama's boy," Dean Craig recalled.

Laboratory schools, introduced into American society in the mid 1800s were a unique type of institution. They were located on college campuses, were small in size, and served two distinct functions: providing a real classroom environment for training future teachers and producing high academic achievement for the primary and secondary student population that attended. College-level students studying to become teachers observed, learned, and practiced expert teaching techniques while working with the latest school equipment as part of their educational process in laboratory schools.[5] Because future teachers were being trained, the faculty members at laboratory schools were generally of high quality and known for successful academic outcomes, benefiting both college-level and primary and secondary student populations.[6]

In addition to quality instruction, valuable characteristics that enhanced academic achievement for primary and secondary students included the personal attention and support they received due to low student-teacher ratios; the continuity in their educational experience across the elementary, middle, and high school levels; and their exposure to a college campus starting in their first year of school, making these students more likely to pursue higher education.[7] As you could probably guess, the students enrolled in these schools were mostly from affluent families,[8] though that was not entirely the case for Lab High.

The students who attended Lab High were from diverse family backgrounds, as defined by their parents' occupational status and educational attainment. Statistics from the class of 1953 identified the three largest occupations held by parents of students at the laboratory school as educators, laborers, and homemakers. Students from these groups comprised over 50 percent of the total population, with the remaining coming from a variety of occupations, including proprietors, clerical workers, service workers, domestics, and farmers.[9] Being an educator signaled prosperity in the African American community. However, the wealthiest family in that group was unlikely to be affluent. As for educational attainment, only 33 percent of the students' parents had graduated high school, and 13 percent had obtained an undergraduate degree. The common threads of the Lab High families were their restricted status in segregated Alabama, progressive family values, and the importance they placed on education. As a result of these common threads, enrollment criteria at Lab High were somewhat informal; however, it gave priority to the children of the faculty and administrators at the school.[10]

The number of laboratory schools in the United States peaked at approximately two hundred before experiencing a steady decline in the 1960s and 1970s. Laboratory schools during the late nineteenth and early twentieth centuries, associated with prominent universities and normal schools that also served as teacher training institutions, included Hunter College (1870), the University of Chicago (1896), Teachers College at Columbia University (1917), and the University of Missouri (1857).[11,12] Lab High was one of thirteen laboratory schools known to operate on Historically Black Colleges and Universities' (HBCUs') campuses such as Talladega College, Atlanta University, Virginia State, Southern University, and West Virginia State.[13] These schools provided a high quality liberal arts education to their students, a significant achievement for African Americans in the South during the Jim Crow Era. Mrs. Craig was fortunate that such a school existed for a portion of Alabama's black children and that she could enroll Quiester in Lab High. However, given its history, it's remarkable that the school survived and developed to ultimately benefit Quiester Craig.

From the establishment of Alabama State College in 1867 as the first state-supported liberal arts HBCU in the United States, its early leaders resisted attempts by state authorities requiring them to offer industrial training aimed at preparing students for jobs as farmers, carpenters, brick masons, cooks, seamstresses, laundresses, or housekeepers. Instead, they upheld the liberal arts mission, equipping students for higher education and professional careers as ministers, lawyers, physicians, and, of course, exceptional liberal arts teachers. A common thread among the leaders was their struggle to keep the school's doors open, but they never wavered in their commitment to grow the model school into a college to train teachers and educate students in the liberal arts.

William Burns Paterson was appointed president of State Normal School, later renamed Alabama State College for Negroes, in 1878 and served for thirty-seven years until 1915. He solidified the school's liberal arts mission, organized a model school where seniors gained in-classroom teaching experience as part of their curriculum, and relocated the school to the city of Montgomery after racial tensions peaked in the town of Marion, its original location. Paterson emigrated to Alabama from Tullibody, Scotland, after the Civil War and established a school in Greensboro, Alabama to educate blacks to teach in the liberal arts. He demonstrated early determination toward his mission, even carrying a gun to defend his school from the Ku Klux Klan, who opposed its existence.[14]

John William Beverly succeeded Paterson after his death in 1915, as the first African American to lead the school. Educated in the liberal arts by Paterson, Beverly graduated from Brown University in 1894 with a Bachelor of Philosophy degree. Using his training at Brown, he transformed the model school into a four-year, degree-granting liberal arts high school and teacher certification program. As Beverly saw it, producing well-qualified liberal arts teachers was the best way to enhance the lives of the greatest number of black

Alabamians. However, after just five years, he was abruptly dismissed and replaced by George Washington "G.W." Trenholm.[15]

G.W. Trenholm served from 1920 to 1925. He established the laboratory school as a primary and secondary institution and grew Alabama State into a college. He noted that his laboratory school "differed from other kinds of schools in emphasizing the how and why, as well as the what, in liberal scholastic attainment." His untimely death at age fifty-four tragically curtailed the achievement of his vision for the college and the laboratory school, to improve education for all African Americans.[16] Although G.W. Trenholm's time was brief, his only child, Harper Councill "H.C." Trenholm, who had worked alongside him, replaced him as president of Alabama State from 1925 to 1962 and carried out his father's vision.[17] Under H.C. Trenholm's leadership, Alabama State College and Lab High prospered during Quiester's enrollment.

Starting in the first grade, Quiester took the public bus across town to Lab High, twelve years before the Montgomery Bus Boycott. Taking the bus daily exposed him to the realities of segregation. When he and his classmates tried to board the bus, the white bus drivers would open the front door so they could pay their fare. Before they could walk to the back of the bus, enter, and take their seats, the drivers would close the doors and drive away. When older black men in the community heard about this, they waited with the children at the bus stop. When the bus arrived, they stretched their arms across the back door to give the kids enough time to pay their fare, get on at the back of the bus and take their seats. "That's an experience I'll never forget," Dean Craig shared. "When things like that happened, we just focused on the good and positive aspects of our lives, like school, church, and home life, in the particular area."

Growing up in those conditions, Quiester could do little more than conduct himself in a way that kept him safe. Not only was he exposed to these situations at the bus stop, but they also infiltrated his community.

On Saturday evenings, when he and his friends played in the streets near their homes, teenage boys from the other side of town would cruise through their neighborhood, hanging out of car windows, yelling things he wouldn't repeat—but the intent was clearly to intimidate them. "This was their idea of Saturday evening fun," Dean Craig recalled. With a vigilant eye on their children at all times, the mothers would dash out of the house during these incidents, find their kids, and hurry them inside for safety.

As a means of survival, there was little to no discussion about these situations at home or at school. The emphasis at home was on getting an education to improve one's life, attending church, and enjoying quality time with family and neighbors. Adults in the African American community focused on preparing their children, hoping they would have an opportunity for a life better than theirs, something Quiester's parents constantly impressed upon him and his siblings. The teachers at Lab High focused on classroom lessons, not on the latest boycotts, segregation issues, or their unfriendly neighbors. Instead, the teachers spent their time discussing topics like "self-realization, leadership, cooperative strategies, self-directed problem-solving, and civic responsibility."[18]

Quiester's teachers at Lab High were professional educators who were well-trained and required to hold at least a four-year degree. In the 1947–48 school year, there were twenty-three teachers on staff. Twelve of them taught both at the college on campus and at the laboratory school; eighteen had completed some level of graduate work; and fifteen, or 65 percent, had earned graduate degrees. In comparison, during this time, only 28 percent of black teachers and 49 percent of white teachers in the state held four-year college degrees.[19] Also, Lab High's faculty established themselves as recognized leaders in education through their professional activities. They took part in statewide and national studies on black secondary education, hosted statewide and regional teachers' conferences and workshops, and created educational materials used by other teachers in the state.[20]

By enrolling Quiester at Lab High, Mrs. Craig provided him with the opportunity to receive a comprehensive, rigorous, first-class liberal arts college preparatory education. English encompassed grammar, essay writing, and literature, taught as a core subject for all four years. The sciences included biology, chemistry, and physics, while the math curriculum comprised freshman mathematics, geometry, and algebra. The history and social studies curriculum featured world history, American history, African American history, social studies, and geography. Lab High also offered physical education and foreign languages. Students were required to take a set number of special courses in art, music, home economics, and manual arts as extra electives. Qualified students could also enroll in advanced courses in math, science, and foreign languages at the college.[21] While this may seem normal for a school, it was challenging for black kids growing up in the South during the Jim Crow Era to receive such a comprehensive liberal arts college preparatory education.

Quiester's favorite subject was literature. He particularly appreciated the integration of black history into the course. The stories he read about black achievers like George Washington Carver, Frederick Douglass, Paul Laurence Dunbar, Langston Hughes, and Paul Robeson, along with their contributions to society, filled him with racial pride. Given the circumstances these individuals were born into—which were significantly worse than his own—their accomplishments especially impressed him. He learned from his study of black achievers that with hard work and focus, you could accomplish great things.

Although Quiester loved literature, he actually preferred recess because he enjoyed talking and socializing with his classmates. He fulfilled his foreign language requirement by studying French. During his time at the school, the foreign language program earned high praise. In 1953, the Southern Association of Colleges and Schools (SACS) evaluation committee commended the faculty for their strong academic preparation, the effective use of the languages they taught, and their effective teaching methods.[22]

The students at Lab High faced challenges set by their teachers to perform their best individually while also supporting their peers. Teachers encouraged students to engage in peer teaching or tutoring to help classmates struggling with academic rigor avoid falling behind. It often affected the entire class if one student failed to complete their work. At the laboratory school, tutoring was viewed as helpful for both parties. The prevailing belief was that tutoring deepened the tutor's understanding of the material and offered valuable insights into the tutee's perspective. The Lab High educators believed that tutoring strengthened student relationships and built a stronger sense of community. With his academic success, Quiester frequently tutored and studied with his classmates.[23]

A variety of robust extracurricular activities enhanced the college preparatory academic program. Administrators and teachers believed these activities offered a "brilliant opportunity for self-expression, individual distinction, and cooperative creativity."[24] Students took part in sports such as tennis, basketball, and track; academic competitions; classical drama productions; and clubs like debate, music, the student newspaper, and the student council, where Lab High students often learned alongside college students. The school celebrated the National Honor Society with great fanfare and frequently hosted formal evening events for its members. Students also engaged in daily religious devotion, attended weekly assemblies, and took part in lyceums, plays, and musical performances sponsored by the college and community organizations as part of their personal development.[25]

Years later, Dean Craig recalled the excitement he felt when professional heavyweight boxer Joe Louis, known as the Brown Bomber, visited the campus. He had learned about Louis's accomplishments by reading about him in *Jet* magazine. Louis was recognized as the first African American to be considered a national hero for defeating the German boxer Max Schmeling in 1938. Dean Craig sat behind Louis, and years later he still remembered the clapping, shouting, and excitement of that day. He remembered Joe Louis encouraging him and his classmates to pursue their education, saying, "We all need tools." And, raising his fists, he added, "This is my tool, but you kids need to get your education. Don't depend on this."

Lab High was similar to laboratory schools at traditionally white institutions of higher education in many ways, but where it differed most was in its resources, which were scarce. As part of a state-funded black public institution, the school's leaders consistently struggled to keep the doors open from its inception. Montgomery County covered only the teachers' salaries, while Alabama State financed all the other operational costs of the laboratory school. From the very start, contributions from philanthropic organizations and the African American community supplemented state support for the school, a practice that was common in black education throughout the Southern States during that time.

The persistent funding issues at Lab High were most evident in the school facilities. By the time Quiester reached high school, the once beautiful and stately Tullibody Hall, where Lab High was situated, had deteriorated from heavy use. When comparing the facilities of the two most prestigious high schools in Montgomery—Lab High and the all-white Sidney Lanier High School—the funding disparities were apparent. Tullibody Hall had had few updates since it was built in 1907, featuring fourteen cramped classrooms and an auditorium shared with the college. Toilet facilities were added in the basement in 1933. In contrast, Sidney Lanier High School, referred to as "The Million Dollar School," was a modern facility built in 1929. It boasted an expansive stone structure, a gym, locker room facilities, multiple indoor restrooms, a shop, an auditorium, and a cafeteria, among many other amenities.[26] Despite inadequate facilities and funding challenges at Lab High, the leadership and faculty remained committed to providing a high quality liberal arts education for their students, and both parents and students regarded the educational experience as a privilege.[27]

To ensure that parents had some investment in their children's education and to support the school's budgetary needs, students were charged a nominal tuition fee of $12.50 per semester and $25 for the entire year to attend Lab High, and they were required to purchase their own books. This amount was significant for many black families due to occupational restrictions in segregated America. Fortunately, several students at Lab High, including Quiester Craig, received multiple scholarships for their academic performance, enabling them to attend school free.[28]

"Every little bit helped," Dean Craig shared. "I was proud to contribute towards my education. It was also an opportunity to become known by President Trenholm. He presented the scholarships each year, so I got to know him since I received scholarships for about nine or ten years."

Once enrolled, students had to maintain satisfactory records in their academics, conduct, and attitude.[29] Meeting these criteria came easily for Quiester. He was academically gifted and showed promise early on. His classmate, Jessica Pettus Rankin, shared that he was the smartest student in the class and even agreed to help her with her nine times tables when they were in primary school. Due to their time studying together and other academic achievements, they presented as sixth graders at Lab High's annual commencement ceremony. At the ceremony, thirty-seven diplomas were awarded to high school students, twenty-five certificates to junior high students, and thirty-two certificates to elementary school students.[30] This attracted a large audience of students, parents, teachers, and professors in the auditorium, including Mr. and Mrs. Craig. For Quiester, the greatest success of that evening was the pride he brought to his parents. He recalled, "Mama was as proud as a peacock, and Papa—I can hear his soft laugh. It was a laugh filled with pride, and I could hear it every time he felt proud of me. I used to speak often in church. When I was eight years old, I memorized the names of all sixty-six books in the Bible in three weeks. The day I recited them in church, I heard Papa's soft laugh as well."

Another practice at Lab High was that "good discipline should be considered a product of good teaching."[31] Students were expected to strictly follow the established rules. These rules were enforced rigorously, yet everyone understood that discipline was applied thoughtfully and that teachers truly cared about the students' well-being. As a result, teachers were remembered and appreciated for many years for the numerous lessons they imparted to their students beyond just reading, writing, and arithmetic.[32]

In addition to the academic rigor and variety of high-quality extracurricular activities at Lab High, Quiester also benefited from the progressive educational movement of the 1920s, which, aside from teaching literacy, helped students understand their citizenship and social responsibilities. Educational reformists John Dewey, George Counts, Harold Rugg, and others introduced innovative philosophies into school curricula to shape school culture and the character of their students. As a result of this movement, educators instituted changes in the "character, purpose, and direction of American education,"[33] and the leaders at black laboratory schools, including Lab High, integrated these philosophies, "sculpting their own form of progressive education" to include beliefs of African American reformers such as W.E.B. Du Bois, Carter G. Woodson, Charles Johnson, and others.[34] At its core was the belief among the Lab High community—students, parents, teachers, and leadership—that "education was an investment that would bring advancement to the individual, and, thus, to society as a whole."[35] The academic program, extracurricular activities, and school culture at Lab High were designed to instill that belief in its students.

These philosophies also taught students the importance and strength of community, defined by their connections to each other, their families, the school as a whole, the larger African American population, and the nation. Students were entrusted with the responsibility to help each other succeed, graduating from Lab High with an understanding of what America's promise of democracy meant and that they, along with all citizens, had the right to enjoy it.[36] The result of these teachings, as was customary at the time across the country, created a new generation of socially minded youth who became activist leaders in the 1960s and 1970s.

The exposure Quiester gained at Lab High helped shape his character. Nearly seventy years after graduating, he viewed his school as a gem, stating, ". . . We were taught to be change agents,"[37,38] something that became evident as he advanced in his career.

At home, it was no different for Quiester Craig. Mr. and Mrs. Craig taught values and created an environment of fun as a family. Since Mr. Craig worked for the railroad, he wasn't home two or three nights a week, and sometimes longer. After his siblings left home, Quiester took on the responsibility of being the man of the house, but only when his papa traveled for work. One thing he missed after his siblings were gone was the fun they used to have as a larger family. When everyone was home, the house was filled with life and engaging conversations at the dinner table. Each of his siblings had unique talents and, as young people, found their own ways to challenge the household rules. With more people around, Mrs. Craig had a multitude of situations to manage, resulting in less focus on him. This was the main thing Quiester missed after his brothers and sisters left home. He also longed for their presence, so after they were gone, he wrote letters to two of his siblings every week on a rotating basis to keep them updated on what was happening at home.

He was thrilled whenever any of his siblings returned home for visits. His brother Ralph came home every Thanksgiving for the Turkey Bowl and always arrived around 2:00 a.m. Mrs. Craig would wake everyone up to greet him. His sisters, who stayed in Alabama, visited most often. Mr. Craig would pick them up in his big blue Buick that looked like a gangster car. It had a gear stick on the floor, two spare tires on the side, and running boards on each side for getting in the car. "Papa was very proud of that car," Dean Craig recalled. "He made it my job to keep the inside clean. Mama was an experienced cook and, looking back on those days when my siblings came home, she made all of her high-cholesterol meals," he shared with a laugh. "Those were great family times."

Quiester also traveled to visit his siblings who had moved out of state. One of his most cherished experiences as a teenager was taking summer trips to Cleveland, Ohio, spending one week with his brother Ralph and another week with his sister Doll. He could only go after the Commander-in-Chief was convinced that he could travel alone on the train from Montgomery to Cleveland and back. The Chief Justice had to step in to make that happen, overruling the Commander-in-Chief's decision. Reflecting on his siblings, Dean Craig said, "We all stayed very close throughout our adulthood. Ralph was the one I looked up to. We resembled each other strongly, and whenever people saw us together, it was clear we were brothers. Ralph often used humor, which I admired, so I always tried to emulate that characteristic."

Mr. and Mrs. Craig instilled a sense of responsibility in their children. Quiester had several chores at home, especially when he was the only boy there. One of his tasks involved gathering coal, wood, and kindling from the yard each evening to bring inside for the freestanding stoves used to warm the house during the cold season. Every morning, he woke up to the voice of the Commander-in-Chief, who would call out to him, saying, "Get up." He would simply lie in bed until her second call prompted him to get up immediately. He would make the fire, hop back into bed, and pray that it caught. Fortunately, Montgomery had mild weather, which meant the fire-making season was brief.

He also worked a paper route from sixth to eleventh grade, delivering the *Montgomery Advertiser*, against the wishes of the Commander-in-Chief. He started the paper route after noticing that his friend, Washington Sankey, always had money. When Sankey mentioned he was making six to eight dollars a week delivering newspapers, Quiester decided to join the business. In retrospect, he said, "That was my first managerial experience, in the particular area. That job provided me with my first experience in business."

He described the job as a significant experience in his life because he learned a great deal from it. Each day, he began by tuning in to the weather report to prepare himself. He gained insights about people and how to manage relationships. One customer called the paper house to complain about him, a situation he had to handle. Another customer, Mrs. Pettus, who was his classmate's mother, baked him cookies. He had to pay for the newspapers upfront and collect his earnings from customers on Saturday. One customer consistently forgot to pay him, leading him to develop a reputation. That customer said, "If you want your paper, you better pay Quiester." No matter the circumstances, he had to deliver the newspapers in the heat, in the rain, and while dodging dogs, always aiming for the perfect throw to land the paper on his customer's porch.

When he received his first tip, he felt motivated to work harder. He learned to save and used his earnings to buy his first car during the summer before eleventh grade, a transaction the Commander-in-Chief did not approve of. Once again, the Chief Justice intervened on his behalf and he purchased a 1942 black Plymouth and named it Buzzy. "Papa was proud of my initiative in taking on the newspaper route and buying a car. He wanted me to be responsible and explore other opportunities because he didn't want me to follow in his footsteps and work on the railroad," Dean Craig stated.

Although Mrs. Craig needed convincing about her baby boy owning a car, she took advantage of him having it. All summer, he drove her around, taking her to church and running various errands, but the Commander-in-Chief would say no if he wanted to use the car to take a young lady to a movie. On the first day of school, dressed in a shirt and tie, Quiester grabbed the keys to Buzzy to head off to school. Speaking in her charming, soft, yet disapproving voice, the Commander-in-Chief asked him, "Where do you think you're going with those keys? Put them on the table," she instructed.

He replied, "Mama, I don't want to be late for school."

And she replied, "That's not why you bought the car." To his dismay, he was not allowed to drive Buzzy to school for the first two weeks of the semester.

Meanwhile, Mrs. Craig sent him on errands, sometimes even on school nights. He delivered sewing patterns to her friend, Mrs. Sally, who lived directly across the street from Lab High. For the life of him, he couldn't understand why his mama thought it was acceptable for him to drive to Mrs. Sally's house at night, but he couldn't drive to the same place in the morning light. "I waited for what I believed was the right moment and called on the Chief Justice for a ruling on the situation," he explained. Quiester received a ruling in his favor from his papa, who described him as "a mature young man who could be trusted until he demonstrated otherwise." That's how he was allowed to drive Buzzy to school for the rest of the year.

In rendering that decision, his papa must have forgiven him for what he discovered when he took him to get his driver's license. When Quiester was about fifteen years old, Mr. Craig bought a new '48 Chrysler New Yorker with an automatic transmission. He decided it was time to teach his baby son how to drive. It's not surprising that the Commander-in-Chief was against him learning to drive, but once again, she was overruled by the Chief Justice. Unbeknownst to his papa, Quiester already knew how to drive. For years, he had watched his papa behind the wheel and practiced his skills using a friend's car. Although he successfully pretended to learn to drive from his papa, when they went for his driver's license, it turned out that Quiester Craig had been there six months earlier and had failed the driving test. "When Papa found out, it was not a pleasant moment for me. In retrospect, it was a good thing I failed the driving test," Dean Craig recalled.

Mrs. Craig applied the same rigor to guide his activities at school as she did at home. She had him learning to play the piano, a skill useful for church. He wanted to learn an instrument so he could march in the school band. For years, he had watched how much fun it was to be part of a band during the community celebration of the Turkey Day Classic, one of the oldest HBCU football classics starting back in 1924. It took place every year on Thanksgiving Day when Alabama State faced their rival, Tuskegee University. Most of the games occurred in Montgomery, marking it homecoming for Alabama State.

"The Turkey Day Classic was the highlight of the year for the black community," Dean Craig reflected. "People came from everywhere, filled with pride for our black colleges, and it was a great celebration. All the black high school bands took part in the parade, generating a lot of excitement. To join these activities, I successfully negotiated a trade with the Commander-in-Chief and switched to the clarinet to become part of the band. We wore gold sweaters, black pants, and a black beret as our uniform."

Quiester fell in love with basketball as his sport. He was well suited for it, with a tall stature like his father's. He always stood taller than everyone in his class. To play basketball, he needed permission from the Commander-in-Chief, and he also had to outline a plan for balancing basketball with his studies, chores, and newspaper route. After intense negotiation, he received approval and joined the Lab High varsity basketball team in his junior year, playing both center and forward. "We didn't win a lot, but it was fun," Dean Craig recalled. Unfortunately for Quiester, the playing schedule was informal. Lab High did not have a formal sports program because of insufficient funding. Despite the informal schedule, he enjoyed basketball so much that his grade point average dropped to the second highest in the class that year. For most of his years at Lab High, he had maintained the highest grade point average in his class.[39] "I had to deal with the Commander-in-Chief regarding my grades, and I needed to improve them to remain on the team," he shared. "With my grades worked out, I was selected to be captain of the basketball team going into my senior year. I was thrilled about that opportunity and looked forward to leading the team on the court before each game."

Meanwhile, another significant development occurred during his junior year. He and three classmates took an all-day college entrance exam for early admission to college under an experiential program sponsored by the Ford Foundation. Students who demonstrated "high academic promise," as indicated by their school records and achievement tests, could skip their senior year and enroll in one of twelve participating colleges. Some of the options included Fisk University, Morehouse College, Columbia University, the University of Chicago, the University of Wisconsin, and Yale University.[40]

This opportunity for Lab High scholars to be considered for early college admission likely arose due to H.C. Trenholm's tireless leadership of Alabama State College and Lab High. One of his significant achievements included advocating for and securing access to regional accreditation for black secondary schools and HBCUs in 1929, a concept that became part of the American educational system starting in 1855. Obtaining regional accreditation signals that educational institutions uphold high quality educational standards, as established and verified by an independent association. SACS, the regional accreditation body for the Southern States, had barred black secondary schools and HBCUs from evaluation since its inception in 1895, allowing public perception to shape the views on the quality of segregated black education as exceptionally poor. These views were validated by data released by authoritative sources that excluded institutions like Alabama State and Lab High, which collectively earned the reputation of being the "most influential state teaching institution for African Americans in the nation"[41] under H.C. Trenholm's leadership.

Being educated at Morehouse College and the University of Chicago, a high achiever at an early age involved in leadership in numerous organizations, and pursuing his late father's vision to improve education for all black Americans, H.C. Trenholm recognized that if black high schools, colleges, and universities were ever to be recognized as valued academic institutions, they would have to be "judged, recognized, and respected for their academic achievements"[42] based on the same standards as white high schools, colleges, and universities. He also knew that if black students were to have a chance at being accepted in graduate and professional schools, black-segregated high schools, colleges, and universities would have to be regionally accredited by SACS.[43] Having firsthand knowledge of the quality of education at Lab High and other segregated high schools, colleges, and universities in the South, he also knew it was time for change.

As the self-appointed leader of black education, H.C. Trenholm and his supporters made breakthroughs with SACS after three years of prolonged advocacy, letter writing, and compromise, agreeing that black educational institutions be evaluated but not become full members of SACS.[44] As all things in the Jim Crow South were segregated, the nineteen secondary schools[45] and the seven HBCUs (Fisk University, Johnson C. Smith University, Morehouse College, Spelman College, Talladega College, Virginia State University, and Virginia Union University) that were accredited in 1929 were considered the Negro Branch of SACS and maintained on a separate list for the next thirty-two years, until they were granted official SACS membership in 1961.[46] For achieving what at one time seemed impossible, H.C. Trenholm and Lab High made history.

Had it not been for H.C. Trenholm's tireless leadership in gaining SACS accreditation for Lab High, Quiester may not have been presented with the opportunity for early college admission. Just before the end of the school year, his classmates received responses letting them know they did not meet the requirements for early admission, but his letter had yet to arrive. His classmates teased him mercilessly, insinuating that he, too, would not be accepted into the program. He assumed the worst, but on July 15, 1953, his seventeenth birthday, as he sat on the front porch with his mother, engaged in spirited debate, the mailman arrived and delivered two envelopes: one addressed to his parents and one for him. Without hesitation, he ripped open the envelope, unfolded the letter, and read the words, "Congratulations! We are pleased to offer you. . ."

Although Quiester's self-doubt had been quelled at that moment, he felt conflicted. He had previously expressed to his parents that he wanted to be the captain of the basketball team in the upcoming year, and he was determined to see that through. When he shared this desire with them again over dinner, the Commander-in-Chief plainly told him that she was disgusted by his desire to choose basketball over college.

"I want you to tell me what your plans are," his papa said, but before he could answer, his papa held his hand up and told him to be quiet.[47]

"At that point, I understood that I would not be the captain of the basketball team my senior year, but instead, I would be going to Morehouse College," Dean Craig recalled.

CHAPTER 3

Morehouse College

At seventeen years old and without a high school diploma, Quiester headed to Morehouse College, a liberal arts HBCU in Atlanta, Georgia, as a freshman in the fall of 1953. He was the first among his siblings to break with family tradition by leaving home for college. His four sisters and brother, Sam Jr., attended Alabama State College, where they all became teachers. Receiving a full scholarship allowed Dean Craig to attend the prestigious all-male private Morehouse College, recognized as one of the elite private HBCUs that educated and developed young black men into what became known as Morehouse Men. During the Jim Crow era, Morehouse Men were trained to go forth and become leaders in the black community and make a difference in the world. Many Morehouse Men embraced that challenge, and their success in their chosen career paths contributed to changing conditions for African Americans. One of the most notable Morehouse Men was the Reverend Martin Luther King, Jr., from the class of 1948.

Although the decision made by the Chief Justice and the Commander-in-Chief led Quiester to skip his senior year at Lab High and, more importantly, miss the opportunity to be captain of the basketball team, he was excited to attend Morehouse College. Back in Montgomery, he had observed Morehouse students when they traveled to Alabama State to play football games and was impressed by their demeanor and style. Also, Mrs. Phillips, his sixth grade teacher, whose son Bruce attended Morehouse, encouraged him to go there. Therefore, he had some basis for the decision his parents made on his behalf.

When it was time to leave for Morehouse, he traveled on the train from Montgomery to Atlanta with his parents. They arrived at the famous Graves Hall, the freshman dormitory where he lived during his first year. Graves Hall, now known as Graves House, is one of Morehouse College's most iconic buildings. It is a four-story red brick structure in Victorian style, featuring a wooden porch that stretches across one wing of the front façade. The building, highlighted by its open bell tower topped with a pyramidal roof, was constructed in 1889 and served for years as the main multipurpose building on campus. It was named for Morehouse's second president, Dr. Samuel Graves, who raised funds for the building by appealing to white Northerners in Massachusetts, Connecticut, and Michigan, as well as securing donations from black Georgia Baptists.[1]

As soon as Quiester got in his room, Mrs. Craig got busy spraying and wiping down everything, including the springs on his bed. She made up his bed with her homemade quilts as the covers. Morehouse had strict rules in place back then, so his parents had to leave the building by 7:00 p.m. They stayed for the first week in a room they rented up the street from the college to make sure Quiester acclimated to his new surroundings. Unfortunately, he didn't see much of them because he had to attend numerous freshman sessions, where they taught the history of the college, among other things. His parents came over in the evenings, and Mrs. Craig would shake the covers and straighten up his bed. He asked her not to do that because he was concerned that she made him look like Mama's little boy.

It wasn't long before Dean Craig was on his own and engaged in the Morehouse College traditions. As a freshman, he had to wear his Crab Cap and make it through Crab Week as a first step to becoming a Morehouse Man. His "G" was Jimmy Young from Tryon, North Carolina. During that time, G was a term used at Morehouse to refer to your roommate. Young played on the baseball team and was ultimately scouted by the Brooklyn Dodgers. Quiester and Jimmy stuck together all the time both in class and around campus. In fact, all the young men at Morehouse formed a community, and they constantly looked out for one another.

At Morehouse College, Quiester continued his liberal arts education, which had been offered at the college since its earliest days. However, his academic experience was quite different from what it had been at Lab High. He found that he needed to work harder to be competitive at Morehouse. Of the student population, he observed that there were always four or five students competing to be at the top of the class. Morehouse had recruited top students from all over the country, many of whom had professional parents, and in some cases, their fathers were graduates of Morehouse themselves. These students had been "schooled by their parents" and were clear about their purpose for being there. Their majors were pre-med or pre-law, and often they were following in their fathers' footsteps. Quiester realized that if he wanted to be competitive, he would have to raise his game.

As it turned out, his academic performance at Morehouse was bookended by B grade point averages in his freshman and senior years, with distractions in between. He was suddenly on his own, making his own decisions and managing his own time with a sense of freedom he had not experienced while living under the rules of the Craig household. During his four years at Morehouse, he learned that choices have consequences and the easy choices are not always the best. Sometimes, when easy choices are made, consequences arise that need to be dealt with later. Although he made many easy choices, he always studied enough to maintain his scholarship, so he did not have to face the Commander-in-Chief.

There were plenty of opportunities for distractions while attending Morehouse College. The college, being adjacent to four other

HBCUs—Atlanta University, Spelman College, Clark College, and Morris Brown College, collectively comprised the Atlanta University System (now the Atlanta University Center Consortium). Each of these institutions had different founders and was established for various educational purposes. For instance, Atlanta University was founded in 1865 by the American Missionary Association to serve as a coed liberal arts institution with a strong emphasis on educating black teachers and providing a racially integrated campus experience. When it was initially established, well trained teachers from the Yale class of 1863 were the first teachers.[2] As for Spelman, it was established by two missionary women, Sophia B. Packard and Harriet Giles, in 1881 to uplift recently freed black women by offering them educational opportunities. Originally a seminary, it later expanded to include a model school for training teachers.[3] The common purpose of all these institutions was to provide educational opportunities for the emancipated slaves.

With all the colleges nearby and Mrs. Craig not around to manage his activities, Quiester had to strike a happy balance. There was always an abundance of things to do. He had many choices, and being on his own, he participated in extracurricular activities that the Commander-in-Chief might not have necessarily approved. To make up for missing out on being captain of the basketball team at Lab High, he played intramural basketball during his sophomore year. He was such a talented player that he caught the eye of Frank Forbes, head coach of the Morehouse Maroon Tigers and Director of Physical Education. As juniors, he and his classmate Norfleet Strother were welcomed onto the varsity team in the 1955–56 school year. Coach Forbes was quoted in a newspaper article saying, "They are pretty good additions to the squad."[4] An article from the 1956–57 school year, when Morehouse hosted Fisk University, named Solomon Walker, Quiester Craig, and Sam Phelps as the basketball team "standouts."[5] He also played on the football team in his junior and senior years. Of his sports activities, he kept them a secret from Mr. and Mrs. Craig.

Quiester also met and socialized with the young ladies at Spelman by attending activities on their campus, such as religious meetings, classes, and sweetheart balls. Two of his Lab High friends, Barbara Johns and Helen Sawyer, were at Spelman during his time at Morehouse. Barbara was one of 117 plaintiffs in *Davis v. County School Board of Prince Edward County*, one of the five cases that became the landmark Supreme Court case *Brown v. Board of Education of Topeka*. At sixteen years old, she led her classmates in a strike at her high school in Farmville, Virginia, to bring attention to the poor conditions of the school facilities. Improvements such as a gymnasium, cafeteria, infirmary, teachers' restrooms, and classrooms were needed. After the two-week strike, she was sent to live with her uncle in Montgomery and attended Lab High. Although she inspired this action and sought help from the NAACP, another student's name was listed first in the lawsuit.[6,7]

To avoid the strict visitation rules that were in place at Spelman, and as Quiester became familiar with his surroundings, he spent more time at Atlanta University (now Clark Atlanta University). Since it was a graduate school, he said, "The more mature students were at that college." When asked about college girlfriends he said he had "friends that happened to be girls." With his newfound freedom and extracurricular activities, Quiester was able to find the appropriate balance to manage his studies and benefit from all that Morehouse College had to offer. Much of this success can be attributed to the influence of Dr. Benjamin Mays, who was president of Morehouse during Quiester's time there. Dr. Mays taught others based on what he had learned from his own experiences.[8] In many ways, he was a living example of the African Americans Quiester had learned about in his literature classes at Lab High.

Born in 1894 to parents who were born into slavery and had limited means and minimal education, Dr. Mays pursued education, determined to change his family's trajectory. After one year at Virginia Union University, an HBCU in Richmond, he transferred and earned a degree from Bates College in Lewiston, Maine, graduating Phi Beta Kappa. That degree was followed by a master's and PhD in Christian theology from the University of Chicago. Religion, which he learned about from his mother, was important to Dr. Mays, as he believed it provided "direction to life."[9] He declared himself "a race man"[10] and explained that to mean that he believed in the black man's ability, which he demonstrated in his own accomplishments. He influenced hundreds of young people through his spellbinding speeches and his inspirational writings to do the same.[11]

By the time he achieved professional success at Morehouse, Dr. Mays had become a highly respected, student-oriented educator, and Quiester and his classmates spoke of him with admiration in their dormitories. Regarding his students, Dr. Mays was best known for his many acts of kindness, which included paying school bills for struggling students, providing employment, buying suits and overcoats for them, and inviting students who could not travel home for Christmas to dinner at his home.[12] The compassion and concern he demonstrated were complemented by the life lessons he imparted and the high expectations he set for his students. He blended his personal experiences and knowledge in education, religion, and civil rights to inspire and motivate his students, while advancing the Morehouse tradition of educating socially conscious, exceptional young black men. Dr. Mays coined the term "Morehouse Mystique," which defined five principles that he expected all students to uphold: "academic excellence, the elocutionary arts, high moral values, social commitment, and belief in a higher power."[13]

He instilled a belief in his students that "Morehouse Men were distinctive in their talent and commitment to racial uplift,"[14] something Quiester took to heart and demonstrated later in his life. Dr. Mays used language in a unique way, crafting sayings and metaphors and incorporating quotations to ensure that his teachings could be easily remembered. He often said, "Here at Morehouse, we are not just producing doctors, lawyers, engineers, and preachers; we are turning out men."[15] Another saying was, "He who starts behind in the race of life must run faster or forever be behind."[16] For these reasons and many others, Quiester and his classmates both respected and feared Dr. Mays, as it seemed he walked on water. Quiester regarded him as a supreme individual who emphasized that success would not come from dreams but from hard work. He recalled that Dr. Mays preached confidence, preparedness, presentation, and pride, and he felt honored to be in his presence. Fortunately, Quiester met with him in a small group twice while attending Morehouse. He believed that Dr. Mays's persona and teachings left a lasting impression on him and he remembered his teachings for the rest of his life. As Quiester advanced in his career, he emulated several of Dr. Mays's characteristics and practices to influence and motivate his students.

One of the most significant impacts Dr. Mays had on his students was during his weekly chapel sessions. In these meetings, he addressed the student body on a range of topics, including "freedom and truth, love and justice, mercy and forgiveness, aspiration and motivation, perseverance and endurance, and reform and resistance."[17] Students were required to attend Chapel every first Tuesday of the month and every Sunday at 9:00 a.m. Of course, exceptions were made if needed, but students who missed too many of these chapel sessions would lose academic credit hours. It was clear to students early on that these meetings were a big deal, and they were treated as such. Seniors always occupied the front rows, not wanting to miss a thing, while freshmen had to sit in the balcony as they learned the ropes.

When speaking at Chapel, Dr. Mays always captivated his audience. He had complete control of his voice, and the words he spoke were enhanced by the passion with which he delivered his message. He talked about life, covering many serious topics. And at times, he would discuss proper eating habits, remind students not to put their elbows on the table, warn them against blowing their car horn, and advise them on how to treat a lady. In his chapel lectures, he made clear what he expected from his students. Occasionally, he invited his wife to speak or deans from the college. Each year, he hosted a Religious Emphasis Week and invited visiting ministers. Quiester found that he benefited from Dr. Mays's simple life lessons just as much as from the serious ones. He felt similarly about the guest speakers, as they all had unique experiences to share.

The words Dr. Mays spoke were structured to instill confidence and create high expectations in his students. He has been quoted as saying, "Morehouse can prepare you. If you make an A at Morehouse, you can make an A at Harvard. If you make a B at Morehouse, you can make a B at Oxford." As his graduates pursued professional and graduate education, he wrote letters to their deans to inquire about their performance, serving as a benchmark for the quality of education they had received at Morehouse. He also asked how his former students were doing and shared updates with his current students during Chapel as a source of encouragement and motivation.[18]

Dr. Mays excelled at maintaining complete control over the audience. He had a distinctive physical appearance, standing six feet tall, of a dark complexion, and with a full head of gray hair. If anything got out of hand during Chapel, he would stand on the stage and raise his hand to stop any unruliness. "It was as if God was raising his hand," Dean Craig recalled. There was only one occasion that he remembered when Dr. Mays was unable to control the crowd. One Tuesday in Chapel, a visiting pastor was delivering a serious religious sermon. As he got into it, as black pastors are known to do, he struck his hand on the podium, and his false teeth fell out. Without missing a beat, the pastor caught them and slipped them back into his mouth. The Chapel, however, erupted with hysterical laughter, and that day, even Dr. Mays could not stop the unruliness in his usual manner. He smiled, sat down, and lowered his mighty hand. "Dr. Mays was a brilliant man, a great speaker, and in that situation, he showed that he had a sense of humor," Dean Craig shared.

Similarly, Dr. Mays excelled in his administrative role as well. When World War II reduced enrollment at Morehouse because many college-aged men enlisted, he took matters into his own hands. Faced with declining enrollment, he was confronted with closing the school until the war ended. He feared that if Morehouse shut down, it might never reopen. As someone who confronted challenges directly, Dr. Mays devised an intelligent test for students and traveled across the country recruiting those too young to be drafted, including students as young as fourteen and fifteen years old. Through this initiative, Martin Luther King, Jr. found his way to Morehouse College during his teenage years.[19]

Inspired by Dr. Mays's Tuesday morning chapel teachings on "stewardship, responsibility, and engagement," as well as sayings like "Do whatever you do so well that no man living and no man yet unborn could do it better,"[20] a young Martin would often approach him after Chapel. Dr. Mays described their encounters. It was written that he said, "He would come up and ask me some questions about the speech. Sometimes he'd agree, sometimes he didn't. And I told him, 'Well, let's walk on down to my office and if there's nobody there, we'll talk properly.' Because I didn't give teachers preference over students, if a person came, I saw him. That was the democratic way that I dealt with my teachers and my students."[21] As Dr. Martin Luther King, Jr. rose to prominence as a civil rights leader, Dr. Mays remained close to him as his spiritual advisor and ultimately eulogized him on April 9, 1968, at Morehouse College.

Dr. Mays's life was a shining example of the lessons he taught his students about overcoming the oppressive conditions they faced as black folks in America. Thanks to his personal sense of urgency, he rose to international prominence. He excelled as an author, minister, teacher, civil rights advocate, orator, humanitarian, educator, and administrator, earning more than 250 awards for his contributions. His home state of South Carolina honored him later in life at the age of eighty-four when he received an honorary doctorate from the

University of South Carolina. Three years later, a portrait of him was displayed in the state capital. The final honor from his home state was the naming of an intersection as Mays Crossroads in Epworth, South Carolina, not far from where he was born. Dr. Mays viewed the honors bestowed upon him by South Carolina as a significant achievement, perhaps indicating that he was finally "understood and appreciated by the white southerner."[22]

Dean Craig felt fortunate to have attended Morehouse while Dr. Mays served as president. He saw Dr. Mays as a role model and found his lessons very powerful, particularly relevant for the times, and profoundly impactful. He carried those lessons with him throughout his life. He relied on the teachings of excellence and preparation as he pursued higher education and imparted these lessons to his students both as a professor and as a dean. Dr. Mays's messages were so strong that even though Quiester was occasionally distracted during part of his time at Morehouse, it was clear that he absorbed the principles of the Morehouse Mystique.

It was at Morehouse that Quiester developed an interest in pursuing a career in business and set his goal of securing a job in corporate America. Many of the young men at Morehouse were on the path to becoming ministers, doctors, dentists, and lawyers—professions chosen by their families. Teaching and preaching were the careers familiar to Quiester's family, and anything else was considered unusual. When he first entered Morehouse, he was thinking about becoming a pharmacist and returning to Montgomery, as there were only a few in the city at that time. His mother, on the other hand, dreamed of him becoming the next Reverend Ike. This was a reasonable thought, given that he was raised in Lilly Baptist Church, was a believer, that there were two ministers in the family: his papa and his brother Sam, and that he was attending Morehouse College, which was founded as a Baptist seminary.

Mrs. Craig had high hopes that her baby son would become a minister, and he helped plant that seed. One Sunday, Quiester arrived thirty minutes early for the Baptist Training Union Ministry, which taught church members about the tenets of the Baptist faith. With the church empty, he entered the pulpit and began to preach, making the sounds and movements he had so often observed during Sunday service, working up a sweat in the process. He was going for a while until he noticed a lady from the church watching him. Once he saw her, he jumped down from the pulpit. The lady informed Mrs. Craig about what she witnessed, and from that conversation, she got the idea that he would become a preacher. "Mama held on to that idea for a long time, but she soon realized that it was not the career path I would pursue," Dean Craig stated.

Quiester became knowledgeable about and interested in business as a profession by spending time at the Yates and Milton Drugstore, a black-owned establishment near the Morehouse and Clark College campuses. The drugstore featured an elegant soda fountain, where students from all the colleges gathered to hang out and eat hamburgers, especially on Sundays when only breakfast and a light lunch were served on campus in the early evening. It was there that he made friends with students from Clark College, Morris Brown, and Atlanta University. They introduced him to the *Atlanta Constitution*, the city's daily newspaper, which listed a wealth of advertisements for business careers. These advertisements and conversations with his friends sparked his interest in finance and economics. When the time came to declare his course of study during his sophomore year, he chose business and took a mixture of classes in business, economics, accounting, philosophy, and religion.

Quiester's interest in business was further stimulated when he met Jesse Blayton during his junior year in 1955 while taking his first accounting course. Blayton was an accounting professor at Morehouse and a prominent businessman in Atlanta. One of his ventures was a CPA firm that provided accounting services to companies and organizations within the African American community. In 1928, he became the fourth African American to earn the designation of

Certified Public Accountant (CPA) in the United States, and he was the first African American CPA in Georgia. Blayton became aware of the CPA profession while serving in World War I, when his officer encouraged him to study accounting. Regarding his decision to do so he later said, "There was nothing in my experience or the experience of anyone I knew to indicate that I could succeed in accounting or banking or business. There was absolutely nothing I could look forward to, but I went ahead anyway. I just decided that since I was an American, too, I ought to have the same chance as everybody else."[23]

Meeting Blayton was Quiester's first introduction to the CPA profession. Through Blayton, he learned about the exam that you had to pass to become a CPA, the significance of holding the CPA designation, the services that Blayton offered in the profession, and the critical role of CPAs to business transactions. Blayton allowed students to work at his CPA firm, where they gained valuable first-hand insights into the profession. He also inspired and encouraged many of his students to pursue accounting as a career, earning him the title of the "Dean of Negro Accountants."[24]

While he admired Blayton's accomplishments and regarded him as a role model and mentor, Quiester was not inspired to specialize in accounting during his time at Morehouse. From Blayton, Quiester also learned about the challenges of obtaining a CPA license and the limited career paths such as bookkeeping for small black-owned businesses. At that moment, he could not envision a future as a CPA based on what he heard. His interest in accounting developed later in his career. Nevertheless, meeting Blayton was valuable for Quiester, as it planted the seed for his understanding of what a CPA was. However, he was interested in a career in business and hoped that his education at Morehouse would pay off.

After several years of discussing job advertisements with his college friends at Milton and Yates Drugstore, Quiester set his sights on a job in corporate America. As he approached graduation from Morehouse, he began applying for positions advertised in the *Atlanta*

Constitution. From what he saw in the newspaper, he believed plenty of jobs were available for young men skilled in economics, accounting, and finance. After all, he and some of his classmates chose business as their majors largely because of those advertisements. It didn't take long before his optimism faded. "We had been reading the ads for some time," Dean Craig recalled, "so we were shocked when we started applying for those jobs and came to realize that those ads were not meant for us black students. Since we could buy the paper, we believed we had an equal chance. We were optimistic and naïve in that particular area, although we should not have been. I received a few calls for potential employment, but when the recruiters found out that Morehouse was an HBCU, that was the end of the inquiries."

What Quiester experienced was not at all uncommon. During the Jim Crow era, most African Americans who earned degrees in business disciplines found it difficult to secure jobs in their field within large corporate enterprises. They primarily worked in banking and insurance firms, which were the larger black-owned enterprises, and smaller black-owned retail and service businesses; taught business courses in segregated high schools and HBCUs; and sometimes found employment at Federal Government Agencies. In the spring of 1957, the year Quiester graduated, Morehouse College celebrated its ninetieth anniversary, and, in its self-evaluation, a list of professional positions held by former graduates was completed. Although many men had careers as educators, presidents of colleges, mechanics, farmers, bankers, insurance brokers, general managers of manufacturing companies, motel owners and operators, pharmacists, chemists, physicists, and mathematicians, the business ventures were mostly black-owned, and no one was catalogued as working in business and industry in any of the business disciplines.[25] Unfortunately, these career opportunities were similar for African American students, regardless of whether they received their business degree from an HBCU or a prominent traditionally white college or university.

The first breakthrough for African Americans in securing management careers in corporate America came in 1940 as a result of the rivalry between the two cola companies, Pepsi and Coke. But as you can see with Quiester's experience in securing employment in corporate America, by 1957, it had not taken root. Sales at Pepsi had stalled, and the company was going through its most troubled financial times.[26] To get Pepsi in a positive financial position, the company's president, Walter S. Mack, broke societal norms and devised a strategy to go after the African American market to boost sales. He understood that Pepsi was already the choice of African Americans because it provided more soda at the same cost as Coke (twelve ounces to Coke's six). In order to tap into the spending power of African Americans, which equaled about $10 billion at the time, Mack put together a sales team of three African Americans to execute his marketing strategy in 1940. The sales team eventually peaked at twelve members in 1951 and consequently broke more societal norms, when African Americans were portrayed for the first time in a positive light as "stylish, fun-loving, middle-class consumers, in advertisements in the black press drinking Pepsi living the American dream."[27]

Although the sales team achieved success for Pepsi, boosting sales by as much as 13 percent in market cities,[28] they experienced a great deal of humiliation in performing their duties. As they moved throughout the South, they were subject to Jim Crow laws that affected where they could sit on buses and trains as well as where they could access hotel facilities. The black salesmen were more educated than their white colleagues. They all had college degrees, but they were paid less, and they worked seven days a week, morning and night, for weeks on end. The most egregious humiliation occurred when Mack himself made an offensive remark at a bottler's convention in 1949, saying to his audience, which included some of his black sales force, "We're going to have to give Pepsi a little more status, a little more class—in other words, we're going to have to develop a way whereby it will no longer be known as a nigger drink."[29] The Pepsi experiment concluded when Mack departed from the company, leading the new leadership to shift the strategy toward the overseas market. All of the black salesmen left the company except for Harvey C. Russell, who, in 1962, became the first African American promoted to the position of vice president in a major corporation.[30] *Ebony* magazine tagged Russell as "the top Negro in American big business" while the Ku Klux Klan "mounted a vicious, though unsuccessful, boycott effort" against Pepsi.[31]

It was that environment that limited opportunities for Quiester and his classmates to join corporate America in 1957. Although he did not leave Morehouse with a corporate job, he left with something even more priceless: the teachings, discipline, and religious influence from his home life and the intellectual training and self-development he received at Lab High, which had been further enhanced through the observance, interactions, teachings, and influence of a very powerful man in Dr. Benjamin Mays. Dean Craig felt blessed to have spent four years under Dr. Mays's leadership. He remembered that the environment was "all about success."

CHAPTER 4

Atlanta University

While at Morehouse, Quiester matured into a young man and assumed responsibility for the important decisions in his life. Since he did not find employment after graduating, he decided to get his Master of Business Administration (MBA) from Atlanta University. He rationalized that if he got his MBA, he would be better qualified for his dream job in corporate America.

His parents agreed with his decision to pursue further education for two main reasons. First, he had been successful at Morehouse, and they felt comfortable with him continuing in the Atlanta University System. They knew he would be safe there and that he would be engaged in learning. Quiester applied, and he was accepted. The second reason for their approval was that he received an out-of-state graduate tuition grant from the state of Alabama to pay part of his tuition and fees. They appreciated the financial assistance, as did Quiester. It wasn't until later in his life that he fully understood the origins of the grant, characterizing it as "pacifying money."[1]

The out-of-state graduate tuition grants originated from a strategy created by state legislators in an attempt to live up to the equal part of the dual system of separate but equal higher education that existed legally across the Southern States until the 1954 landmark ruling *Brown v. Board of Education of Topeka.* Under this program, state legislators believed they could satisfy the black community by financially supporting their youth to obtain graduate and professional education at traditionally white colleges and universities outside of the Southern States or at private black colleges and universities: Atlanta University, Fisk University, and Meharry College in Tennessee; Tuskegee University in Alabama; Hampton University in Virginia; and Howard University in Washington, DC.[2] State legislators believed this approach was more economical than expanding academic programs at public black colleges to offer degrees beyond the bachelor's level. Little consideration was given to the costs and inconveniences that African Americans would face in leaving their home state to pursue graduate and professional degrees.

As Dean Craig regarded these graduate tuition grants as "pacifying money," so did the black leadership, who used them to defeat Jim Crow segregation in public accommodations. However, from their inception until their termination, they were used by African Americans to obtain higher education at traditionally white colleges and universities outside the South or at various programs offered at the private HBCUs. With his acceptance and funding secured, Quiester was ready to start the MBA program at Atlanta University in the fall of 1957.

To occupy his summer, he took part in a program sponsored by Morehouse College that provided work opportunities for students at different locations in the North, enabling them to earn money to help pay for their education. The summer of 1957 marked Quiester's third year participating in the program. The summer after his freshman year at Morehouse, he worked on a tobacco farm in Connecticut. Following his sophomore year, he worked in Rochester, New York, at Birdseye Frozen Food Company, where he loaded cooked food into a freezer and unloaded it once it was frozen.

With his newly earned Bachelor of Arts degree from the esteemed Morehouse College, he boarded the train alongside about one hundred freshmen and sophomores from Morehouse and headed back to the tobacco farm in Connecticut for his summer job. Dean Craig explained that decision, "As I grew into a young man, I took those summer jobs because I had outgrown the strict rules of the Craig household. I relished my freedom and no longer wanted to abide by Mama's rules. Therefore, I decided to head north instead of returning to Montgomery for my summer breaks."

Although tobacco is primarily recognized as a product of the Southern States, Quiester found himself working on a tobacco farm in Connecticut in pursuit of his personal freedom. It's an intriguing story: To compete with foreign markets after the Civil War, the U.S. Department of Agriculture sought farmers to cultivate a thin leaf of tobacco for use as the outer layer of cigars. Experiments in Florida yielded no results, but in 1899, W.C. Sturgis, a botanist in Connecticut, succeeded in growing the thin leaf tobacco plant. And by 1910, tobacco shade farms had become well established in the state. To address the seasonal labor shortage, the National Urban League connected Marcus Floyd, president of the Connecticut Tobacco Company, with John Hope, president of Morehouse College.[3] Drawing from his own experiences, Hope recognized the importance of working to fund one's education, as it was often the only way to attain it. He had worked in banquet halls in Providence, Rhode Island, to finance his education at Brown University.[4]

By the summer season of 1916, Hope arranged for the first group of Morehouse students to work on Connecticut tobacco shade farms during their summer breaks. To facilitate this arrangement, the corporate growers constructed residential buildings on their tobacco shade farms to accommodate students traveling north to work. A Morehouse dormitory was built on the border of Simsbury and Granby, ten miles northwest of Hartford, in 1936. Several notable African Americans worked on these tobacco shade farms, including Arthur Ashe, the first African American professional tennis player to achieve a number one worldwide ranking and win the men's singles title at Wimbledon and the United States Open; Mahalia Jackson, one of the most revered gospel singers; Hattie McDaniel, the first

African American to win an Academy Award for her role in *Gone with the Wind*; Thurgood Marshall, the first African American Supreme Court Justice; and Dr. Martin Luther King, Jr.[5] During his summers there, a young Martin led weekly religious gatherings while grappling with what he perceived to be a calling on his life to become a minister. It was on a Connecticut tobacco shade farm that he decided to answer that calling. He was quoted as saying, "I finally decided to accept the challenge to enter the ministry. I came to see that God had placed a responsibility upon my shoulders and the more I tried to escape it the more frustrated I would become."[6]

Dean Craig was not aware of the tobacco shade farm's significance in history, particularly concerning the African American notables who worked there as youths. However, he remembered that the work was extremely labor intensive. Temperatures could soar to 110 degrees Fahrenheit under those tents, and the workday was long, lasting from 7:00 a.m. to 5:00 p.m. The workers comprised a team of three: two pickers and one puller. Quiester served as a picker, which meant he had to carefully break the tobacco leaves off the stems, starting from the bottom up. Being tall made his job even more challenging, especially given the narrow space between the rows. The puller transported a basket along the tight rows to collect the tobacco leaves harvested by the two pickers. Each leaf that went into the basket had to be flawless, with no holes, tears, or blemishes. Workers had their pay docked for any damaged leaves that ended up in the basket. "To avoid losing pay, we got clever and buried the damaged leaves in the ground," Dean Craig confided.

Before heading to work each morning, the workers received what Quiester and his fellow workers referred to as the big three: bologna, peanut butter, and cheese, along with six slices of bread for their daily meals. They quickly learned that this food wasn't just breakfast. At first, they swore they wouldn't touch it, but by midday, the big three took on the allure of ribeye steak, smothered chicken, and lamb chops. They devoured it eagerly. They earned sixty-five cents an hour for day work, and after three weeks on the job, they were paid based on the amount they picked. "Getting paid for what we picked made us work like superheroes," Dean Craig shared with a laugh. "We would quit after making fifteen dollars in a given day. While the work was tough, the experience taught me teamwork, how to work quickly and intelligently, and how to avoid making the same mistakes."

Quiester also learned the art of managing money through his summer jobs. With the earnings from his first two summer jobs, he saved a little for spending and then bought a money order to send home to his mama in her name. When he returned South to school and wanted to access his savings, the Commander-in-Chief required him to justify how he intended to use the money. He offered reasons such as having grown taller, needing new pants, or requiring a religious suit. When she would not accommodate him, he called on the Chief Justice to intercede. Mrs. Craig then kept a record of every dollar she returned to him.

Quiester got smarter during his last summer on the tobacco shade farm. This time, he made the money order out in his name and sent it home in a self-addressed envelope. When he returned home, his mama said, "There are letters here addressed to you, and they are in your handwriting." While Quiester had strategized to keep his earnings, he still needed to prove to the Commander-in-Chief that he was not wasting his money. As his papa observed this exchange, he said to Quiester, "My boy just taught me something." Of all the lessons he learned during his summer work experiences, the most important one was his need for an education—a message his parents had emphasized to him and his siblings throughout their lives. After working at the tobacco shade farm that last summer, he looked forward to returning to Atlanta University to start working on his MBA, so he could once again pursue that corporate job.

Atlanta University was very familiar to Quiester given its proximity to Morehouse and its affiliation with the Atlanta University

System. He had spent a lot of time there while at Morehouse. There was only one dormitory, Ware Hall, located about half a mile from campus. Upon entering Ware Hall, one would find a large baby grand piano in the front lobby. The cafeteria was in the center of the building on the first floor, separating the female living quarters on one side from the male living quarters on the opposite side. As Quiester knew, there were numerous opportunities for friendships and camaraderie at Atlanta University. Several of his friends from Morehouse had also gone directly to graduate school there, so he already had some established connections. Being there full time allowed him to concentrate on his studies, make many new friends, and mature further as a young man. Although it was a small environment, by his own account, Atlanta University proved to be highly beneficial to his development.

Atlanta University was the first HBCU to establish graduate courses in economics and business administration, leading to a master's degree. To broaden its course offerings, the Atlanta University Graduate School of Business Administration was founded in 1946. The graduate school was started at a time when the city of Atlanta was ripe with opportunity. It was the largest market of African Americans in the southeast, with a population of 150,000 in 1940. The city had the largest black professional class in the southeast and, at the same time, it had a very large number of workers engaged in domestic service.[7]

Graduate courses in economics and business administration began at Atlanta University as a small program in 1929; however, its size did not hinder its contributions to the African American community. From the initial organization of the program until the mid-1940s, only thirty-five degrees were awarded, and twenty-nine of those graduates secured work in their respective fields. Among the thirty-five graduates, there were seven treasurers, business managers, and bursars of colleges; five accountants; five business owners; five teachers of economics and business; four serving in the army or listed as missing in action; two owners of newspapers or periodicals; two economists or executives in government agencies; two managers of housing projects; one manager of a community cooperative; one college registrar; and one whose status remains unknown. One thesis completed during that time supplied the research on non-cola beverages that led to the establishment of a flourishing bottling works company in at least three cities.[8]

Another success of Atlanta University's graduate studies in business was its strong connections with the Atlanta African American business community. The program was recognized for significantly enhancing black-owned businesses and enriching Atlanta's civic life, largely due to the leadership of Lorimer D. Milton and Jesse Blayton. Encouraged by Dr. W.E.B. Du Bois while he was a faculty member at Atlanta University, Blayton, Georgia's first CPA who taught accounting at Morehouse, helped establish the Graduate School of Business Administration to expand the range of courses available in the business disciplines. Du Bois's interest in business education and its relevance to the city dates back to 1899, when he coordinated a survey of black-owned businesses in Atlanta with the help of two Atlanta University students as part of his efforts to create a pathway to black economic empowerment and independence.[9] Du Bois was a staunch advocate for the higher education of black men and women and suggested they use their "passion, expertise, and knowledge" to uplift the black community economically, politically, and socially.[10]

The early twentieth century laid the foundation for a more robust type of entrepreneurial activity in Atlanta's black community. Most of it was attributed to the "passionate vision and untiring efforts"[11] of Heman E. Perry, who arrived in Atlanta penniless in 1908, just two years after the infamous Atlanta Race Riot. As a result of the Atlanta Race Riot, a new consciousness emerged within the black community, manifesting into a movement to consolidate the black business community in the city's northeastern sector along Auburn Avenue. Black leaders in Atlanta mounted a vigorous campaign to increase financial support and patronage of black-owned businesses to overcome the economic disadvantage prevalent among the African American community during that time.[12]

Between 1913 and 1924, Perry established eleven businesses in Atlanta,[13] drawing entirely on the economic resourcefulness of the black community.[14] The most valued enterprise in his portfolio was the Standard Life Insurance Company, the first black-owned firm to sell only ordinary life insurance and the third black-owned insurance company to achieve legal reserve status, joining Mississippi Life and the North Carolina Mutual Life Insurance Company.[15]

Between 1917 and 1925, Perry's eleven businesses operated at different times with an estimated value of around $11 million. In 1923, at their peak, it was reported that they had over 2,500 employees.[16] Perry even founded The Service Foundation to support colleges and universities that specialized in training black men and women in business disciplines for employment in black-owned businesses. He aimed to impact the economic lives of African Americans by replicating the Atlanta model in other Southern cities with large African American populations.[17]

As life would have it, though, Perry did not remain at the helm of his enterprises. By 1924, his portfolio of companies experienced serious financial difficulties, and by 1925 many of his businesses were in the hands of new owners. The intertwining of funds and transactions from the regulated Standard Life Insurance Company with his other companies proved unfortunate. The end result was that his prized enterprise, Standard Life, was ultimately absorbed into a smaller, white-owned insurance company after a series of complex negotiations and transactions.[18]

Black Atlantans who had invested in and believed in Perry were distressed by the downfall of Standard Life. They felt betrayed and believed he had handled their hard-earned investments irresponsibly. They also felt he drew unnecessary attention to himself by appearing in a *Forbes* magazine article in February 1924 titled "The Largest

Negro Commercial Enterprise in the World."[19] It was reported that in the article, Perry was described as "a man of humble origin who, by virtue of his uncanny vision, courage, and Napoleon-like leadership, is building a gigantic commercial institution whose very spirit is already beginning to revolutionize conditions for the Negro in the South."[20] The article also highlighted the white collar employment Standard Life "provided to black men and women as clerks, stenographers, bookkeepers, statisticians, accountants, and executives."[21]

There were several reasons cited for Perry's downfall, including a lack of support, given the racial climate, to remedy his business problems;[22] lack of access to capital to finance his business from the start; lack of management skill to complement his energy, resourcefulness, and abilities as an organizer and marketeer; an unwillingness to take the advice of others;[23] and of course bringing attention to himself by agreeing to be interviewed for the *Forbes* magazine article. Whatever the reason for Perry's downfall, his example inspired other African Americans, most notably Milton, Blayton, and their partner Clayton Yates, to establish businesses in Atlanta. Together in 1933, they purchased 75 percent of the stock of Citizens Trust Company, Perry's bank, and managed it to become the first black-owned bank to be a member of the Federal Reserve System.[24]

This partnership, along with their separate entrepreneurial interests, became an influential force in Atlanta's black business community, adding a fire insurance company, a bottling company, a nightclub, an accounting firm, a radio station, and a trade school to the local black economy.[25] Most of these businesses were concentrated on Auburn street, which, in 1956, *Fortune* magazine named "The Richest Negro Street in the World."[26] Given the strong presence of black-owned businesses in Atlanta during that time, it was only fitting that Atlanta University became the first HBCU to offer an MBA program. It remained the sole institution in the Southern States where African Americans could pursue an MBA until the mid-1960s under the dual system of separate but equal higher education.[27]

As business owners and civic leaders, Milton and Blayton had a vested interest in providing professional business training to the black community. These pioneers recognized the importance of expertise in business disciplines for launching, growing, and sustaining enterprises. They actively contributed to developing a robust, segregated economy for black residents in Atlanta, using their businesses as practical training grounds for students on the business machines of that era. They hired students as interns and welcomed graduates as young executives. Because of their example, many Atlanta University MBA graduates pursued entrepreneurship and started their own businesses in the city.

When Quiester enrolled at Atlanta University for the 1957–58 school year, the MBA program had grown substantially but still served only a small number of students. Forty-six students pursued MBAs that year—forty-one men and five women. Students seeking MBAs represented only 7 percent of the 699 students enrolled at the university. The students enrolled at Atlanta University that year came from twenty-three states, the District of Columbia, and eight foreign countries.[28] Ninety-seven percent of the students enrolled had completed their undergraduate studies at HBCUs; 2 percent at traditionally white institutions, and 1 percent at institutions of higher learning in foreign countries.[29]

One benefit Dean Craig fondly remembered about Atlanta University was the sense of community fostered by the small student population. Each day before class, the students gathered in the cafeteria for breakfast and spirited conversation. The topics they discussed typically revolved around their various fields of study, which led to engaging discussions. After finishing breakfast, they walked to class together. At the end of the day, they reconvened in the cafeteria for dinner and continued their spirited conversations.

The MBA program was led by Dr. Samuel Z. Westerfield, Jr., who served as dean of the Graduate School of Business Administration after Milton's retirement in 1955. Westerfield was also a professor of economics. He graduated from Dunbar High School in Washington, DC, a notable black liberal arts high school comparable in quality to Quiester's school, Lab High. He studied economics at Howard University and later earned an MA in 1949 and a PhD in economics in 1950, both from Harvard University. Before joining Atlanta University, he held positions as an economics professor at Howard University, West Virginia State College—a land-grant HBCU in Institute (now West Virginia State University)—and Lincoln University (Missouri), where he also chaired the Department of Economics and Business Administration. Additionally, he served as a visiting professor at Harvard's Graduate School of Business Administration (now Harvard Business School).[30]

The aim of Atlanta University's Graduate School of Business Administration during Quiester's enrollment was "to give thorough training in the fundamental principles which determine the conduct of business affairs for those who look forward to places of responsibility and management in business and in government."[31] There were five fields of study: Production offered two courses; Marketing offered three; Finance offered four; Control offered six accounting courses, a business mathematics course, and a business statistics course; and Management and Administration offered nine courses. There were fourteen courses offered in the Economics Department.[32] Again, Quiester pursued a course of study in general business and economics. He took several accounting courses and developed a stronger interest in the topic, along with the confidence that he could manage the subject matter. He also enrolled in money and banking, marketing, and management courses. Nevertheless, most of his credits were in economics, which was designated as his area of specialization.

Quiester quickly recognized that in his MBA studies, he was now playing in the "major leagues." The expectations for graduate students were significantly different from those he experienced as an undergraduate at Morehouse. To succeed in the MBA program, he quickly realized that he couldn't do it alone. He went down the hall and studied with his friends and classmates. In hindsight, he viewed those experiences as invaluable training in teamwork. Like at Morehouse, the professors were supportive, and when necessary, they would occasionally call him aside or tap him on the shoulder. They held office hours, and when he visited, they would simply chat.

Typically, it took a student two years to fulfill the requirements of the MBA program. Students who had not previously studied business subjects or whose previous studies were deemed insufficient were required to complete two years of coursework. However, students who had completed business courses at an accredited college and met Atlanta University's requirements could earn their MBA in one year.[33] Students enrolled for two years were required to complete thirty semester hours of business courses in their first year and twenty-one semester hours of business courses, plus nine hours of electives, in their second year. They were expected to select their subject matter specialization during the second year, and in their final semester, they had to complete a thesis on a topic related to their area of specialization. Also, administrators at the Graduate School of Business Administration aimed to assist their graduates with finding employment. While making no promises, the university's bulletin indicated that graduates had experienced little difficulty in securing "congenial employment."[34]

With the business courses he had taken at Morehouse, Quiester was able to complete the MBA program in one year, from August 1957 to August 1958. "To my own admission, in my first semester, I did not study as hard as I could have," he shared. "The same distractions I encountered as a student at Morehouse followed me to Atlanta University. I played intramural basketball during my first semester, but by my second semester, I realized that wasn't why I was there. Once again, I was confronted with choices, and I had already learned my lesson about choices at Morehouse. With choices, there are consequences."

By the second semester, a new level of maturity had set in for Quiester, so he quit basketball to focus on his studies. Another factor that motivated his change was his papa. He had been involved in a terrible accident while working on the railroad and underwent various surgeries but was never the same afterward. Realizing the severity of his condition, Quiester understood that his mother would need support in coping with the situation. Therefore, he shifted his focus, dedicated himself to his studies, and completed his thesis. Once he developed that serious persona, he maintained it throughout the rest of his life.

His thesis was titled "A Critical Analysis of the Recessions of 1945, 1949, and 1953." When it was time to defend it in front of four highly qualified faculty members, including his advisor Dr. Westerfield, he was shaking and extremely nervous. He managed to get through it successfully. As part of the MBA program, students were also required to take a comprehensive English proficiency test, which they needed to pass to earn their degree. While he passed the English proficiency test without any issues, it was on that test that he realized he could not spell the word meaningful. He spelled it "meaniful," and continued to do so until he learned a memorable lesson later in his educational pursuits.

With everything in order for his MBA graduation from Atlanta University, Quiester felt both happy and sad. His parents could not attend the ceremony due to his papa's condition. He was particularly upset that his mother would miss the cherished Atlanta University tradition of placing the hood on her graduate. In her absence, he asked Delores, a "friend who happened to be a girl," to perform the honors. She was a first-year student at Atlanta University pursuing a degree in social work.

After the graduation ceremony and the heartfelt goodbyes to the close-knit community that he had been part of for the past year, he returned home to be with his parents. His papa was growing weaker, and he could hear the concern in his mama's voice. So, he left Atlanta without a job. "When I got home, I found Papa in bed. I showed him my diploma, and he placed it under his pillow in his room. When his friends visited, he would pull out the diploma and share it with them. Papa was tough. I knew he cared. He never got out of that bed again," Dean Craig somberly shared.

The time leading up to and following graduation from Atlanta University was challenging for Quiester. What should have been a celebratory period was overshadowed by Mr. Craig's illness and Mrs. Craig's concern for her husband. This burden weighed heavily on him, and his concern was magnified because he had not yet determined his future. Fortunately, after just two weeks at home in Montgomery, he received a call from Dr. Westerfield, his advisor. He asked Quiester two questions: How far was he from Orangeburg, South Carolina, and what would he be doing the following week? As it happened, Dr. Westerfield had recommended him for a position as a professor, teaching business classes at South Carolina State College (now South Carolina State University), a land-grant HBCU in Orangeburg, South Carolina.

Quiester was pleased that Dr. Westerfield had thought of him, but teaching was not part of his plans. When he thought it over and rationalized why he called, he thought that Dr. Westerfield might have been impressed with his thesis presentation, particularly the conclusion. When he presented his thesis, he pointed out that the same policies had been repeated during each of the three recession years. In his concluding statement, he posed the question, "Why would they implement the same policies repeatedly?" Whatever the reason that prompted Dr. Westerfield's call—which was likely related to fulfilling the promise of helping graduates find "congenial employment" and building a pipeline of college professors in business disciplines at HBCUs—Quiester expressed his gratitude to Dr. Westerfield for his thoughtfulness and the referral, but he knew he was not interested in teaching. "Teaching was not my aspiration," Dean Craig confided. "I had applied for more corporate jobs before I left Atlanta, and I was hoping something would come through for me."

A few days later, he received a call from the chair of the business department at South Carolina State College, who extended him an opportunity to come down to Orangeburg for an interview. After some consideration, Quiester decided to go. After all, he had no other upcoming interviews or job offers to consider, and his pride was getting the better of him. This was especially true when the older adults in his church and community shared their opinions. They found it hard to understand that he had attended Morehouse College and Atlanta University, had two college degrees, but was without a job. Dean Craig stated, "Given all the circumstances, I felt I had to do something." So, he borrowed the family car and asked his friend Sankey to accompany him on the five-hour drive from Montgomery to Orangeburg, South Carolina. Upon arrival, he was welcomed by Archibald Brown, who was anxiously looking for someone to start the job immediately.

"Teaching was never something I dreamed of doing. I had not taken an education course in my life. I never envisioned myself as a teacher of students, but I was proud and confident. As a Morehouse Man, I was trained to believe I could achieve great things. So, when I was offered a position to teach at South Carolina State College for $350 a month, I accepted it. I often wondered what career path I might have taken if I'd stayed in Atlanta," Dean Craig concluded.

PART III

BECOMING QUIESTER

The members of the staff are: Mr. E. J. Daniels, Mrs. Carrie Ward, Mr. Archibald Brown, *Head of the Department;* and Mr. Quiester Craig.

Quiester Craig while on the faculty at Lincoln University (Missouri) from the 1959–60 to the 1968–69 school years. From left to right: 1960, 1965, and 1969.

CHAPTER 5

South Carolina State College

In the fall of 1958, Quiester Craig joined the business department at South Carolina State College. Although becoming a teacher was not part of his career plan, this move began a long and exceedingly productive career as an HBCU business school professor and dean.

South Carolina State College, located in the city of Orangeburg, sat on about eight square miles of rural land at the time of Quiester's arrival. In 1958, Orangeburg had a population of approximately 13,000, and student enrollment at the college totaled 1,860 students.[1] The college was situated in the black section of town. Quiester took the train from Montgomery to Orangeburg and arrived at a stop right by the school's entrance. The entrance consisted of a red brick archway, topped by a white arch with the words "State College" in large black letters. On the opposite side of the railroad tracks was a small strip mall with black-owned businesses, including a barbershop and several small retail stores. The campus was small, with several newer classrooms and residential buildings.

Underfunding had long been an issue at the college, contributing to a housing crisis in the Orangeburg black community. Almost 40 percent of the student population lived off-campus due to severe overcrowding in the campus dormitories.[2] With so many students residing off-campus, available housing for sale or rent was in short supply. The situation was so dire that just four years before Quiester's arrival, twenty-nine male and female faculty members lived in the dormitories alongside their students.[3] The housing crisis started with veterans returning from World War II; they were provided makeshift housing in the form of huts. Due to overcrowding, many veterans could not take advantage of the tuition benefits offered by the GI Bill.[4] The housing crisis was just one of several challenges faced by college administrators. Another issue was faculty salaries: They were lower than those at other HBCUs, which complicated efforts to hire and retain faculty.[5] This was likely why Mr. Brown was so eager to hire Quiester just before the start of the fall semester in 1958.

The underfunding that existed at South Carolina State College during that time was prevalent at all the black public colleges across all the Southern States. State public HBCUs were generally funded at only a fraction of that of traditionally white public institutions of higher learning. This was the case even though public HBCUs were given the responsibility to solve the illiteracy problem of the emancipated slaves who were prohibited by law from being taught to read or write for over a century up to the Emancipation Proclamation. The state of South Carolina enacted the first such literacy laws in 1740,[6] and all the Southern States followed suit.

Quiester lived in Nix Hall, a male faculty dormitory that was one of the newer buildings on campus, conveniently located near the football field. It featured a living space on the second floor and a community kitchen on the first. In addition, there was newly built housing for single female faculty nearby, along with accommodations for faculty with families located at the base of campus.

Nix Hall provided housing for twenty-four single male faculty members. It was constructed as part of a significant campus development project that included housing, classroom facilities, and other buildings,[7] and was completed just a few years before Quiester's arrival. The state legislature had allocated $3 million to improve the school's infrastructure. It was the most that had ever been spent on improvements since the school's founding in 1896.[8] This building boom occurred under the leadership of Governor James F. "Jimmy" Byrnes, who succeeded Strom Thurmond as governor of South Carolina after his election in 1950. Byrnes was a political powerhouse, having served in the state and federal government's legislative and executive branches, including a term on the U.S. Supreme Court.[9] The $3 million that was spent for improvements at South Carolina State College was done only as a means to hold off desegregation of higher education in the state, which was imminent based on actions by the African American community.

Finding the state tuition grants as an unacceptable means to pursue professional education and advanced degrees, starting in the 1930s, many lawsuits were filed by African American students seeking admission to traditionally white colleges and universities in their home states. The National Association for the Advancement of Colored People (NAACP), under the leadership of Charles Hamilton Houston and Thurgood Marshall, defended the students. The most notable lawsuit that the Maryland Supreme Court ruled in favor of the plaintiff was *Murray v. Pearson*. Significant lawsuits that the U.S. Supreme Court ruled favorable on for the plaintiff were *Missouri ex rel. Gaines v. Canada*; *Sipuel v. Board of Regents of the University of Oklahoma*; *Sweatt v. Painter* in Texas; and *McLaurin v. Oklahoma State Regents*. Each of these cases redefined "equal," to mean that states must provide the same legal education for black and white children within the borders of their states. These rulings were the first significant steps toward dismantling legal segregation and laid the groundwork for the landmark U.S. Supreme Court case *Brown v. Board of Education of Topeka*.

During the process of these lawsuits, Governor Byrnes rationalized that if he financed capital improvements, faculty salaries, and education beyond bachelor's degrees at South Carolina State College, segregated education in the state would prevail. Providing perspective to Governor Byrnes' beliefs, historian William C. Hine, a professor of history at South Carolina State College for forty years, wrote:

"The sixty-eight-year-old governor was confident almost to the point of arrogance that the separation of the races was so time tested and logical that the U.S. Supreme Court was all but certain to reject any challenge to segregation."[10] While the lawsuits won by the NAACP proved Byrnes wrong, the financial investment at the college was more than welcomed, as it was long overdue.

This was the social and political climate Quiester found himself in when he arrived at South Carolina State College in the fall of 1958. Despite this atmosphere, there was a strong sense of togetherness among the college administrators, faculty, and the black community. Everyone took immense pride in the school. Quiester appreciated the closeness that existed and how everyone collaborated for the common good. This spirit of cooperation made him feel at home, reminiscent of his upbringing in Montgomery and his college years in Atlanta. He lunched with his colleagues daily in an impressive faculty dining room constructed during the building boom. A lovely family-style meal was served, which he valued since he was living alone then.

He had a lasting memory of the warmth he felt within the South Carolina State College community. This warmth became a hallmark of HBCUs and contributed to their enduring legacy, as African Americans cultivated a strong sense of pride in their institutions. Their churches, black-owned businesses, schools, colleges, universities, sororities, fraternities, sports teams, and bands fostered goodwill within their communities and instilled hope in the entire race during the Jim Crow Era. This was particularly true for South Carolina State College. As historian Hines wrote: "No public institution in South Carolina has meant more to the state's African American residents than the school that became South Carolina State University . . . It was for seven decades the state's only public institution of higher education open to black people. . . . But because by law, South Carolina State could enroll and employ only black people, it became their college. They developed an affinity for it, they were proud of it, and they could exert a measure of control over it."[11] Black administrators could exert only "a measure of control" over their college since for the first seventy years of the school's existence, its board of trustees consisted solely of white men.[12]

As Quiester settled in, he had to come to terms with his new status in life as a college professor. He had little insight as to what would be expected of him as a teacher, so he was apprehensive about what he was getting into. He felt anxious and was scared stiff especially after he was assigned to teach courses in business law and finance. This was his first real job, and his only job offer, so, as he saw it, he had a lot riding on this opportunity. Although he was concerned about his ability to deliver in his new position, he accepted the challenge like a Morehouse Man was trained to do. He was fortunate to have a couple of other new, young faculty members, just like him. They supported each other, being that they were all in the same boat. After he received the books for the courses he would teach, he immediately got to work on developing an approach to present the material to his college students.

He described his first year of teaching as "no picnic." He found the job quite challenging, so much so that he questioned what he was doing. He was in a position for which he had not been formally trained, teaching subjects he didn't know much about. His knowledge of business law and finance was limited to what he had retained from his undergraduate and graduate studies. Meanwhile, he had books, a classroom, and a room full of students looking to him for knowledge that, in his mind, wasn't very deep at that point. "I had to read, study, and learn to plan the lessons I would teach in the classroom. There was a lot of self-development in teaching business courses at historically black colleges back then," Dean Craig recalled.

His approach to self-development was to concentrate on understanding the why and how of the subject matter he needed to teach—concepts he had learned during his time at Lab High. As he prepared, explaining the why to himself helped clarify the how. Before going in front of the classroom, Quiester needed to be ready to explain the material to others. Thus, he had to study thoroughly to present confidently. Many of the business school students were slightly younger than he was, with a few being older. When the students became aware of his age, he felt the need to assert himself to maintain control of the classroom. He realized that his presentation was crucial. Therefore, he drew on Dr. Mays's teachings of confidence, courage, and pride to enhance his delivery and manage the classroom effectively. During his first year, the easiest days were those when he felt prepared. As time passed and his anxiety lessened, he began to view his job more as a potential career opportunity, although he wasn't fully convinced just yet.

He did recognize, however, that he enjoyed teaching, the learning he had to do to prepare for it, and, even more importantly, the relationships he developed with his students. He noticed that his students depended on him, and he came to realize that he could have an impact on their lives. With a large portion of his students coming from rural areas and growing up on farms, he understood the significance of their desire for a college education. They were not much different from him in that respect. He also observed that his students were smart and talented; they had courage and drive and were very committed to furthering their education. Several of them planned to continue their business studies at Atlanta University, and he happily shared about his educational experiences there.

When Quiester was not teaching or studying to prepare for his classes, he kept track of what was happening back home in Montgomery and found time for social activities in and around town. Going to the movies was one social outlet he enjoyed. One evening, when he went to the Orangeburg movie theater in town to see *The Defiant Ones,* he was reminded of the social conditions in the South during that time. Living and working on an HBCU campus somewhat shielded him from that aspect of life. However, this movie served as a reminder, as did the protocols, with whites seated downstairs in the theater and blacks sitting upstairs in the balcony. The film illustrated the lack of unity in America at that time. The storyline followed two escaped convicts, one black and one white. Sidney Poitier portrayed the black convict, and Tony Curtis played the white convict. They were chained together and had to learn to get along to avoid capture. As the characters disagreed and fought while on their journey to mutual respect, the whites cheered for the white convict, while the blacks cheered for the black convict. After the movie ended, blacks were required to remain in the balcony until the whites left the theater.

Weekend trips to Columbia, the state's capital, offered another social activity for him. He, along with several colleagues, would occasionally travel there on weekends. Columbia was a larger and more sophisticated city than Orangeburg, making it a welcome change. "Leaving Orangeburg allowed us to observe African Americans living a more prosperous city life, which was inspirational," Dean Craig recalled. "We also enjoyed fun and stimulating activities at Claflin University, a private HBCU located next to South Carolina State."

For years, South Carolina State College was known for its dynamic football program within the Colored Intercollegiate Athletic Association, now called the Central Intercollegiate Athletic Association (CIAA). As a sports fan, Dean Craig attended games on weekends. He remembered watching a football player who would come to be known as David "Deacon" Jones, who was playing his first year of college football while Quiester was in his first year as a professor. Jones had exceptional talent in football and was one of the early black athletes to make it to the National Football League (NFL), later being drafted by the Los Angeles Rams. He achieved this distinction as a result of divine intervention. His talent was not widely recognized since black college sports were not covered in the white press. He was discovered by chance when two scouts for the Rams were reviewing the film of an opponent and noticed him outrunning the players they were scouting. They recommended him as a sleeper pick, and he became one of the finest pass rushers in the NFL.[13] "For a long time, a lot of great black talent went undiscovered," Dean Craig shared. "The same thing happened with blacks in business careers. Talent gets lost when the opportunity isn't available."

While in Orangeburg, Quiester took several road trips back to Montgomery to check on his papa. Knowing exactly when he should arrive, his mama was always waiting for him. As expected, the visits were filled with spirited conversations and, of course, his mama's delicious, high-cholesterol cooking. His papa's health—well, it continued to slip, so he traveled home as often as he could. On one of his drives back from Montgomery to Orangeburg, he met a stranger, and from this encounter, he recounted what he called a life-changing event.

It was around 11:00 p.m. on a cold, rainy Sunday night in the spring of 1959. He was traveling back from Montgomery to Orangeburg in his old 1948 Plymouth. He had bought this used car when he first moved to Orangeburg. The car quit on him on the highway in the middle of nowhere. He was closer to Augusta, Georgia, further away from Aiken, South Carolina, and a very long distance from Orangeburg. With Augusta being the closest, he decided to walk in that direction and ended up at a gas station. Using the telephone at the gas station, he called a friend in Orangeburg for help; however, his friend couldn't give him a ride. He explained that his tires were in poor condition and that he didn't want to risk driving in the rain. This left Quiester in a tough spot, so he lingered at the gas station, hoping for a miracle.

While waiting, he assessed the situation and determined that his best option was to walk to the nearest bus station in Aiken. Not quite ready to head out on foot, he decided to hang around the gas station a bit longer. As he chatted with the owner, the owner gained confidence in him and became interested in assisting him. When the next car pulled up to the gas station, heading in the right direction, the owner solicited a ride for him. The driver, an African American man traveling with his wife, declined to give Quiester a ride, explaining that there was no room in the car because his wife needed to stretch out in the back seat, and the front seat was needed for their belongings. Having no other options, he got a cup of coffee and set out on foot toward Aiken in the cold, rainy darkness of the Jim Crow South. "That was the first time in my life that I had a cup of black coffee without sugar," Dean Craig recalled. "It was cold, I was tired, and I was on foot. Unsweetened black coffee, which I would not usually drink, was my only comfort that evening," he shared with a laugh.

After about a mile into his walk, he noticed that the man and his wife were driving back toward him. Quiester felt a moment of happiness, thinking that the man had a change of heart. However, his brief joy turned to disappointment as the man slowly drove up beside him and quickly pulled away. Obviously, he considered the man's actions cold-hearted. He continued walking, and a half-hour later, a white man dressed like a farmer, husky in stature, and sporting a pleasant smile, pulled up in a pickup truck and offered him a ride. With no other options available, Quiester graciously accepted, though not without suspicion. Before getting into the truck, he quickly bent down, picked up a couple of rocks, and tucked them into his coat pocket as a safety precaution. As they traveled and talked, the farmer revealed that the gas station owner told him to look out for him alongside the highway and suggested he give him a ride to the Greyhound bus station in Aiken. When it was time for Quiester to exit the truck, he thanked the driver and offered him money for his assistance and kindness. The driver refused the money but asked him to promise to help someone else someday. He then drove off and continued on his way.

"From that day forth, the feeling of gratitude was crystalized in my life," Dean Craig shared. "I always remembered the man with his friendly smile who gave me a ride on that cold, rainy night when I was stranded. I also learned that sometimes in life, things happen that mean something in the particular area. For me, this was one of those times. That experience led me to commit to helping others, to honor the challenge presented to me. My only regret was that I never got the driver's name and contact information. I always wished I could have contacted him to thank him again."

Building on that experience, Quiester later adopted the gospel hymn made famous by Mahalia Jackson, "If I Can Help Somebody," as his favorite song. The main line in the song says that a person's life won't be in vain if they help somebody while they are here on earth. As Quiester progressed in his life, he honored that challenge and helped so many people in so many ways. After that ordeal, he made another commitment. He promised himself that he would never purchase another used car, something he stuck to for the rest of his life. After several more paychecks, he purchased a new 1958 Ford with a four-hundred horsepower engine. At the end of the summer of 1959, he packed up his new car and headed to Jefferson City, Missouri, where he had accepted a faculty position at Lincoln University, adding another $100 to his monthly pay.

CHAPTER 6

Lincoln University (Missouri)

Quiester Craig vividly remembered the call he received in July 1959 from Dr. Westerfield, his former advisor and dean at the Atlanta University Graduate School of Business Administration. At that time, he was back in Montgomery during South Carolina State College's summer break, helping his mama care for his papa. When Dr. Westerfield informed him that he had recommended him for two faculty positions in the business departments at Lincoln University in Missouri and West Virginia State College, Quiester was pleasantly surprised. Although he wasn't yet convinced about becoming a career professor, Dr. Westerfield educated him on the need for African Americans with MBAs and PhDs in the business disciplines to develop business education at HBCUs. At that time, they were exceedingly rare. Based on Dr. Westerfield's conversation, Quiester understood that his business school education, as well as that of PhDs in the business disciplines, was urgently needed to build business programs at HBCUs.

Hiring professors with doctorate degrees in all fields of study posed a challenge for HBCUs during this period, as few African Americans had obtained the credential in the first half of the twentieth century. Over seventy-five years, from 1876 to 1951, a total of 673 doctoral degrees were awarded to African Americans, with 292—or 43 percent—of those degrees conferred in an eight-year span between 1944 and 1951.[1] Doctoral programs at HBCUs were established after 1954, with Howard University being the first to confer a doctoral degree in 1957, followed by Atlanta University in 1968. Together, these universities awarded twenty-eight doctoral degrees in 1972, a number that grew to 75 by 1982. Additionally, three other HBCUs awarded a total of twelve doctoral degrees in 1982. The public HBCUs established their doctoral programs even later, with only two awarding their first doctorate degrees in 1982, while three others established new doctoral programs. Many of the doctoral programs offered by HBCUs focused on the education and biological science disciplines. In contrast, professional programs were established in the early 1900s, when HBCUs began training black doctors, dentists, lawyers, veterinarians, pharmacists, and ministers to serve the segregated black community.[2]

Due to those statistics, the demand for African American PhDs greatly exceeded the supply, creating fierce competition among HBCUs to hire and retain faculty with that credential. The shortage of PhDs benefited Quiester and made his MBA a valuable asset to HBCUs that were developing business programs, and Dr. Westerfield played a significant role in presenting him with opportunities. He was becoming Quiester's guardian angel by showing interest in him even though they were not in a formal mentor-mentee relationship. During their conversation, Dr. Westerfield encouraged him to consider a career as a business school professor.

With two new potential job opportunities, Quiester had a decision to make. He considered both options seriously. The first thing he did was look up Jefferson City on the map to find its location relative to Orangeburg. It was 900 miles northwest of Orangeburg. As an avid baseball fan, the next thing he did was to see how far Jefferson City was from Kansas City and St. Louis. Both cities were quite far from Jefferson City, but St. Louis's Busch Stadium was twenty miles closer, and the St. Louis Cardinals had a record of having signed one black player, Thomas Edison Alston, from Greensboro, North

Carolina. Quiester shared a love for baseball with his papa, and that love was solidified when he was a junior in high school and they went to see the Jacksonville Braves, the farm team of the Atlanta Braves. That year, Hank Aaron broke the color barrier in the South Atlantic League and earned League MVP honors. Conversely, West Virginia appealed to him because it was closer to Ohio, where his brother Ralph and sister Doll lived.

With Major League Baseball within reach in Missouri and proximity to two of his siblings as competing factors, Quiester had compelling reasons for leaving South Carolina State College after just one year. What ultimately persuaded him was his telephone interview with Cletus Stamper, the Chair of the Department of Economics and Business Administration at Lincoln University. Stamper piqued Quiester's interest when he outlined his plans for the business program. They were significantly more substantial than the plans at West Virginia State College and his current employer, South Carolina State College.

Although Dr. Westerfield had given Quiester sound advice on pursuing a career as an HBCU business school professor, he still was not thinking long term about his career when he accepted the position at Lincoln. However, he felt blessed for the opportunity presented to him and was eager to begin his new role. Nevertheless, by his own admission, his career plans lacked specificity, and he recognized that teaching would still be challenging for him since he had only one year of self-taught experience. Despite his concerns, he arrived at Lincoln University in Jefferson City, Missouri, the night before his first day of work in August 1959.

When Dean Craig arrived for the early morning faculty meeting at Page Library the next day, Charlene, the administrative staff member greeting the faculty, would not let him enter the building, and no reason was provided. She called Stamper, who came out and asked, "Are you Mr. Craig?" Quiester replied yes, and Stamper promptly welcomed him and escorted him to a large room in the library where the meeting was taking place. The entire college faculty was present, so he engaged immediately in meeting some of the faculty members. He was pleased to find that in some ways they were similar to the faculty and staff at South Carolina State College, Atlanta University, and Morehouse. They were supportive, friendly, and part of a close-knit community. After getting to know Charlene, he playfully teased her for years about the welcome she gave him on his first day at Lincoln. While she remained apologetic for her mistake, he never found out why she didn't think he was a faculty member.

As Quiester acclimated to Jefferson City and Lincoln University, he encountered a few surprises—some familiar and some different from what he experienced in Alabama, Georgia, and South Carolina. "In those states, black people received no respect, had to work harder, and had to fight for everything they earned," he shared. "I somehow thought that by moving so far north to Missouri, I was leaving all of that behind, but I soon realized that I was still in the South. That was one surprise about my new life in Jeff City."

Quiester received an early wake-up call during his first month in Jefferson City when he walked into a downtown drugstore and sat at a soda and ice cream fountain to order a malt milkshake. Time passed, and no one had attended to him. He soon realized he was being ignored. Initially, he thought it was just bad service, but then it dawned on him that he wasn't supposed to be sitting at the counter. Although he was no longer physically in Alabama, he was still socially in Alabama. He thought he was free from the Jim Crow South, but the reality was that he was still trapped there. This aspect of Jefferson City was very disappointing to him. Another surprise came when winter arrived. Jefferson City was quite hilly, and Lincoln's campus sat atop a hill overlooking the Missouri River. It was here that he experienced his very first snowstorm. Having grown up in Alabama and never living north of South Carolina, he was unaccustomed to the cold weather and driving on ice and snow. This was a new environment that Quiester had to learn to navigate.

His biggest surprise was that Lincoln University had both an integrated faculty and student body. This was different from what he expected because he thought he was coming to work at an HBCU in the traditional sense and had not anticipated the changes he encountered. "With all the surprises I faced when I arrived in Jeff City, I realized that I hadn't done my homework in the particular area," Dean Craig shared with a laugh.

Having an integrated faculty and student body was a significant shift from the original resolution adopted by Lincoln University's founders. The idea of a school for freed slaves in Missouri came from Lieutenants Richard Baxter Foster and Aron M. Adamson, who requested to lead colored troops during the Civil War. Both the officers and the enlisted men of the 62nd and 65th United States Colored Infantries made small yet meaningful contributions, collectively raising $6,000 in seed funding to establish Lincoln Institute in 1866, which was later renamed Lincoln University and reorganized into a land-grant college. The enlisted men, many whom were slaves, could barely sign their names on the resolution, having been denied, by law, the privilege of learning to read and write as children.[3] Even with their limited learning, they understood the necessity for and urgency of educating the black race, and they contributed their earnings as soldiers in the Civil War to help make it happen.

The integration at Lincoln University resulted from the legal efforts of the NAACP, initiated by Charles Hamilton Houston in the early 1930s and continued by Thurgood Marshall. After successfully securing the right for African Americans to pursue graduate and professional education at public white colleges and universities in their home states during a time when such education was not accessible at black public colleges, Marshall led the next strategy: using the courts to obtain better elementary and secondary educational opportunities for African American children. Lawsuits were filed, with the NAACP's support, by brave African Americans from five communities to challenge the status quo through the courts. The most notable lawsuits included *Briggs v. Elliott* of Clarendon County, South Carolina; *Davis v. County School Board of Prince Edward County* of Farmville, Virginia; *Bulah v. Gebhart* and *Belton v. Gebhart* of Wilmington County, Delaware; *Bolling v. Sharpe* of the District of Columbia; and *Brown v. Board of Education of Topeka*, in Kansas. All of these lawsuits were combined into the landmark Supreme Court case *Brown et al. v. Board of Education of Topeka* in 1954, which ruled that separating children in public schools based on race was unconstitutional and marked the end of legalized racial segregation in all of the nation's schools and in public accommodations.[4]

In anticipation of changing times and prior to the *Brown* decision, Missouri, along with Maryland, West Virginia, Oklahoma, and the District of Columbia, opened their traditionally white public colleges and universities to black students. Additionally, white students began to enroll in public black colleges in five states—Delaware, Maryland, Kentucky, West Virginia, and Missouri.[5] Two months following the *Brown* decision, Missouri's Attorney General made it official when he announced that "the state's school segregation laws were null and void."[6] In turn, the Lincoln University Board of Curators announced that "all persons, regardless of race or creed would be accommodated at the beginning of the summer session."[7]

With this announcement, integration took place at Lincoln University in a manner contrary to what had been expected. White students enrolled in large numbers at the historically black Lincoln University, partly due to the closure of the city's public junior college by the Jefferson City school board.[8] It was these factors that contributed to Dean Craig's surprise of the racial makeup of Lincoln University upon his arrival. Years later, in 1999, an article by Arlene Levinson in the *Washington Post* shared reflections on Lincoln's integration from African American graduates Hazel Birth, a retired guidance counselor living in Minneapolis from the class of 1954, and Adrienne Hoard, class of 1970 and a fine arts and art education professor at the University of Missouri.[9]

Birth recalled, "That summer we had an influx . . . and the complexion of the university was changed overnight with white women arriving in shorts, smoking, shattering Lincoln's then strict rules. Faculty were silent . . . It was like they were almost afraid to offend them. Lincoln was going to hell in a handbasket."[10]

Levinson reported that in the early years of integration, students mingled freely in social activities. White students joined black students to integrate Jefferson City's bowling alleys, movie theaters, restaurants, and the Missouri Hotel. Additionally, the emergence of activism on campus marked a shift from the "obedience and respect for authority" that students had been conditioned to uphold throughout Lincoln's history. Activism for civil rights led to student demands for better cafeteria food, improved dormitory conditions, lower prices at the campus bookstore, keys for women to access their dormitories, and a more relaxed dress code, allowing students to wear shorts to class. Hoard commented, "It was new. In the '60s, people were more open to doing the uncomfortable . . . but it did not last. Society is still segregated," she said. Levinson reported, "The '60s also brought chaos to Lincoln. A fire during a protest in 1969 gutted the student union." Of that incident, Levinson reported, "'We shall overcome' dissolved into 'You go your way, I'll go mine.'"[11]

There were both advantages and disadvantages for the white and black communities due to Lincoln's integration. Integration provided white residents of Jefferson City and its surrounding communities access to a public college that was much closer to their communities since the University of Missouri was thirty miles from the state's capital city. Lincoln also offered lower costs than the University of Missouri. In 1957, tuition and fees at Lincoln University were $600 compared to $1,300 at the University of Missouri.[12]

From the perspective of Lincoln's administrative team, the integration presented an opportunity to secure additional funding for essential program development and capital improvements while also diversifying the faculty by potentially hiring more PhDs.

Unfortunately for Lincoln, full integration subjected its Schools of Law and Journalism to scrutiny, which, like the capital improvements that occurred at South Carolina State College, had been hastily established by state authorities to hold off desegregation. Due to budget constraints, the Lincoln University board decided to close the law school, requiring that students complete their studies at the University of Missouri. At the same time, the School of Journalism was restructured into the Department of Journalism. These adjustments saved an estimated $254,000, funds that were needed for more urgent expenses.[13]

The school's integration also transformed campus life and introduced cultural and social challenges at the university. Black students, primarily from St. Louis and Kansas City, lived on campus and formed close-knit communities through their involvement in student government, sororities and fraternities, and sports teams. Meanwhile, most white students were day and evening students that commuted and were hesitant to engage in sports and school activities. Black students participated on the football team and constituted the majority of the basketball team, while the golf team was entirely composed of white members. In the late fifties, both school administrators and coaches were optimistic, encouraging the participation of all students in school activities. However, by the mid-sixties, student division was commonplace and became an "understood tradition," leading to a saying that characterized Lincoln University as: "White by Day, Black by Night,"[14] according to Levinson's reporting.

Despite cultural differences and social challenges, white students leveraged the advantages offered by Lincoln University, which was evident in enrollment statistics. Before desegregation in 1954, enrollment totaled 776.[15] By 1958, total enrollment climbed to 1,184, with white students making up 32 percent.[16] This growth trend continued, and by 1959, the year Quiester joined the faculty, total enrollment had reached 1,487, increasing to 1,652 by 1965,[17] when white students became the majority population for a period from 1960 to 2017.[18] Many of the white students were evening students, and the demand for evening courses became the norm. By December 1957, enrollment in evening courses exceeded 200, with anticipated enrollment for the second semester expected to be over 250.[19] The impact of increased enrollment and the growing pressures to accommodate the rapidly changing student body were just some of the challenges the administration faced. There was also an urgent need for capital improvements for a student union, a stadium, dormitories, and additional parking.

While Quiester recognized the cultural and social norms influencing the student population, he was more focused on how the integrated university would affect his own life experience. After his time at the soda fountain, he wasn't exactly sure what to expect at the university. However, he was certain of one thing: His role at Lincoln had broadened his experience beyond the segregated world he was accustomed to. He shared, "I had always suspected that at some point, the changes that occurred in baseball would happen in society, but Lincoln's integration caught me by surprise. This was the first time in my life that I had to interact with whites in an up close, personal, and 'meaniful' way."

Quiester faced more than that concern as he approached his new role. Regarding his classroom performance, he was acutely aware of his limited experience as a teacher. At that time, he had only one year of self-taught experience, which made him anxious, and he realized that the trembling and shaking he experienced when starting at South Carolina State College had made the trip with him to Lincoln University. Another worry for him was that, although he was in his second job, he had yet to develop a career plan.

Setting aside all of his concerns, he focused on fulfilling his responsibilities both in the classroom and beyond. One of his early experiences at Lincoln University involved participating on a faculty committee tasked with addressing the parking issues stemming from the increased enrollment. With a significant proportion of the growing student population being commuters, there was a heightened demand for student parking. Due to an insufficient number of parking spaces, cars ended up parked in various locations, including in no-parking zones and along curbs, which made it challenging for drivers to navigate and maintain traffic flow. This situation led to considerable chaos for everyone, including the administrative staff, faculty, and students.

As a member of the parking committee, Quiester, along with other faculty members, was tasked with developing a plan to better manage the parking problem. After the rules they established were approved by the administration, they were put into effect. One of the rules stated that violators would be towed after three offenses. Quiester was an enforcer of the rules and was perfectly suited for the position because he had developed a philosophy regarding his responsibilities. He believed that if you accept a job, you'd better be prepared to do it. This was a part of his work ethic, which had developed over the years from his home upbringing, his church, his education, his summer "internships," his paper route, and of course, from his role as a Morehouse Man. This philosophy was part of his DNA.

When he joined Lincoln University, he shared an office with his colleagues in the business department. They were located on the second floor of Young Hall, which provided him with a direct view from his window of one of the problematic traffic areas. One day, he observed a car parked on the curb, blocking other cars from passing. Quiester left his office to take care of the situation. During his investigation, he learned that the car blocking traffic belonged to Dr. Dowdy, a professor who was also the head of the biology department. He was a mature faculty member and occupied a large office in Young Hall. Quiester approached him and asked if he would please cooperate with the rules of the parking committee and not park on the curb. He replied, "I will do my best."

On a second occasion, Quiester noticed his car parked on the same curb and confronted him again. This time, he said, "Could you please set an example for others by doing your part to resolve the parking issues?"

Dowdy replied, "When I have things to do, sometimes I cannot comply." The third time Quiester saw Dowdy's car blocking traffic, he had it towed. For that action, Quiester was called to President Dawson's office and reprimanded. When they spoke, he defended his actions, confirming that he followed the approved rules and towed the car after giving Dowdy two warnings. As the news spread about what he had done, his colleagues called him crazy.

As it turned out, Dr. William Wallace Dowdy, Jr. was a well-known and well-respected faculty member, and like many of Lincoln's instructors, he was a long-term employee. He gained international recognition for his research in ecology and entomology, bringing prestige to Lincoln University. As a research scientist, he developed and conducted experiments to study insects in their natural habitats and scheduled field trips for specific days of the week and at the same time each day, regardless of the weather, to collect specimens and take measurements. He diligently adhered to his schedule,[20] which likely led him to inadvertently violating parking rules, resulting in Quiester having his car towed. With guidance from his colleagues and a reprimand from the university president, Quiester learned an important lesson. He became more aware of the different roles people play in their professional lives and the levels of prestige they hold due to their responsibilities, positions, and accomplishments. By his own admission, this was a growth opportunity for him, and it helped shape how he balanced his responsibilities and actions with his relationships moving forward. Nevertheless, he remained steadfast in his beliefs about work ethic, and he continued to enforce the rules as they were written.

Regarding his work in the classroom, Quiester approached it with an open mind. After all, this was just his second job, and he had not yet settled on a career plan. Nevertheless, he was committed to his role at that time. When he joined the faculty, Lincoln had a solid business program. In the 1959–60 school year, the eight courses offered included Principles of Marketing; Fundamentals of Real Estate, Retail, and Insurance; Statistical Analysis; Business Law I & II; and Business Organization and Control.[21] As enrollment increased, Stamper led the expansion of the business program to meet students' needs. The business administration major, excluding accounting, grew from eight courses to thirteen over the span of ten years. In 1965, a course in corporate finance was added. Marketing management and three courses in human resource management were added in the 1969–70 school year.[22]

In response to the students' demands, two new majors—Secretarial Science and Accounting—were added to the Business Department in 1960. Prior to this change, secretarial training had been incorporated into the business education major since 1942, following the opening of job opportunities for blacks in this field during World War II. This addition provided three options for students interested in secretarial training: majors in Secretarial Science, Business Education, and a two-year certificate program in secretarial practice.[23]

To accommodate a major in accounting, the number of courses offered increased from three to nine. Six courses—Principles II, Intermediate II, Advanced Accounting II, Auditing, Cost Accounting, and Income Tax Procedure—were added to the original course offerings of Principles I, Intermediate I, and Advanced Accounting.[24] In 1963, Governmental Accounting was also added to the accounting program, bringing the total credit hours up to thirty.[25] In the 1967–68 school year, the accounting program became its own department, and later, Managerial Accounting and Consolidations were added to the course offerings.[26] As Lincoln University developed a comprehensive accounting program, Quiester's teaching load in accounting courses increased, leading him to ultimately discover his career path.

Although the curriculum was expanded to address student needs, the changing demographics at Lincoln University did not guarantee stability for the institution.[27] Funding continued to be limited despite the racially diverse student body. Like all historically black public colleges in the Southern States, Lincoln had always faced inadequate financing and was subject to the "personal predilections and political goals" of the state's political leaders.[28] The Missouri General Assembly, in an effort to undermine desegregation, had even proposed to close Lincoln, citing duplication of programs with the white state public institutions.[29]

The new demographics did, however, inspire support for Lincoln University within the broader community. Several editorials in local newspapers advocated for the university, marking a shift from a previous eight-decade streak of negative publicity. Editorials in the *Jefferson City Tribune* criticized the efforts to cut funding at Lincoln University and pointed out how little Lincoln's faculty earned, with some making less than unskilled laborers. Another editorial in December 1958, titled "Lincoln U's Requests Deserve Consideration," served as a plea to the Missouri Legislature to approve the university president's request for funding. These editorials signaled a new attitude toward the institution as the appeals for funding indicated that Lincoln now represented an investment for its citizens.[30]

Quiester's student population at Lincoln was very different from what it had been during his year at South Carolina State College. His students at Lincoln were primarily mature, working individuals, some of whom were married with families. Again, to his surprise, most of them were white. Coming from Montgomery, known as the Cradle of the Confederacy, he had few opportunities to develop relationships with white people, a situation that had been consistent throughout his life since he had only attended segregated black schools up to that point. Now, he found himself a professor in a classroom filled primarily with white students who were likely also experiencing for the first time in their lives being in such a personal setting with a black man. They all adapted without any issues. In other words, his experience mirrored what was depicted in a March 1958 article in *Ebony* magazine, which showcased Lincoln University as a model of integration by presenting readers with a photo spread of black and white students interacting freely in classrooms, activities, and organizations.[31] Dean Craig recalled, "The students were there to learn, and I was there to teach. They were serious about their education, with a strong willingness and desire to learn, and I could see they were counting on me. Just like at South Carolina State, I worked hard to be prepared and to earn their confidence, in the particular area."

When Quiester joined the department, there were six other faculty members on staff. The following year, the department went down to four and remained at that number for several years. Quiester developed close-knit relationships with his boss and colleagues in the Department of Economics and Business, including H. Monroe Purnell, T. Charles McKinney, and the department head, Cletus Stamper, whom he remembered as "personable, a good leader, patient, and tolerant." Each professor, including Stamper, taught a primary subject and filled in with courses from other disciplines as needed.

Purnell's primary responsibilities included teaching business education and secretarial training, and he frequently assisted with courses in economics and business administration as well. Quiester described Purnell as a "fun guy, a church guy who had the gift of singing." McKinney's main teaching duties were in economics while he pursued a doctorate in the subject. Consequently, Quiester became the primary instructor for the accounting courses. Initially, when the accounting program consisted of only three courses, he also helped teach several business administration and business law classes. Having accounting as his main area of responsibility was challenging for him, especially as the program expanded. He had only one year of self-taught teaching experience and had completed just a few accounting courses at Morehouse and Atlanta Universities.

When he first started teaching at Lincoln University, Quiester applied the same self-development techniques he had used to navigate his first year of teaching at South Carolina State College. Drawing on what he learned in his college accounting and business classes and his one year of teaching experience, along with his gift for retention, he focused on the how and why of the topics he was teaching to better understand and deliver the subject matter. This time, he implemented a new strategy since he was also teaching accounting courses. He worked through every problem in the chapter he was teaching before class, marking how far he had progressed with an X on the page for any given day. No matter what the students asked in class, he refrained from discussing topics for which he had not prepared. He did not allow his students to take him beyond the X simply because he was unprepared to teach that particular subject matter. "Preparation, patience, and pride" became his mantra at Lincoln University.

Recognizing the challenges he was having on the job, Quiester was determined to succeed. He reasoned that while his teaching skills were still developing, he possessed some intangibles that he could draw upon as well. Once again, he relied on the self-discipline he learned in the Craig household, the faith he nurtured in his church, the confidence he gained at Lab High, and the belief instilled in him about what he could achieve as a Morehouse Man. He grew up understanding that his opportunities were limited, and so far, that had proven true in his life. His dream job in corporate America had not come to fruition, and he had received only one job offer from the Internal Revenue Service during his first year at Lincoln. He declined that opportunity because he enjoyed teaching, but he still had not mapped out a clear career path. However, he understood he had two options: He could quit or keep pushing harder. He chose to keep pushing harder. As the years went by and the accounting program expanded, he was assigned more accounting classes to teach, and at that point, Quiester Craig came to a few important realizations.

One realization was that he enjoyed teaching accounting and other business subjects to both him and his students. He shared that he "found accounting fascinating." As the accounting program expanded, he taught a full load of accounting courses each semester and developed an interest in becoming an assistant professor and achieving tenure. To pursue these two goals, Quiester recognized that he needed an additional twenty hours of study in business disciplines. He also recognized that Lincoln needed expertise in accounting, and since he was already teaching all the accounting courses, gaining the additional twenty hours in that field just made sense. Looking back, Dean Craig confided, "At that point, I wasn't thinking long term about my career as I should have been. I was just trying to hold on to my job and gain tenure. My thoughts were focused on job security and trying to move beyond being tied to a year-to-year contract. Job security was important because during my time at Lincoln, I started my family."

To earn an additional twenty hours in accounting, Quiester started taking accounting courses at the University of Missouri in his spare time. He maintained a full teaching load, which consisted of twelve to fifteen hours, translating to four to five classes depending on the semester. The classes he taught varied each semester, requiring knowledge of a wide range of accounting topics. Some of his classes were scheduled during the day, while others took place in the evening, sometimes from 6:00 p.m. to 7:15 p.m. and from 7:15 p.m. to 8:50 p.m.

To achieve his goal, Quiester began "schedule hopping," planning his time around his full-time teaching obligations. While teaching daytime classes at Lincoln University, he enrolled in evening courses at the University of Missouri, and when he taught in the evenings at Lincoln University, he attended classes during the day at the University of Missouri. Over the course of two years, he completed two accounting courses. He enjoyed the classes he was taking, and as he spent more time there, his classmates in the accounting doctorate program began inviting him to lunch. Through their conversations, he became part of their supportive group, which consisted of about six members, with him being the only African American. They encouraged him to pursue the accounting PhD program and introduced him to Dr. Joseph Silvoso, a professor and the chair of the accounting department. Silvoso had been a long-time employee of the University of Missouri and was deeply engaged in the accounting profession, making significant contributions to the development of the university's accounting program.

As Quiester got to know Silvoso, he found him to be a friendly, kind-hearted person who welcomed him and encouraged him to take full advantage of the opportunities offered by the accounting program at the University of Missouri. He continued his part-time studies and schedule-hopped for the next six years. In the 1965–66 school year, he achieved his first goal by completing the twenty hours required to attain the title of Associate Professor and tenure, which allowed him to finally move beyond year-to-year contract negotiations.

The growth of the accounting program at Lincoln University worked to Quiester's advantage. As his understanding of accounting subject matter deepened as a result of his studies at the University of Missouri, his teaching performance improved. He grasped concepts that had previously troubled him and became more capable of presenting them with increased confidence. With the enhancement of his teaching, he developed a greater appreciation for both accounting and education, realizing that the subject matter was not as challenging as he had initially thought. His demeanor improved, as did his relationships with his students, leading to greater enjoyment in his role as a college professor. As an added bonus, he ended up in the PhD accounting program at the University of Missouri, where the faculty collaborated with him, demonstrating patience and understanding because he was a part-time candidate. They offered their full support. In reflection, Dean Craig remembered the environment as "very supportive and positive" and noted that he was "challenged to strive for excellence" in every way throughout the program.

As it relates to excellence, the faculty at the University of Missouri focused on even small things. Quiester used the word "meaniful" in a writing assignment in his advanced auditing course. Silvoso was his professor, and he also happened to be the author of the auditing textbook used in the course. One day in class, he told Quiester that he made a meaningful score on an assignment, and he threw the dictionary at him. He then asked him to look up the word "meaniful," but Dean Craig could not find the word, as he spelled it, in the dictionary. When Dr. Silvoso revealed the correct spelling to him, he felt ashamed, and it was duly noted. "'Meaningful' was a word I never misspelled again," Quiester shared. "The learning I took from that experience was an understanding of the need to always strive for perfection."

During his time at the University of Missouri, Quiester also learned a great deal about his work in comparison to others in the accounting field, and he applied that knowledge toward his professional development and that of his students. It was there that he encountered other college accounting instructors who were not teaching as many different accounting subjects as he was. Generally, he taught eight different accounting courses each year, leading four different accounting classes each semester as the primary instructor. He also gained valuable insights into the accounting profession beyond what he had learned from Jesse Blayton, Georgia's first African American CPA, while at Morehouse College and Atlanta University. Several of his classmates in the PhD program were CPAs who had worked for large CPA firms. Most of the faculty at the University of Missouri were CPAs with PhDs in accounting, and like Silvoso, were influential within the profession.

Quiester's exposure to the PhD program broadened his understanding of career paths for CPAs, as he learned about the Big Eight accounting firms and their roles in business. This new knowledge was an eye-opener for him, extending well beyond the professions of "teach, preach, and bury," which were most familiar to him as a young boy growing up in Montgomery. He absorbed everything he was exposed to at the University of Missouri and took what he learned back to his classroom, introducing the CPA exam as an option for his accounting students at Lincoln University. His students worked hard and several passed it after leaving Lincoln University, and they reached out to let him know.

In addition to enhancing Quiester's knowledge, the expanded business and accounting programs at Lincoln University also paid dividends to its students, and employers. Graduates not only became CPAs, but they capitalized on opportunities in a variety of fields. By the late 1960s, recruiters from major corporations and governmental entities were looking for business administration and accounting majors for career opportunities across a broad geographic area. Recruiter schedules were placed in the school newspaper for entities such as IBM, Ford Motor Company, Ford Motor Credit Company, Mobil Oil Company, the U.S. Department of Agriculture, and the Internal Revenue Service, to name a few.[32] Even the American Institute of Certified Public Accountants (AICPA) advertised in the *Lincoln Clarion* with a large eye-catching advertisement entitled "Where are the black CPAs?" explaining the status of the profession and its recruitment strategy going forward.[33] Little did they know that while Lincoln University was an HBCU, it had very few black accounting students at that time.

During Quiester's time at Lincoln, Stamper managed the department through a period of growth and received a fair amount of media attention publicizing the department's accomplishments. By 1970, the Department of Economics and Business Administration was the largest on campus, boasting an enrollment of 503 students, representing 22 percent of the total university enrollment.[34] *Jet* magazine featured Stamper in a December 1970 interview, where he attributed the growth trend to "the structure of today's society." *Jet* magazine quoted Stamper as saying, "It is not too surprising that we should have such a large number of students as compared to some other departments on campus. We live in a business-oriented society, and the socio-economic background of our students has a strong influence on their major field selection."[35] Being a black magazine, *Jet*, like the AICPA, recognized Lincoln University as an HBCU but perhaps had little knowledge that its business program had few African American students.

Despite assumptions about the demographics of the student population, Cletus Stamper, Quiester Craig, and their colleagues made significant contributions to business education at an HBCU during that time. In 1970, Stamper critiqued the department in a newspaper article in the *Jefferson City Post Tribune*. He outlined the program's impact on its students: "Our graduates have written a whole new chapter of success stories. Many hold high positions in state and local government and run their own businesses. Some of the most successful real estate brokers in Jefferson City prepared for the real estate business by taking courses in our department. Our past graduates usually occupy middle management positions when they begin their occupation. Graduates from the department can expect starting salaries between $7,500 and $10,000 per year."[36] With employment opportunities and career success as positive outcomes, Stamper and his team expanded and restructured the department to achieve favorable results for its students.

During the process of expanding and restructuring the Department of Economics and Business Administration at Lincoln University, with accounting as his primary focus, Quiester continued to pursue his PhD in accounting and noticed that many people "washed out of the program." This observation made him somewhat anxious. So, he sought out the requirements for CPA certification in Missouri, discovering that his MBA qualified him to sit for the CPA exam. While considering his options, he concluded that taking the CPA exam was a much shorter path than the PhD to obtaining his professional credentials, which he referred to as his "union cards." In his view, completing his PhD in accounting as a part-time student was a much longer endeavor. He discussed his plan with his advisor, who strongly recommended that he finish his PhD first, then pursue his CPA certification. Despite making significant progress toward his PhD, Quiester chose to disregard his advisor's advice and take the CPA exam first. His reasoning was that by taking the shorter path, he would at least have one union card and not be at the mercy of the PhD process.

Quiester set his goal and executed his plan quietly. He secured several old CPA exams and got busy studying them. After months of studying and feeling comfortable with his progress, he decided it was time to take a shot at sitting for the CPA exam. To further prepare, he purchased the *Journal of Accountancy*, the trade magazine for the accounting profession. It projected the topics that would be on the upcoming CPA exam. "The projection included the topic of trust and estates; however, my research revealed that this topic was rarely on the exam. So, I decided not to study it," Dean Craig confided.

The CPA exam was administered at the Gateway Hotel in St. Louis, Missouri that year. When he showed up at the hotel, he was stopped at the door. He said to the gatekeepers, "I am here to take the CPA exam." As he handed them his admission slip, people observing his entry started to laugh. As he entered the room, he saw that it was filled with one hundred or so folks. He looked across the crowd and did not see anyone else who looked like him. Being the only African American, he stood out. He found a chair in the middle of the room and sat down. People were snickering all around him. At 1:00 p.m. sharp they started to outline the rules for the first part of the exam, which was accounting practice.

During this time, the uniform CPA exam tested an accountants' aptitude in four subjects: accounting practice, accounting theory, business law, and auditing. The exam was conducted in five segments, comprising a total of 19.5 hours of testing, which began at 1:00 p.m. on Wednesday afternoon and concluded around 5:00 p.m. Friday evening. Various topics from the entire body of knowledge for each subject tested were included in the scope of the exam. Topics considered major to the profession were on the exam more frequently than topics that were considered minor, and they were rotated to cover the entire body of knowledge over a five-year cycle.[37] Individuals taking the CPA exam had a better chance of passing if they were fully prepared in the complete body of knowledge for the tested subjects. A score of 75 on any part was considered passing, and passing a minimum of two parts was required to retain any parts as completed.

Quiester had two mechanical pencils, one blue and one red. He felt confident and prepared to tackle the CPA exam until he reached the first question in the accounting practice section. It dealt with trusts and estates, the very topic he assumed would not appear on the exam and chose not to study. To make matters worse, he wasted too much time trying to answer that question, causing him to forgo answering the last question in the accounting practice section due to a lack of time. What happened on Wednesday diminished his confidence and affected him as he approached Thursday and Friday, when he would take the remaining four parts. During that time, less than 15 percent of the candidates taking the CPA exam passed. So, all Quiester Craig could do was hope for the best.

As he understood it, his future as a CPA would now be determined by the size and shape of the envelope he would receive several months later from the AICPA, the membership organization for the profession that administered the exam. If he received a small, longer envelope in the mail, that was an indication that he had passed. A large envelope from the AICPA would have an application to apply to retake the exam.

With the CPA exam behind him, Quiester got right back to work on his PhD. Being busy with teaching and his part-time studies, the exam was no longer at the forefront of his mind until the day he received a large envelope in the mail from the AICPA. As he looked at the envelope, he had an aching feeling in the bottom of his stomach, as if a rock had hit it. He sat down for ten minutes, staring at the unopened envelope. He then said to himself, "Craig, you are a Morehouse Man," which is something he said when he needed a push to survive. He mustered up his energy, opened the envelope, and discovered that he passed three parts: Auditing, Law, and Theory. His score on accounting practice was a 63, just twelve points short of a passing grade. Quiester embraced the good news; three parts were completed and one part to conquer.

Eager to get accounting practice out of the way, he set his sights on the next CPA exam date while continuing his PhD studies and managing his teaching load. This time, he became an expert in trust and estates, and he dared the AICPA to have it on the exam. Months later, when he received the small envelope in the mail, he opened it right away, and he was ecstatic. He had earned his first union card and could now identify as a CPA in the state of Missouri. Filled with excitement, he marched around his apartment in celebration.

Quiester shared his success with his family, Stamper, his colleagues, his friends at Lincoln University, and his PhD advisor, Dr. Eugene Zieha. They were all proud of his accomplishment. Individuals who passed the CPA exam in Missouri were listed in the local Jefferson City newspaper. When his classmates saw his name, they asked, "Is that our Kister?" "They were surprised because I kept it quiet while I worked on my goal to secure my first union card," Dean Craig shared with a laugh. "It was very gratifying to see my name in the newspaper: *Quiester Craig, Certified Public Accountant.*"

It wasn't unusual for Quiester's classmates to mispronounce his name. This happened all the time since his first name is uncommon. He confessed that, because his name was such a tongue twister for most people, he often thought about using his brother Ralph's name to avoid having to teach people how to pronounce his name. When asked about the origins of his first name, Dean Craig laughed and excitedly said, "I don't know! I don't know!" He had heard all kinds of wise tales about the origins of his name from family members.

One story suggested that someone was trying to spell Quincy. Of all the wise tales told, he considered the one about his paternal grandfather the most realistic. His grandfather, like many black folks in the old days, used initials as his name and went by Q.C. Before he was born, his family considered naming him after his grandfather, but his sister Doll insisted she couldn't have a brother with initials for a name. So, as the story goes, she came up with Quiester. Among all the family wise tales, he found Doll's story to be the most believable.

Quiester may have never known the true origins of his unique name, but he used it to signify a change in his life, both personally and professionally. Seeing his name in the newspaper with CPA at the end of it was significant for him. Knowing that CPAs hold the most prestigious credential in the accounting profession, it represented progress and achievement, and he began to see himself differently. "When I arrived in Jeff City, I was Baby Bro. While I was there, I became Quiester," he shared proudly.

The life lesson Quiester Craig learned while at Lincoln University was that "You can accomplish a lot if you apply yourself." He believed he was truly blessed for ending up there and for all that he was able to do while he was there. "I owe a great deal of gratitude to Dr. Westerfield," Dean Craig shared, "because just like he set me up with South Carolina State, I ended up in Jeff City at Lincoln University because of him."

CHAPTER 7

The CPA Profession

Quiester Craig earned his CPA in 1969, making him the second African American CPA in Missouri. His achievement was significant, especially when viewed in the context of the development and growth of the CPA profession itself, its importance as a foundational element that drives the economy, and the plight of the pioneering African Americans who obtained the CPA credential.

The CPA profession dates back to 1896 when the first Certified Public Accountants bill was passed in New York, called an act to Regulate the Profession of Public Accountants.[1] The legislation stipulated that only individuals who passed an exam could use the title of Certified Public Accountant. Candidates also had to be at least twenty-five years old with at least three years' experience in the office of an expert public accountant.[2] One year after the legislation was enacted, those who received CPA certificates formed the New York State Society of CPAs as a membership organization. Over time, every state in the Union recognized the profession, enacted regulatory laws similar to New York's, and established their own state society membership organizations[3] affiliated with the American Association of Public Accountants[4] (now the American Institute of CPAs, or AICPA), the national body representing certified public accountants across the United States.

The CPA profession started its rise with the post-Civil War economy when corporations proliferated, transferring ownership of companies to absentee stockholders. Since stockholders were not involved in the day-to-day management of the business, they needed assurance that the corporations they invested in were meeting their financial expectations. This assurance was provided through audits: external reviews of a corporation's financial statements by independent CPAs who attested to their accuracy. These audits strengthened investor confidence in the corporate entity, enabling businesses to raise capital to grow and evolve into the mammoth corporations that we know today.[5]

The early auditing work conducted in the United States was carried out by Scottish and English Chartered Accountants who settled there after the Civil War to oversee British interests. These pioneers included Edwin Guthrie, Arthur Young, James T. Anyon, John B. Niven, Ernest Reckitt, George Wilkinson, Arthur Lowes Dickinson, and George O. May. Notable Americans who established significant accounting firms in the late 1890s and during the first two decades of the 1900s were Alwin C. Ernst, Charles Waldo Haskins and Elijah Watt Sells, Robert H. Montgomery, and Arthur Andersen.[6]

These individuals played a crucial role in establishing the public accounting profession in the United States, which relies on the expertise of CPAs. By 1900, six public accounting firms had been founded, contributing to what became known as "The Big Eight": Arthur Andersen, Arthur Young, Coopers & Lybrand, Deloitte, Haskins & Sells, Ernst & Whinney, Peat Marwick Mitchell & Co., Price Waterhouse, and Touche Ross. Today, these firms are referred to as "The Big Four" due to mergers: Ernst & Young, Deloitte, KPMG, and PricewaterhouseCoopers. These firms dominate the public accounting industry, generating billions in revenue.

While the post-Civil War economy, supported by corporations needing regular audits, established the public accounting profession, its "survival and growth" stemmed from significant social and economic events in the decades that followed.[7] These events included the enactment of the first federal income tax laws in 1913 by the U.S. Congress,[8] the financial advice given to the U.S. government and manufacturers of wartime products during World War I,[9] and the complex nature of accounting systems and tax laws that developed in the 1920s and 1930s.[10] By 1933, the profession grew further due to a series of events that disrupted the economic system, including the 1929 stock market crash and fraudulent activities involving the New York Stock Exchange (NYSE) listed company, Kreuger and Toll.[11]

These events led to requirements for companies seeking a listing on the NYSE to submit an audit certificate prepared by an independent CPA alongside their financial statements. In further response to these disruptive events, the market for the public accounting profession expanded when Congress enacted the Securities Acts of 1933 and 1934, which were administered by a new government agency known as the Securities and Exchange Commission (SEC).[12] The 1940s and 1950s introduced new business opportunities for the CPA profession during World War II. By this time, the public accounting profession had established its position in the American economy with a "specified area of expertise, government-granted monopoly over this expertise, and strict rules of entry and conduct."[13]

By the end of the twentieth century, the CPA profession had grown to 400,000 CPAs, yet less than 1 percent were African Americans. This low representation stemmed from the profession's early exclusivity, mirroring the limitations of established fields like law and medicine, which favored wealthy white men. Candidates were required to pass the CPA exam and fulfill an experience requirement by working under a licensed CPA. Naturally, acquiring the necessary comprehensive accounting knowledge was essential for passing the CPA exam, which in its early years was largely gained through on-the-job training.

These entry requirements for the profession, especially the experience needed under a licensed CPA, created barriers to entry for African Americans. For much of the twentieth century, very few white employers would hire and train African Americans to become CPAs. Fortunately, due to their ingenuity and determination, African Americans were able to overcome these obstacles during the Jim Crow era to become CPAs, but not in significant numbers. By 1965, there were only 103 CPA-credentialed African Americans: five in the 1920s, four in the 1930s, thirteen in the 1940s, thirty-six in the 1950s, and forty-five up to 1965.[14]

Three of the first five African American CPAs overcame the experience barrier by taking the CPA exam in states that had not yet enacted laws requiring work experience under a CPA. John W. Cromwell, Jr. traveled from his home in Washington, DC, to take the exam in New Hampshire, and in 1921, he became the first African American CPA in the nation. Arthur J. Wilson obtained his CPA license in 1923 in Illinois, and Jesse B. Blayton, Sr. earned his in Georgia in 1928. These men were fortunate to finish their CPA exam when they did, as finding employment under a licensed CPA was extremely difficult, though not impossible. Wilmer F. Lucas successfully found employment in New York City with Daniel L. Levy & Company, and in 1929, he became the fifth African American CPA in the nation.[15]

Determined to obtain the CPA credential, Chauncey L. Christian, who became the third African American CPA in the nation, employed a different strategy to sit for the CPA exam after studying accounting through a correspondence course. Since Kentucky did not permit African Americans to take the CPA exam, he utilized his mixed heritage to navigate this obstacle. Acting on a friend's advice, Christian submitted his application to take it on the latest possible day to evade a background check. On the day of the exam, he concentrated less on the test itself and more on whether the monitors would recognize him as an African American, given his nearly white complexion. Christian was one of seven out of fifty individuals who passed the CPA exam in Kentucky in 1926.[16]

With these five as the pioneers, more African Americans became aware of the profession, were inspired to pursue it, and received support from several of the first African American CPAs to fulfill the work experience requirement. Of the 103 African American CPAs in 1965, the largest concentration, at twenty-eight, was in Illinois.[17] During the Jim Crow era, African Americans seeking their CPA certification moved to Chicago, which had a thriving community of substantial black-owned businesses.[18] Wilson made it a point to assist them in meeting the experience requirement, including Mary T. Washington, who became the first African American woman CPA in the nation in 1943.[19] Once she obtained her CPA, Washington was dedicated to helping others fulfill their work experience requirements as well. By 1965, New York State had a total of sixteen African American CPAs, the second highest in the nation.[20] In the late 1930s, Lucas partnered with CPA Alfred Tucker to establish Lucas, Tucker & Co., the first black-owned CPA firm in New York, which served as a training ground for many aspiring CPAs in that state.[21]

Educators like Blayton, who taught accounting to Quiester Craig at Morehouse College and Atlanta University, and Orlando C. Thornton, an accounting professor at Howard University, encouraged students to further their studies at predominantly white institutions with more comprehensive accounting programs and make it their goal to become CPAs. Blayton inspired many students to pursue their CPAs, earning him the title of "Dean of Negro Accountants."[22] Many students relocated hundreds of miles from their homes to attend colleges and universities, aiming to improve the accounting education they received at their respective HBCUs. Further education was necessary because the curriculums at HBCUs were not fully developed, a consequence of the low participation of African Americans in the profession, and, of course, underfunding of their business programs. After obtaining a comprehensive education, many of these individuals traveled great distances to take the CPA exam and secure employment under an African American to fulfill the experience requirement. Once they earned their CPA certification, they faced exclusion from state membership societies for decades, which made it challenging to stay current with developments in the profession.

Many pioneering African American CPAs obtained their accounting education from top-tier, traditionally white colleges and universities outside the South. Since their training was classroom-based rather than on-the-job, they received a more robust education in accounting compared to many of their peers.[23] It wasn't until 1938 that New York State led the charge to elevate educational standards for the profession, aiming to enhance both its status and performance on the CPA exam. This change required every CPA candidate to graduate from an approved course of study at the collegiate level, in addition to holding an approved four-year high school degree. Eventually, all states raised their educational standards, though not quickly. As late as 1945, the national organization's Committee on Education continued to recommend that all candidates have at least a high school education.[24]

The early African American CPAs pursued the CPA profession despite the obstacles and challenges they encountered. They applied their knowledge and skills to uplift the black community. Although denied employment after passing a test administered by the Internal Revenue Service, Wilson became an expert tax preparer and was able to help many small black business owners reduce their tax liability and increase their disposable income. Due to his expertise in tax law, he was recognized for helping to expand the black middle class in Chicago.[25]

Blayton's accounting expertise proved invaluable during the Civil Rights Movement, as he collaborated with Dr. King's lawyers to address a felony tax evasion charge brought by the State of Alabama, marking the first such charge in the state's history. Blayton managed the situation efficiently, demonstrating that the deposits into Dr. King's bank account were redeposited unspent funds from travel, not unreported income as claimed by the state. Thanks to Blayton's exceptional work, an all-white jury acquitted Dr. King, much to everyone's surprise. Additionally, Blayton utilized his skills to help raise funds for the Southern Christian Leadership Conference (SCLC) that Dr. King led, aiming to foster societal change.[26]

Unfortunately, the economic opportunities for the early African American CPAs sharply contrasted with the growth of the CPA profession for others. They operated their CPA practices in the evenings and on weekends while holding full-time jobs in black-owned businesses or government positions. They served businesses in the African American community that were primarily small retail and service establishments.[27] In contrast to the growth and development of the CPA profession, African American CPAs achieved their first breakthrough in business development when President Lyndon B. Johnson launched his War on Poverty initiative, which allocated significant funding to black community organizations and they could afford to access CPA services.[28]

Regarding employment at Big Eight firms, Robert E. Hill was the first African American who broke the color barrier and secured employment at Athur Young. Hill was an avid reader who developed an interest in accounting as he stumbled across an accounting textbook while browsing the shelves in a bookstore. Shortly thereafter, he relocated from Kansas City to Los Angeles and began studying accounting at Los Angeles City College, followed by the University of California, Los Angeles. As graduation approached, Hill was encouraged by his classmates to apply for positions at Big Eight accounting firms. Although he was not very familiar with the field, he knew that Big Eight firms typically did not hire African Americans. Nevertheless, he wanted to become a CPA, and even though he was a top student, he quickly noticed a change in the recruiters' demeanors when he arrived for his interviews.[29]

Some of the recruiters he met with were more candid than others. Two revealed their surprise at interviewing an African American, while another acknowledged that his firm was not ready for integration. The representative from Arthur Young shared that his firm had not yet hired any African Americans, but he believed the time had come for them to do so. He promised Hill he would bring the issue up with his superiors; however, the only job offer Hill received was for a government position at the California State Tax Board. Naturally, he was disappointed, as his goal of becoming a CPA would be put on hold. When Hill's professor, Harold Simms, learned of his job-hunting experiences, he was outraged and reconsidered whether he even wanted to continue a career in the profession. Hill never discovered if Simms's anger influenced Arthur Young's decision to extend him an offer, but regardless, the recruiters agreed to hire him and finally integrate the firm.[30]

As Hill and a few other African American CPAs broke the color barrier in the mid-1960s, the AICPA held its first discussion about whether to formally integrate the profession in 1965. This effort likely responded to the Civil Rights Act of 1964 and all that transpired leading up to it. The pioneering work of Charles Hamilton Houston and Thurgood Marshall, which ended "legal" segregation in education with the landmark *Brown* decision in 1954, to the 1968 March on Washington, provided hope and inspired African Americans to mobilize and continue fighting for full citizenship. The 1964 Act legally ended segregation and discrimination based on race, color, religion, sex, or national origin, and Title VII prohibited employment discrimination on the same grounds.[31]

This was important legislation for the African American community, as it granted them full citizenship rights and opportunities to escape economic oppression, although they knew that resistance would persist. The attitudes, beliefs, and actions of people did not change overnight.

Despite the expectation of ongoing resistance, the new laws encouraged African Americans, including Quiester Craig, to explore new possibilities for themselves. These possibilities, which he had kept caged in his mind as a protective measure, suddenly surfaced. He wasn't entirely sure what these changes would mean for him personally, but he could at least sense that change was on the horizon. "Growing up in Montgomery, I understood the struggle well," he shared. "Although I was attending Morehouse during the Montgomery bus boycott, I recognized that the lack of black riders placed a significant economic burden on the city. From that experience, I understood the goal, recognized it wouldn't be easy, and I was determined not to give up."

When the March on Washington took place, Quiester was back in Montgomery during Lincoln University's summer break. He watched Dr. King deliver his famous "I Have a Dream" speech with a group of childhood friends and Lab High schoolmates at Theodore Chilson's home. Dean Craig recalled their feelings. "We all wondered, is this possible? Will this really happen? Will we truly be judged for our character rather than our skin color? There were many reasons for us to be skeptical, but we all felt hope and inspiration, though it was cautious hope and cautious inspiration."

He continued, "At that time, no one could have ever convinced me that I would accomplish what I did professionally. When you start off behind, it's hard to catch up. You have to make up ground and run harder, longer, and smarter. For that, I needed energy. My stubbornness also kept me from giving up. I was raised by Betty Craig, who put me in situations where I always felt I had a power stronger than myself, so I had faith. I needed to believe in myself."

Even against the backdrop of the 1960s Civil Rights Movement and the passage of the Civil Rights Act of 1964, making the decision to integrate the CPA profession was not an easy choice for its members. The discussion seemed somewhat one-sided when the issue was initially raised in 1965 by AICPA council member Hugh K. McKee from Alaska, who was white, born, raised, and educated in Mississippi, and a graduate of Ole Miss. Recognizing the implications of noncompliance with the new employment laws, McKee bravely suggested that the membership adopt the following resolution:[32]

"Whereas we recognize that most CPA firms have long since ceased unwarranted discriminatory practices, it still seems desirable that this Council go on record on that subject. It is Therefore Resolved that it is the consensus of this Council that there should be no discrimination because of race, creed, color, sex, or national origin in the employment practices of individuals or firms engaged in the practice of accounting."

McKee followed up his resolution with a speech addressing the expected pushback from his colleagues, urging them to pay attention to the historic events unfolding that clearly indicated the "winds of change were blowing." He encouraged his colleagues to act rather than wait to be forced into it. He expressed his conviction that the evidence of discrimination was evident, though challenging to prove or disprove, and referenced a quote to support his point: "To him who believes, no explanation is necessary; and to him who does not believe, no explanation is possible."[33]

In keeping with meeting protocols, the AICPA council president requested a motion to second McKee's resolution. He received none. Another member, Mr. Wallace, stated, "Mr. President, I think this is a matter of the individual firms in this area, and accordingly, I move that the motion be tabled." A member seconded Wallace's motion. It was then put to a vote. The motion was tabled, and the organization remained silent on the issue of discrimination for the next four years.[34]

Meanwhile, the struggle of African Americans for full citizenship and the resistance from those who opposed it persisted well into the late 1960s. More tragic events unfolded in 1965 with the assassination of Malcolm X, followed by Bloody Sunday. A glimmer of hope for some came with President Johnson's signing of the Voting Rights Act. The year 1968 was marked by sorrow, with the assassinations of presidential candidate Robert F. Kennedy and the anointed and revered leader of the Civil Rights Movement, Dr. Martin Luther King, Jr. These events led to civil disturbances across America's major cities. Once again, America found itself in turmoil, and social consciousness reached unprecedented levels. Many institutions reflected on their practices, just as McKee had urged the AICPA to do four years earlier and concluded that the time for change had arrived. This time, the public accounting profession also stood ready for change.

In October 1968, the topics of discrimination and integration arose once again at the AICPA Council meeting. The discussion was led by President Ralph Kent along with a Committee on Recruitment from Minority Groups, which included committee chair Edwin R. Lang, a recruiting partner for Haskins & Sells, as well as ten other members. Five committee members were African American, including Robert E. Hill, Lincoln Harrison from Louisiana, and Bert N. Mitchell from New York. All of these men faced significant challenges to earn their CPA, ranging from being barred from the examination room due to segregation laws to continual employment rejections despite having the necessary credentials.[35]

After a period of study, the Committee on Recruitment from Minority Groups developed a resolution that Chairman Lang presented to the AICPA Council during its May 1969 meeting. In his presentation, Lang emphasized the necessity for the organization to take a stand against discrimination by highlighting the conditions that excluded minorities from the profession. Voluntary compliance with the Civil Rights Act of 1964, rather than waiting for federal enforcement, was also a key point in this discussion. Finally, Lang discussed the impact of client relations, noting that at least one client had asked what his firm was doing to hire African Americans.[36]

The response Lang received was very different from what McKee experienced during his presentation four years earlier. Although there were some objections regarding whether African American CPAs were capable or adequately educated, and consequently whether they would weaken the profession, the group ultimately voted in favor of integration through a voice vote. The resolution was subsequently sent to presidents, deans, and chairpersons of business and accounting departments throughout the academic community to inform them of the CPA profession's desire to hire black students with "high potential."[37] High potential was a compromise among the members, added to the resolution even though it had been debated and acknowledged that the profession did not always hire students with high potential from any segment of society.[38]

Reflecting on the integration discussion, Dean Craig was not surprised to hear such opinions. These thoughts reflected his life experiences up to a point. He noted, "Such ideas are instilled at birth, so it takes a lot to alter what people believe. We would have to walk in their shoes to truly understand how they feel. However, as you can see, there are always those who help and those who hinder. While the decision to integrate the profession was praised, the notion that blacks had to be high potential was merely another barrier."

Dean Craig continued, "To overcome the false barriers, I learned to adjust, avoid overreaching, wait, and always have confidence in myself. I believed in myself despite the odds. I couldn't give up or fall into the hands of the detractors. The path forward is to believe in God, trust in yourself, and move through life without fear. I learned through experience that being prepared helps one to conquer fear. With that said, the AICPA and the Big Eight, now Big Four, put a lot of muscle behind their efforts to diversify the profession."

The AICPA's Committee on Recruitment from Minority Groups immediately started working toward its goal of integrating the profession. In 1969, they visited several HBCUs to assess the needs of the accounting programs. As a result of their findings, $350,000 was raised from AICPA members and awarded to various HBCUs to enhance their libraries, provide internships for faculty, and hire CPAs as part-time faculty at the colleges.[39] As a result, the number of African Americans pursuing careers in the profession increased. In 1968, the major firms in New York employed only eighteen African American accounting professionals, but by 1970, there were more than 100 African Americans in the same offices.[40] However, offices of Big Eight firms in the South were a bit slower to welcome African Americans.

Overall, the Civil Rights Act of 1964 significantly altered the career trajectory and economic circumstances for many African Americans. The white-collar professional jobs in corporate America that Dean Craig once aspired to, which had been out of reach for nearly a century since the management profession first emerged in America as the post-Civil War economy developed, were now accessible to people like him. Additionally, other benefits that contributed to the growth of business education at HBCUs included substantial gains from the Higher Education Act of 1965. Federal funding for all colleges and universities tripled, and HBCUs received a fairer share than before, with an increase from $18 million in the 1962–63 school year to $123 million in the 1968–69 school year.[41] During this period, several states also increased appropriations to HBCUs, and funding from the Ford, Carnegie, and Rockefeller foundations saw a dramatic rise.[42] The long-overdue larger share of funding for HBCUs was effectively utilized.

As Quiester Craig's career progressed and he eventually moved into leadership as dean of the School of Business and Economics at A&T, he took full advantage of everything the AICPA, Big Eight, philanthropic organizations, and others had to offer to build the accounting program. He facilitated scholarships, internships, full-time employment, and personal and professional development opportunities for both faculty members and students. Like Blayton and Thornton, he sought to influence every student studying accounting at A&T's business school to obtain the most respected credential in the accounting profession. While the exact number of CPAs he produced is unknown, it is believed that he graduated more African American accounting students who became CPAs than any other business school in the United States. One reported statistic indicated that by 1998, over three hundred of his graduates had earned their CPAs. This represented more than 5 percent of all African American

CPAs in the nation.[43] The path to an integrated CPA profession was not easy to navigate, and no one understood this better than Quiester Craig. He was committed to making the most of the new opportunity for economic progress in the black community.

While African Americans made progress in the CPA profession during the 1970s, growth slowed in the 1980s due to policy changes in the Reagan Administration regarding affirmative action. This led to a 25 percent decline of African Americans in the profession. The 1990s saw stabilization as clients became more diverse and looked to firms to have more diverse teams. Like the earlier years, African American educators pushed forward, expanding their programs at HBCUs, and together with the National Association of Black Accountants (NABA), they continued to work to increase the number of students pursuing accounting degrees to become CPAs and expand opportunities within the CPA profession.[44]

"We all had to be ready to take advantage of the opportunity when the time came. I am so proud of my students and what they accomplished. As a people, we have come a long way, and we still have a long way to go. There is still a lot of catching up to do to increase the number of African Americans in the profession," Dean Craig concluded.

CHAPTER 8

Farewell, Lincoln University

Despite the expanded opportunities that the CPA certification could have offered Quiester Craig, he never contemplated leaving the classroom. He continued teaching at Lincoln University, although not for long. Within a few months, Mr. W.A. Hamilton, the business manager at Lincoln University, presented him with an opportunity that helped accelerate the completion of his PhD. Hamilton lived in the same community as Quiester, and over the years, they developed a friendship. "He was well respected in his corner," Dean Craig shared. "He became a strong supporter of me while I was at Lincoln University." Hamilton was much like most of the people Quiester met there: kind and supportive. During his ten years at Lincoln University, in various ways, his boss, colleagues, and friends had all contributed to his professional and personal development.

With Quiester's consent, Hamilton arranged an interview for him to learn about a fellowship from the Ford Foundation that would enable him to take a leave of absence from teaching and focus on his doctorate full-time. He was fortunate to have another chance to pursue an educational grant from the Ford Foundation, which had financed his undergraduate education at Morehouse College. He was interviewed and selected to apply for the fellowship. Traditionally, this fellowship had been awarded only to science-related majors at Lincoln, but Hamilton intervened and persuaded the

Ford Foundation to interview Quiester Craig as a candidate pursuing a PhD in accounting. This was likely an easy decision for the Ford Foundation. They had invested significantly in reforming business school education over eleven years, from 1954 to 1965, spending $46.3 million, which is roughly equivalent to about $486.6 million in 2024. Half of this funding was allocated to business schools, while the remainder was designated for fellowships, research projects, workshops, and publications. During their reform initiative, they recognized the need for analytical, research-oriented PhDs in the business disciplines, so they funded candidates to expand the PhD pipeline.[1]

Quiester took a leave of absence from teaching from the fall of 1969 to the end of August 1970, during which his salary from Lincoln continued, allowing him to focus on his PhD studies in accounting at the University of Missouri. He had one year to dedicate his full attention to the program, and the fellowship also classified him as a full-time registered student, which he needed to fulfill a requirement of the program. Lincoln University had a longstanding tradition of supporting its faculty in pursuing higher education, and Stamper, along with his colleagues, offered their support as well. Having been at Lincoln for nearly nine years and having played a significant role in developing their comprehensive accounting program, Stamper was particularly supportive, especially since Quiester focused his studies on accounting. After all, having a PhD faculty member in accounting would have been a major boost for Lincoln's accounting program.

For years, Quiester had taken partial course loads, but now as a full-time student, his goal was to complete all of his remaining courses and prepare the proposal that needed approval for his dissertation topic, which was quite a task. The aim of the dissertation was to contribute new literature to the accounting profession, so he had to choose a topic that had a basis for research. The topic he chose also had to interest a faculty member who would agree to be his dissertation advisor. In tackling this aspect of his doctoral requirements, he sought ideas from several faculty members, eventually settling on cost control and managerial accounting. While teaching at Lincoln, cost accounting became his favorite subject. He then approached the only faculty member of color in the business school and asked if he would be his advisor. His name was Dr. William Campfield.

In 1951, Dr. Campfield became the first African American in the United States to earn a PhD in accounting, awarded by the University of Illinois. Ten years earlier, he had become the twelfth African American CPA in the nation and the first in North Carolina.[2] In 1933, he earned his undergraduate accounting degree from New York University and, after a couple of years of work, obtained his MBA from the University of Minnesota in 1937, becoming the institution's first MBA graduate.[3] While there, he also became the first African American inducted into Beta Alpha Psi, the national honor society for accounting students.[4] Dr. Campfield's professional accomplishments were equally impressive, as he served his community as a teacher, local business consultant, HBCU business school controller, and government accountant. As a new faculty member at the University of Missouri that year, he caught Quiester's attention due to his being African American. Consequently, he approached Campfield and asked if he could become his advisor.

Quiester quickly learned that Campfield was a visiting professor at the University of Missouri, there for only one semester, which meant he could not serve as his advisor. However, he had the chance to participate in the faculty meeting when Quiester presented his dissertation topic, "Controllable Cost," for approval. During this presentation, a faculty member aggressively questioned Quiester, struggling to understand the significance of his research. No matter how he responded to the questions fired at him by that faculty member, he could not satisfy the inquiry. As the conversation persisted, Quiester grew tense and a bit irritated, puzzled by the faculty member's aggressive questioning and the dissatisfaction with his answers. Eventually, Campfield intervened, posing a few questions to the faculty member that ended his resistance. "It quieted the issue," Dean Craig remembered. "Dr. Campfield knew his trade."

Due to the rescue, Campfield became Quiester's hero. Afterward, he went to his office to thank him. He felt supported by Campfield and years later remembered his encouraging words: "Always do your best, and you will be okay." As Quiester advanced in his career, he came to know Campfield well and always valued his support. He described him as a trailblazer recognized for his many professional involvements and achievements. "He was well-spoken, brilliant, and a highly qualified government accountant. He was also well-known in the accounting profession, and everyone respected him," Dean Craig remembered. He found him both encouraging and motivating, feeling honored to be acquainted with him. In reflection he said, "I was trying to achieve what he had already accomplished, so it was an amazing experience to meet him and get to know him."

Throughout his career, Campfield was undeniably a heavyweight in the fields of accounting and business education, with numerous accomplishments to prove it. One notable achievement was his ranking from 1921 to 2005 as the twenty-first most prolific publisher in *The Accounting Review*, the leading journal for accounting academics.[5] For his extensive research that broadened knowledge in the accounting field, he became the first African American inducted posthumously into the American Accounting Association's (AAA) Accounting Hall of Fame in 2019. He was the ninety-eighth inductee.

While Quiester viewed Campfield as his hero, he also found an advisor on campus in Dr. Eugene Zieha, a professor of cost accounting. As they collaborated on his dissertation, Zieha proved to be a valuable asset to the process, supporting him tirelessly. They worked diligently on Quiester's dissertation, and he was fortunate to receive additional support from his managerial accounting professor, as well as Silvoso, the chairman of the Accounting Department.

During the process of studying for his PhD, Quiester finally returned to his old self and started to perform at his personal best, reminiscent of his Lab High days. He had tangible goals, which changed his focus. Achieving his goal of becoming a CPA reignited his ambition, and he now sought his second "union card," especially after meeting Campfield, who possessed the credentials he aspired to obtain. Additionally, he was in a doctorate program with mature, accomplished students who were serious in their pursuits. Some had prestigious undergraduate backgrounds, some held CPA certifications, and some had worked for Big Eight firms. Being part of this supportive group of mature individuals with clear goals provided motivation and focus for Quiester. Regarding the support group he noted, "We supported and encouraged each other. It took a batch of Cs to succeed in the PhD program: courage, confidence, competence, and compassion. Some of the toughest faculty I encountered in the program were the most supportive."

Throughout his research, Quiester's love for cost accounting grew. He was intrigued by cost accounting as a tool for management within a company to utilize it for budgeting, as well as establishing policies and programs to enhance a company's profitability. This differs from financial accounting, which is the primary focus of public accounting firms. Quiester was curious why cost accounting allowed some companies to thrive while others failed, prompting him to consider how businesses managed their costs and how cost accounting influenced their management decisions. This elevated level of thinking was a departure from the classroom and he thoroughly enjoyed it, alongside the camaraderie of his fellow accounting PhD students. But as all good things must come to an end, by August 1970, Quiester's leave of absence from Lincoln University ended. He had completed all his coursework and most of his dissertation, leaving just the final chapters to finish. He observed the career opportunities his classmates were receiving, and they were all moving on to do much bigger things. Watching them made him wonder about the possibilities that lay ahead for him. After much contemplation, he decided to explore the types of opportunities available to him.

During this period, many traditionally white institutions sought to diversify their faculties in response to the desegregation changes sweeping across America in higher education. Credentialed African Americans were being pursued for faculty roles at these institutions, leading to intense competition for business programs at HBCUs. That year, Quiester Craig was the only African American candidate completing a PhD in accounting in the country. Unlike when he graduated from Morehouse College and Atlanta University, his opportunities were plentiful. He received over forty invitations to visit schools from all parts of the country. Most of the invitations came from Big Ten schools. Only seven or eight of his offers were from HBCUs, and only one was from a traditionally white institution in the South. A couple of faculty members at the University of Missouri had passed his name on to a few schools as well. Intrigued by the opportunities he received, he decided it was time to leave Lincoln University. However, his final decision was contingent upon gaining approval from his advisor to complete his dissertation away from the University of Missouri.

Dean Craig noted, "When I received concurrence from Gene that I could continue my dissertation from out of state, I made my final decision to leave Missouri. I just needed to find the right opportunity."

By that time, Quiester had accepted that teaching business at the collegiate level was his career path. However, he had other considerations in determining where he would go. The first factor in finding the right opportunity was whether to move to a traditionally white institution or to remain at an HBCU. He interviewed with several traditionally white institutions and was tempted by some of the offers, as they were much more financially attractive than those from the HBCUs. Regarding the HBCUs, he sought a school committed to developing a strong business program. Admittedly, he preferred HBCUs and believed he could add more value at one by helping to establish a quality business program. He had also grown accustomed to the culture of togetherness prevalent at HBCUs, and he recognized that although they faced challenges with program development due to funding issues, they compensated with genuine care and support for their student's success. He was concerned that with the recent societal changes, he might be seen as a token at a traditionally white institution, while at an HBCU, he would likely have a greater opportunity to make an impact. Despite these pros and cons, he remained open-minded to the new opportunities that arose.

Another consideration was his family. He thought about opportunities that would bring him closer to Cleveland, where Doll and Ralph lived. By this time, he had lost both his parents. His father passed away in 1960, shortly after Quiester started at Lincoln University. After his papa's death, his mother moved to Cleveland to live with his sister Doll. During his breaks from school, he had visited her there until she passed away in 1966, six years after his beloved papa. At the time of her death, his siblings were scattered across various cities: Magnolia in Denver, Cary in Detroit, Iona in Chicago, and Sam in Palms, California; and of course, Ralph and Doll in Cleveland. While he wanted to be close to family, he knew he could rely on their annual family reunions to maintain their closeness as they grew older.

Now that he had decided to leave Lincoln University, he needed to narrow down his choices. He had accepted that teaching would be his career path and recognized that his aspirations leaned toward HBCUs. Except for the University of Missouri, his entire education had been at HBCUs, and he spent the first twelve years of his career teaching at these institutions. Although Lincoln University was different, its culture resembled that of an HBCU. Quiester understood that HBCUs were important to him and that they offered more to the African American community than just education; they served as a community where people lifted each other up and supported one another.

To narrow his options, he concentrated on what he perceived to be the plans for the business program at the HBCUs where he had interviewed. Only one HBCU stood out with its ambitious plans. Dr. Sybil Mobley, the chair of the accounting department at Florida Agricultural & Mechanical University (FAMU), a land-grant HBCU located in Tallahassee, had substantial goals for her program. He became acquainted with Mobley when she called him one evening while he was at home in Jefferson City. After introducing herself, she explained that she was reaching out on behalf of her boss, Dr. Adams, to invite Quiester to visit FAMU's campus and learn more about the accounting and business programs. She informed him about the programs, the strategic plans for the departments of business administration and accounting, her leadership style and personal commitment to the program, and the type of faculty they were looking to hire. Mobley's plans for the accounting department were ambitious, and she piqued his interest.

Fortunately, the call came during the time that Quiester was contemplating his next move. He had not committed to any specific course of action, but he was weighing the pros and cons of his options: teach at a Big Ten school or teach at an HBCU. When he visited FAMU, he met Adams, Mobley, and other faculty members. Everyone was well-versed in the big plans for the business and accounting program and again, Quiester was even more impressed. He was well aware that FAMU's accounting and business programs and budget were much smaller compared to the Big Ten schools he had visited. Having experienced life at a "big boy school" at the University of Missouri, he understood the differences. Regarding his personal situation, the traditionally white institutions were offering more money and smaller teaching loads, and some were located closer to his siblings in Cleveland, making the Midwest appealing to him. In making his final decision, Dean Craig felt conflicted. He was still undecided until three FAMU students helped him reach his final decision.

After his interview at FAMU, three seniors—black males in the accounting program—drove him to the airport for his return trip to

Jefferson City. During their conversation, he shared his life experiences, including the range of colleges and universities he was considering joining as a faculty member. These young men encouraged him to think about them in his decision. They specifically asked him—and this is something Quiester said he never forgot: "If qualified guys like you all go to those schools, what about us?"

"That question rocked me," Dean Craig shared. "I could not answer it."

On the flight back to Jefferson City, that conversation deeply troubled him. It didn't make him feel guilty for considering his opportunities more broadly; instead, it prompted him to reflect on his upbringing in Montgomery, Alabama. Those experiences reminded him that we, as black people, must support one another. "I couldn't forget their question… What about us?" Dean Craig reflected. "That conversation rocked me and left me dumbfounded. As I contemplated it, I realized I am 'us.'" That conversation marked a turning point for Quiester. "Those young men made me think. They helped me recognize that I belonged at an HBCU. In making my final decision, I was drawn into the Morehouse tradition," he concluded. Of the nine African American PhDs in accounting in the United States at that time, six were employed at HBCUs.

With his decision made, the next step for Quiester was to communicate his intentions to leave Lincoln University to Stamper, his boss. This decision was difficult for him and filled him with regret in some ways. What weighed on him most were the long-term relationships he would be leaving behind—friends who were faculty, students, administrators, and neighbors he had developed over his ten years in Jefferson City, along with those he had also made at the University of Missouri. When he informed Stamper of his plans, Stamper urged him to stay. Both the administration and Stamper did their best to keep him on the Lincoln University faculty. Stamper even visited him at home to persuade him about the future of his career with Lincoln.

While Stamper presented a compelling case, Quiester had his own perspective on his future at Lincoln. He remarked, "The university was facing a budget crisis, and there were changes in the leadership at the top. We had developed quality business and accounting programs, but the program was small, and I was teaching most of the accounting courses in the particular area. Changes were happening, but they were gradual. Lincoln had aspirations but lacked the budget. The University of Missouri was the big boy in town, and the leadership in the business department at Lincoln was stable. It was difficult to envision a path for myself," Dean Craig admitted. Well, his assessment of his career mobility was spot on. Stamper enjoyed a lengthy career with Lincoln University, and when the business program transitioned into the Lincoln University College of Business, he served as dean from 1977 to 1983. In 2002, the building that housed the College of Business was named Cletus Stamper Hall in his honor.

"Leaving Lincoln was a very hard decision, but when I look back, it was the right thing for me to do," Dean Craig concluded.

PART IV

MAKING THE MOVE TO LEADERSHIP

From left to right: Jannette Suggs meeting with Dean Craig, circa mid-1970s. Dr. Danny Pogue, Assistant Dean, conferring with a student, circa 1980s.

One of Dean Craig's early actions as a leader was to assemble his core team, consisting of Jannette, Evelyn McKeathen (not pictured), and Dr. Danny Pogue, which he called The JED Principle; he attributed much of his success to their unwavering support.

Dean Quiester Craig teaching cost accounting at North Carolina A&T. Due to limited resources at the business school, upon becoming dean, he also assumed roles as Chair of the Accounting Department and professor, teaching accounting courses, 1972.

CHAPTER 9

Florida Agricultural and Mechanical University (FAMU)

In the fall semester of 1970, Quiester Craig joined the faculty of FAMU's Department of Business at the invitation of Dr. Lucy Rose Adams, a long-term FAMU employee who earned her PhD in business education from Ohio State University. When Adams assumed leadership of the department, Bachelor of Science degrees were offered in Accounting, Business Administration, Marketing, Business Education, and Secretarial Training. Courses in the Principles of Salesmanship, Advertising, Statistics, Investments, Real Estate, and Retailing were offered in alternate semesters to meet the needs and interests of the students. Under Dr. Adams's leadership, the business program largely remained the same from 1958 to 1970, with the most significant change being the elimination of the marketing curriculum.[1] By the late 1960s, FAMU's business program was in transition. With the desegregation of Florida's high schools, the demand for black teachers in business subjects rapidly declined. FAMU also began to realign its business program to prepare students for the new opportunities emerging in corporate America as a result of Title VII of the Civil Rights Act of 1964, which prohibited workplace discrimination.

These factors caused a shift away from the business education and secretarial science programs of study. Over a four-year period, enrollment in the Department of Business increased by 258 percent. In the 1962–63 school year, there were 180 students; by the 1969–70 school year, that number had risen to 644. During the same time frame, the number of baccalaureate degrees awarded in business also grew. In the 1962–63 school year, twenty-eight baccalaureate degrees were awarded, with 50 percent in Business Education and Office Management, and the remainder distributed among Accounting, Marketing, and Business Administration. By the 1969–70 school year, 68 percent of the degrees awarded were in Accounting and Business Administration, with Accounting emerging as the "dominant influence" in part due to the impact of the AICPA's initiative to integrate the CPA profession.[2] In the 1969–70 academic year, a total of thirteen faculty members were employed in the Department of Business. Six faculty members continued to teach Business Education and Office Management, even though only 15 percent of enrolled students were pursuing that area of study.[3]

The sudden changes in society presented significant challenges for the leadership of FAMU's business program. Overnight, the program needed to be fully developed to prepare students for competition in corporate America. Quiester's new boss, Dr. Sybil Mobley, was at the forefront of addressing this challenge for the accounting program. Mobley joined the faculty in 1963 as an assistant professor of accounting and was recognized for bringing to the department an "excellent academic background, exceptional self-confidence, a highly competitive spirit, a cooperative attitude, and an abundance of energy"[4] as she navigated through her supervisor to upgrade and expand the accounting program.

Mobley was well acquainted with FAMU. After obtaining her degree from Bishop College, a private HBCU in Marshall, Texas, she began her career at FAMU in 1945 and held various clerical positions in the business office and dining hall. In 1959, she temporarily left FAMU and her family to pursue her MBA from the Wharton School of Business, which she obtained in 1961. Three years later, she earned her PhD in accounting from the University of Illinois, becoming the seventh African American to achieve that credential. She subsequently became a CPA in the state of Florida.[5]

Born in 1925 in the Jim Crow South of Shreveport, Louisiana, Mobley credited her parents for arranging her life and those of her siblings in a manner that shielded them from social factors that might convince African Americans they were not equal. Her upbringing significantly bolstered her confidence and prepared her for the male-dominated world of business education and corporate America.[6] "She brought a spirit of confidence and a lot of ambition to developing the accounting program at FAMU," Dean Craig recalled, "instilling the same drive in her students and modeling it for her faculty."

Mobley advanced to leadership quickly. After obtaining her doctorate in accounting, she was appointed to lead FAMU's accounting program and immediately began to implement "progressive practices, innovative methods, and creative approaches"[7] to improve program quality. She overcame significant challenges in building a robust accounting program by securing well-credentialed faculty in the accounting discipline; recruiting talented, high-achieving students; and fostering relationships with leaders in the AICPA, Big Eight firms, and leading corporations. Simultaneously, Mobley also elevated her status within the accounting profession by publishing numerous articles on accounting topics in professional journals, which resulted in her peers selecting her as a member of the editorial boards of *The Accounting Review* and the University of Florida Press in the 1970s.[8]

On the issue of upgrading the faculty, Mobley sought out the talent she needed to develop a more innovative accounting program. Apparently, she maintained awareness of African Americans who were pursuing PhDs in accounting. This is how she discovered

Quiester Craig. After hiring him, Mobley stated about her faculty, "There are only nine black PhDs in accounting in the United States. Florida A&M University has two of them and is hopeful in its ongoing negotiations for a third."[9] Due to the competitive landscape for the limited number of African Americans holding PhDs in the business disciplines, she was unable to hire a third PhD in accounting. However, she did upgrade her accounting faculty.

In 1964, the accounting faculty count was three: Mobley; Irene Mandexter, who held a master's in education from the University of Pittsburgh; and Evelyn M. Hodges, who had an MBA from Indiana University. By the spring of 1970, Mobley had added four additional faculty: Quiester Craig; Viceola D. Blackshear and Man Chand Maloo, both MBAs from Atlanta University; and John L. Green, University of Illinois, who subsequently became a CPA.[10]

"Sybil assembled a remarkable faculty," Dean Craig recalled. "We worked diligently, built strong relationships, and socialized frequently." He remembered that he cultivated fruitful relationships with all his colleagues in the accounting department and valued their individual strengths as team members. Blackshear was an exceptional teacher who connected well with her students. She moved on to A&T after a year. Mandexter introduced him to a Florida room, as she often entertained the faculty at her home. Maloo was a graduate of Florida State University, and Quiester got to know his family well. Overall, he particularly noted the care they each demonstrated for their students. "Some were FAMU Rattlers, some were long-term faculty, but the common thread was our shared dedication to the university," he recalled. "We took pride in our efforts to forge a new path for the accounting students. As faculty, we committed ourselves to helping them achieve success."

The classroom environment at FAMU was similar in some ways to Quiester's experiences at South Carolina State College and Lincoln University. Once again, he carried a full teaching load, as did all the faculty at FAMU, due to underfunded budgets and the challenges they faced in hiring qualified faculty in the business disciplines. At that time, it was primarily African Americans who constituted the main pool of faculty teaching at black colleges, and the supply of business school faculty was very limited. With most black colleges responding to the opening of corporate America to prepare their students, recruiting qualified accounting faculty was particularly challenging.

Quiester was assigned to teach Statistics, Intermediate Accounting, Advanced Accounting, and Cost Accounting, subjects he was familiar with from his time at Lincoln University. However, this time, teaching was much easier for him. Thanks to his advanced studies at the University of Missouri and his years as the lead accounting professor at Lincoln, he was now more qualified for the position he had taken. "The shaking and shivering that accompanied me from Orangeburg to Jefferson City did not make the trip to Tallahassee," Dean Craig shared with a laugh. "I knew my material, had greater confidence in my delivery, and enjoyed being in the classroom."

He was thrilled to be assigned to teach cost accounting, his favorite subject. He was also pleased that the culture he encountered at FAMU met his expectations. It was supportive, much like the environment he had grown accustomed to. The faculty and administration were very professional, collegial, and supportive, and they worked together as a team. He needed that because he once again had a lot on his plate with a full teaching load and his goal of completing his dissertation during his first semester at FAMU.

When he left Missouri, he only had the final chapter of his dissertation to complete. His topic was controllable cost. During the early part of the first semester at FAMU, he made significant progress toward completing that final chapter, and by the Thanksgiving holiday, he only had a few loose ends to tie up. Committed to meeting his timeline, he moved out of his house and into the Holiday Inn in downtown Tallahassee for two weeks so he could concentrate on finishing. Quiester had three young kids at home at the time, and he needed an environment where he could focus. He called home daily to stay in touch with his family while still dedicating his full attention to completing his dissertation. Early in the new year of 1971, he traveled to Columbia, Missouri, to finalize the steps necessary to earn his doctorate degree in accounting. To leave Missouri as a PhD, he needed to complete some typing of his dissertation, have it approved, and successfully defend his research before a committee. Although those tasks seemed straightforward, they presented significant challenges for him to complete in a short time.

Fortunately, he had access to the necessary resources at the University of Missouri. A typist was provided to handle all the typing, a skill he never learned. He felt a great deal of stress lift when she informed him that she would also manage the table of contents section of his dissertation. The other person he had to work with was Ms. Ward, a staff member in the graduate office at Jesse Hall. Her role was to ensure the dissertation met the university's specifications. "Ms. Ward looked at people with a sharp eye," Dean Craig recalled. "When I brought her the finished product, she took out her ruler to check the margins to see if they adhered to the specifications, and they did. I was relieved that everything was in good order." With his dissertation in good shape, he was now ready for what he called "the most stressful part," defending his research.

On the day Quiester Craig had to defend his research, he walked into a large conference room that, to him, felt like a courtroom. There were about ten older men sitting around a large conference table, mostly white with a few of international status, and all PhDs from the accounting department at the University of Missouri. Quiester had questioned his classmates who had gone before him to gauge the experience. He assumed they would pose similar questions about the history of accounting, the field of accounting, and of course, controllable cost, his dissertation topic. His classmates had suggested that he remain calm and confident throughout the process. After introductions, someone asked him to explain where he came from, what led him to accounting and to the University of Missouri, and what his future career plans were. Not expecting that line of questioning, Quiester panicked: "To say I was a little shaken would be an understatement," he remembered.

Gathering himself, he began to share his background, including his upbringing in Montgomery, Alabama, his educational experiences, and other personal details with the committee. He thought he could fill the time discussing these topics, but after a while, they interrupted him. They then questioned him about his research. According to Quiester, things seemed to be going well until Silvoso asked, "Mr. Craig, who is the client on an audit engagement?" He hesitated and fumbled slightly, being careful not to fall into a trap. He then provided the obvious answer, stating, "The client, since they are the one who does the hiring and pays the bill." Silvoso responded, "That was a good attempt, but I was thinking more along the lines of the public, the readers of the audit report, such as bankers and investors who rely on that information." At that moment, blood rushed to Quiester's face. He did everything he could to keep it together. Silvoso eased the tension with his sense of humor, saying, "I've been asking that question for years, and I always get the obvious answer. I'm still trying to figure out which one is the right answer myself." This allowed Quiester to breathe a sigh of relief, at least for a moment.

Then came more questions. They asked him what he discovered from his research and whether anything he learned changed his perspective on the topic. After fifty minutes of questioning from various people on different subjects, he was excused and asked to wait in a conference room in the dean's office down the hall. The committee took about thirty minutes to deliberate. During this time, Quiester paced, back and forth, back and forth. The secretary in the dean's office said, "Please sit down; you're making my coffee nervous." He felt shaky and uncertain because he was aware that a classmate who defended his dissertation a couple of days before had been put on hold. His anxiety level was high.

His thoughts about the time he had invested in pursuing his PhD and what he would tell his family if he didn't succeed were contributing to his anxiety. A flurry of thoughts raced through his mind. He had a lot at stake, and he felt the pressure intensifying. Finally, the door opened, and someone came to escort him back to the conference room, saying, "Dr. Craig, they're ready for you." However, his anxiety level was so high that he did not process what his escort said. His focus remained on his feelings. As they walked down the hallway to the conference room, he felt as if his stomach was walking on its own. When he entered the room, reality struck him. He turned around and asked his escort, "What did you call me?"

By that time, everyone sitting around the table was on their feet, congratulating him. "That was a very gratifying moment," he shared. "I was finally able to take a deep sigh of relief. My budget was tight, so the first thing I did when the meeting adjourned was make a collect call home to Tallahassee from Dr. Quiester Craig. I heard a scream of joy from my wife confirming that she understood the mission was accomplished," he shared proudly. On his walk back to the hotel, he felt his stomach come back into his body, but then he felt like he was walking on air. "I felt gratitude, satisfaction, and a great sense of achievement in earning my PhD in accounting," he recalled. With that goal accomplished in 1971, Quiester Craig officially became the first African American to earn a PhD in accounting from the University of Missouri and only the tenth African American in the nation to hold that credential.

With his doctorate settled, he could now fully dedicate his attention to his responsibilities at FAMU. He had already been a strong contributor to the accounting department. Mobley had strong connections, leveraging them in corporate America and academia to enhance the exposure and learning opportunities for FAMU students in the accounting program. One of Quiester's early tasks upon joining the faculty was to assist Mobley with coordinating a distinguished lecture series for the auditing course in the fall of 1970. Featured speakers included professors from major universities and partners at Big Eight firms, such as Robert K. Mautz from the University of Illinois; Howard Stettler from the University of Kansas; Joseph A. Silvoso from the University of Missouri; R. Bob Smith from Peat Marwick, Mitchell & Co.; Felix A. Kaufluian of Lybrand, Ross Brothers and Montgomery; Jack Arrell from Price Waterhouse; and James Gallaner from Haskins & Sells. The lineup also featured Douglas R. Carmichael from the University of Texas, a consultant for the AICPA, and none other than Quiester's hero, William Campfield, who was then a visiting professor at Columbia University.[11] Committed to their goal of integrating the profession and fostering the growth of quality accounting programs at HBCUs, the Big Eight accounting firms, and the AICPA were well represented in this lecture series.

The lecture series provided FAMU's students with quality instruction, fresh perspectives, and significant exposure to the profession as well as to individuals who enjoyed successful careers in accounting. It was so effective that FAMU's accounting department gained prominence at both the state and national levels, enhancing the credibility of Mobley and FAMU within the industry. This also enabled Mobley and her team to build working relationships with some of the leading accounting minds in the country.[12]

"Sybil became very well known in the accounting profession and business world," Dean Craig shared. "She leveraged her relationships to acquire resources for the accounting program. The lecture series was a remarkable initiative in this way. We had presenters who had never heard of FAMU and had little to no knowledge or exposure to HBCUs. It was an excellent program for everyone involved, and the students were encouraged and inspired by these types of events." Silvoso, who had supported Quiester during his time at the University of Missouri, was impressed with his first visit to FAMU. It was reported that he wrote a letter to Mobley stating, "I have visited many places in my life, and my visit to FAMU will always be cherished as one of my most pleasing experiences. You are, indeed, most fortunate to be located with an administrative staff, faculty, and students of such high caliber. We are interested in attracting your students to study with us. I believe that we are able to provide an educational experience which will enable them to make an outstanding career in the accounting profession." True to his word, Silvoso recruited many FAMU accounting students to the University of Missouri, the first of whom graduated with master's degrees in 1973.[13] Looking back, Dean Craig was not at all surprised by the connection Silvoso established with FAMU's accounting department. He always regarded him as a personable and supportive individual and valued Silvoso's assistance during his time at the University of Missouri.

The lecture series was so successful that it became a recurring program for the accounting department. In 1971, Mobley informed the FAMU administration that she was bringing in visiting professors to help with program development as a strategy to address her budget issues. The AICPA sponsored Dr. Kenneth Perry from the University of Illinois. That year, FAMU was the only university to receive an AICPA visiting professorship. Others involved included Professor Herbert B. Miller, a partner at Arthur Andersen & Co.; Dr. Dee Keespie from the University of Arizona; and Professor Guy Darnell from the University of Chicago. Darnell had a diverse skill set and was able to teach a wide range of courses required by accounting majors.[14]

Quiester found it a gratifying experience to work with the participants in the visiting professors' series. He learned a great deal from them due to their diverse qualifications, stature, and methodologies, as they came from more established business and accounting programs. He was particularly intrigued by Perry, who was nationally recognized for preparing students for the CPA exam. Utilizing his test-taking methods, Perry's students consistently achieved top scores on the exam. For instance, in three different years, two of his students secured the top two scores out of 16,444 test takers in 1968; 29,668 in 1973; and 67,269 in 1985.[15]

Even though he had already completed the CPA exam, Quiester often attended Perry's classes because he found his presentations incredibly interesting and learned a lot. Perry was also supportive of and encouraged both women and minorities to pursue accounting as a career. He was a colleague that Mobley met at the University of Illinois, and he became a fixture at FAMU, so much so that they awarded him the Honorary Soul Brother Award, which he cherished along with his many distinguished honors from various universities and professional associations.[16]

The exposure that FAMU's students gained from the visiting professors was invaluable. In addition to the exposure for the students, the program also provided white professors from traditionally white colleges and universities, partners from Big Eight firms, and professionals from other corporate entities the opportunity to experience the lives of black students, black faculty, and a black college. This experience was essential for changing perceptions. Too often, segregation led whites to form opinions about African Americans based on superficial beliefs and misinformation. They defined African Americans according to their own perceptions, shaped by the caste system they imposed. The accomplishments of African Americans like the pioneering CPAs, Mobley and Campfield, and many others clearly demonstrate that, from the very beginning, blacks possessed ample ambition, intellect, determination, and the ability to succeed, even in the face of limited opportunities.

"These interactions were beneficial for everyone," Dean Craig acknowledged. "It was just as important for FAMU's students to meet African Americans with similar qualifications, like Dr. Campfield and Joe Cramer, as visiting professors. Seeing African American PhDs and CPAs provided role models who looked like them and conveyed a message of what the students could aspire to as well. The students were favorably impressed by all the visiting professors, including Campfield and Cramer."

Like Campfield, Dr. Joseph Cramer was part of the small but growing group of African American CPA/accounting PhDs, which included both Quiester and his boss, Mobley. Cramer attained the rank of the sixty-third African American CPA in the nation in 1961 and became the sixth African American to earn a doctorate in accounting when he received his PhD from Indiana University in 1963. He was also the first African American to secure a full-time permanent position and achieve tenure as an accounting professor at a traditionally white institution of higher learning.[17]

To ensure that her faculty had broad exposure as well and could effectively relate classroom concepts to the workplace, Mobley instituted a Faculty Development Program requiring accounting faculty to spend several summers working in corporate America. She did not exempt herself, spending multiple summers at various organizations such as IBM, Price Waterhouse, Chase Manhattan Bank, Union Carbide, and the Internal Revenue Service.[18]

Quiester's participation in the Faculty Development Program finally provided him a chance to experience corporate America as an employee. For two summers, he worked in public accounting in New York City. One summer, he was with Coopers & Lybrand, and the other summer with Touche Ross, both Big Eight firms. He found those jobs to be quite different from being a professor in the classroom. He recalled carrying large trunks filled with working papers and supplies to client offices, a necessity in the days before laptop computers. What he liked most was applying the knowledge he had learned about auditing and accounting in the classroom. He discovered that using his academic expertise in the workplace made the concepts much clearer.

Of the experience working in corporate America, Dean Craig recalled being well-received during his assignments and he felt he was an integral part of the audit team. He found the workload intense and felt challenged to get the job done. The feedback from the audit team leader indicated that he was "too strict in his judgment on various issues." He also viewed those work experiences as essential to his development, gaining a perspective to share with his students to help them understand how to be competitive in that marketplace. Although he enjoyed the experiences and learned a great deal, he knew it wasn't something he wanted to pursue long term.

In addition to developing a quality curriculum and hiring qualified faculty to deliver it, Mobley also needed high-achieving students to realize her goals of making accounting a leading program and preparing students for leadership roles. She employed several strategies to attract "high potential" students, which included restructuring the admissions policy; sending recruitment packages to high schools in urban cities such as Newark, Los Angeles, Philadelphia, Shreveport, and New Orleans; hosting Big-Eight-sponsored recruitment banquets; and reaching out to prospective students via telephone and personal home visits. Mobley's faculty supported her department's recruitment initiatives.[19]

As the recruitment program paid dividends, she then needed financial support for scholarships to help her students fund their education. She was obviously well aware of the "high potential" requirement for targeted students that the CPA profession sought to support. Mobley wrote of her recruitment program in 1969, "Our efforts indicate that our ability to interest high potential students exceed *[sic]* our ability to provide the financial assistance necessary to enroll them in the program." Her next step was to "more intensely encourage" Big Eight firms and other corporate entities to fund scholarships for FAMU accounting students.[20]

Quiester closely observed Mobley and recognized her as an exceptional fundraiser. He gained valuable insights from her in this area. Through her connections, FAMU's accounting program received financial support in various forms from corporate America, beginning in 1968. The Price Waterhouse Foundation offered a special grant of $50,000, their largest to date, as "catch-up" funds for enrichment programs, while the AICPA contributed $50,000 in 1971 for the scholarships program.[21] These were just a few among many others. In addition to scholarships, Mobley arranged internships for her students through many of her corporate supporters. Once more, the CPA profession was holding to its commitment to integration.

The external funding allocated to FAMU was essential because, as a land-grant public HBCU, the Florida legislature provided only minimal financial support. This resulted in underfunding for the Department of Business, of which the accounting program was a part. In 1971, a group of students took the initiative to improve the circumstances and sought to raise funds through a statewide lottery. Unfortunately, their efforts were quickly abandoned due to violations of state lottery laws. Undeterred, the students proceeded with a direct appeal to the Florida state legislature for support of FAMU's Department of Business. They communicated to the legislators that "FAMU did not want permission to be inferior, but the opportunity to be superior."[22]

Impressed with the persistence and determination of the students, the legislators passed a special bill that allocated $150,000 for eleven new faculty positions in the Department of Business. This incident received extensive coverage in local, state, and national newspapers, praising the students' lobbying skills. Mobley, perceived as the catalyst behind the students' actions, was summoned by the administration and reprimanded, since individuals, professors, nor administrators were permitted to lobby without prior permission. However, their dissatisfaction was short-lived when she reported that over $2 million in private donations were generated as a result of the media attention. This new funding established the Arthur Young Professorship in 1971, which provided an annual salary subsidy of $7,500, among other benefits. FAMU became the seventh university to receive this honor, joining the Universities of Chicago, Illinois, Kansas, and Michigan, along with Ohio State and Columbia University. Obviously, it was the first HBCU to receive that award. Meanwhile, Mobley insisted that she had no knowledge of the students' actions.[23]

The appeal to the Florida legislature was not the first time the students would lobby on behalf of FAMU's business department. With the guidance of Mobley, the accounting students sent an unprecedented memo to the AICPA in 1969, entitled "Suggestions for Improvements of Black Accountancy," which presented several topics that warranted further action for the disadvantaged group: the need for fellowships to attend graduate school; funding for students to travel back to their high schools to share the opportunities in accounting at FAMU; internships and employment at public accounting firms, with an emphasis on firms in the South; sponsorships for guest lectures and seminars; honoring the organization's non-discriminatory policies; and including black faces in the AICPA literature and brochures. The memo also asked the pointed questions: "What does the Institute do for accounting firms?" and "Is this done for black firms also?"[24] This was a bold move on the part of Mobley. Her courage was rewarded with the $50,000 gift for the scholarship program that was received in 1971.

Being bold was another lesson Quiester learned from Mobley. He observed her boldness in many situations, but her cunning nature, maybe not so. When asked if he thought she might have had her students lobby him on the ride back to the airport, he laughed and replied, "I admired her, and I wouldn't put it past her. When you're as trailblazing as Sybil was, you can't be shy. She was building an accounting program that was helping students land positions in Big Eight firms and major corporations. These students were gaining the career opportunities I desired when I graduated from Morehouse. This was a new frontier for FAMU, and the perceptions of our schools and students were overwhelmingly negative. We didn't have advanced notice to prepare for these new opportunities, and our accounting and business programs needed development, with resources—financial and otherwise—being a challenge, in the particular area. We had to instill in our students the confidence necessary for success. Sybil emphasized preparation and confidence. The students also needed to learn that they could thrive within the culture of the accounting profession. She ensured they understood that the faculty was committed to supporting them."

He continued, "A lot rested on what Mobley was doing." Being twelve years older than Quiester, she was one of the early African American MBA/CPA/PhDs in accounting who developed a quality accounting program and paved the way for HBCU students to enter the corporate sector. "As you know, first impressions can be lasting impressions, so what she did and what her students did mattered. She took risks to obtain the resources she needed to achieve her goals, and fortunately, they paid off."

Quiester's time at FAMU lasted just two years. With numerous positive changes and new opportunities in the form of professional careers in business, many HBCUs began revamping their accounting and business programs. Enrollment in business programs soared at most HBCUs, and students were eager to pursue corporate careers. In response, several presidents and chancellors at HBCUs prioritized improving their business programs and building business schools. With African American PhDs in accounting and other business fields in short supply, those with credentials were highly sought after, including Quiester Craig.

Toward the end of his first year at FAMU, he interviewed for a position in the accounting department at A&T. During a professional meeting of the American Accounting Association (AAA), the organization for accountants in academia, he met Dr. Theodore Mahaffey, who was then chair of the business program. The African American members of the AAA had a chance to network, and it became known that Quiester held a PhD in accounting. Mahaffey was looking to expand the business program at A&T and was searching for additional staff. He invited Quiester to visit A&T's campus in hopes of hiring him as a member of the accounting faculty. Quiester traveled to Greensboro and met with Mahaffey and Dr. Herbert Watkins, who chaired the accounting program. It was during that visit that he first encountered Mrs. Jannette Suggs, the administrative assistant for the business school. Although he interviewed with Mahaffey and Watkins for a teaching position, they could not reach an agreement on the terms.

Quiester returned to work at FAMU and continued to enjoy his time in the classroom. At that time, he wasn't considering becoming a department chair or an administrator because he had found his sweet spot and loved working directly with his students. He had chosen FAMU because of Mobley's credentials and her ambitious plans, and he was learning a great deal as a member of her team. He felt content there, until he received another call from A&T in the spring of 1972. This time, the call came from the chancellor, Dr. Lewis Carnegie Dowdy. Quiester expressed interest, but before he committed to a visit, he accepted an invitation from Dr. Milton Wilson, the dean of the business school at Howard University. He was invited to visit their campus and learn about their business program. HBCU students weren't the only ones being offered new opportunities; Quiester Craig's "union cards" were opening doors for him as well.

CHAPTER 10

I Stood on Their Shoulders

In the spring of 1972, Dean Craig visited Howard University in Washington, DC, to meet with Dr. Milton Wilson, the dean of the business school. He was excited about this meeting because Wilson was renowned in both business school academia and the accounting profession for his achievements. He was the first African American business school dean to achieve accreditation for an HBCU from the American Association of Collegiate Schools of Business (AACSB), an organization founded in 1916 by deans of the most prestigious colleges and universities to establish standards ensuring the highest quality of business school education. The founding member schools were Columbia University, Dartmouth University, Harvard University, New York University, Northwestern University, Ohio State University, Tulane University, the University of California, the University of Chicago, the University of Nebraska, the University of Pennsylvania, the University of Pittsburgh, the University of Texas, and the University of Wisconsin.[1]

Accreditation by the AACSB signifies that a college or university's business programs not only meet but consistently uphold high-quality programming standards. In the late 1960s, Wilson earned AACSB accreditation for historically black Texas Southern University, the first state-supported HBCU in Houston, Texas. He later took on the role of dean of Howard University's business program with the goal of replicating his success at Texas Southern University. Wilson invited Quiester to Howard University to discuss his goals to earn AACSB accreditation and solicit his interest in joining the faculty to assist with this endeavor.

Quiester first learned about Wilson and became aware of his achievements while attending meetings of professional accounting associations, where Wilson emphasized the importance of AACSB accreditation, especially in the evolving landscape of HBCU business programs. Quiester felt honored to meet him, given his reputation and his role as a leader dedicated to leveling the playing field in business education for African American students at HBCUs. Although Quiester had no hands-on experience with business school accreditation, he recognized the significance of Wilson's achievements, particularly at a time when few people of color aspired to or accomplished goals in this area. Wilson's successes made him the ideal role model for leaders of business programs at HBCUs, and his achievements opened up new possibilities for these programs.

Quiester used the meeting with Wilson as an opportunity to learn more about him and the details of his accomplishments. At that time, he was not well-versed in accreditation, but he was eager to understand Wilson's "travels down that road," the challenges he encountered, what it took to achieve success, and the plans for Howard's business program. Being twenty-two years his senior, Wilson engaged with Quiester as a younger professional, and from that meeting, he became a mentor.

Wilson was born in Paducah, Kentucky, in 1915. His father worked as a Pullman Car Porter, and both his mother and grandmother were public school teachers. He was influenced by his parents to have a strong work ethic and to understand the need for an education.[2] He earned his undergraduate degree from West Virginia State College, where one of his professors inspired him to become a CPA. To pursue this goal, he moved to Indiana and completed his master's degree in commercial science at Indiana University. He became the first African American CPA in Indiana in 1951 by circumventing the experience requirement, since the state allowed graduate education to substitute for work experience.[3]

Wilson's first job as a cost accountant with the Federal Office of Emergency Management in Washington, DC, was short-lived. His supervisor told him that, because he was African American, his opportunities for promotion were limited. Consequently, he became an educator, leading the accounting programs at two HBCUs: first Hampton Institute (now Hampton University) in Virginia and later Dillard University in New Orleans, Louisiana. Wilson was later invited to join the faculty at Texas Southern University to develop a business program. At that time, Texas Southern had been newly established by state authorities with a law school to prevent the integration of the University of Texas's law school.[4] The U.S. Supreme Court case *Sweatt v. Painter*, led by the NAACP, established that the law school for blacks at Texas Southern was grossly unequal to the law school at the University of Texas.

Wilson accepted the challenge to create a business program at Texas Southern University. However, he first returned to Indiana University to earn his doctorate in accounting, becoming the first African American to receive a doctorate from that program.[5] By obtaining that degree, he became part of a group of seven African Americans who, by the mid-1960s, had earned doctorates in the accounting discipline: William Campfield from the University of Illinois in 1951; Milton Wilson from Indiana University in 1951; Lincoln Harrison from Ohio State University in 1953; Broadus Sawyer from New York University in 1955; Larzette Hale from the University of Wisconsin in 1955; Joseph Cramer from Indiana University in 1963; and Sybil Mobley from the University of Illinois in 1964. Coincidentally, these seven individuals also earned their CPA certification, and all but Cramer had MBAs. They formed a small group, and by the end of 1965, they represented a mere 1 percent of the total 573 individuals with PhDs in accounting in the United States.[6]

Like Wilson, most of the seven were older than Quiester and were the African American MBA/CPA/accounting PhD pioneers who earned their credentials prior to the passage of the 1964 Civil Rights Act, a time when social conditions for black people were extremely restricted. They left their home states to obtain degrees at traditionally white institutions of higher education, where being there did not guarantee fair and equal treatment. They were required to live and eat off campus, often finding themselves isolated in their studies. Similarly to Wilson, their career choices were limited, with teaching at an HBCU typically being their only career option.

Quiester Craig was part of the post-Civil Rights African American MBA/CPA/PhDs in accounting, alongside Talmadge Tillman from the University of Southern California (1968), Herbert Watkins from the University of Wisconsin (1970), and Johnnie Clark from the University of Georgia (1973). Together, these four raised the total number of African American PhDs in accounting to eleven. By 1973, these eleven accounted for less than 1 percent of the total 1,525 PhDs in accounting awarded in the United States.[7] As evidenced by these numbers in the early 1970s, there was a significant shortage of African American doctorates in accounting, an issue that extended to all business disciplines. The low supply of African Americans in business disciplines resulted from limited career opportunities in the field. Few black students opted to study business, and even fewer black educators specialized in accounting. These eleven individuals were exceptional in their educational endeavors and became pioneers in diversifying business school education early on.

Being particularly interested in Wilson's accreditation achievements, Quiester learned a great deal about his work at Texas Southern University and his plans for Howard University during their conversation. When Wilson arrived at Texas Southern, he dedicated his efforts to developing the business program. In 1955, this program was named the Jesse H. Jones School of Business in honor of a Houston-based businessman, politician, and philanthropist.[8] One of the most significant insights Quiester gained from their conversation was that having adequate resources was essential for achieving success. The Ford Foundation was among several organizations that provided financial support to help establish a high-quality academic business program at Texas Southern and enhance the infrastructure necessary for training and placing students in white-collar professional careers.

In 1965, the Ford Foundation allocated $600,000 to Texas Southern University. This grant was one in a series of grants totaling $1.1 million "to help prepare Negroes for business and management opportunities." Additional funding was granted to Wilson's alma mater, Indiana University, to provide instructors for faculty-student seminars and advisors to support program development.[9] The Sloan Foundation, and several others who had an interest in training minorities for jobs in business and industry, contributed financial support to this initiative as well.[10]

Infrastructure initiatives that supported the academic program included establishing career guidance and placement centers on HBCU campuses; executing a national media campaign through public service announcements on television, billboards, radio, and in newspapers and magazines to attract black students to pursue business careers; and positioning the National Urban League to act as a liaison between policymakers, corporate partners and administrators and teachers at HBCUs.[11] Both the funding and infrastructure improvements were needed to assist Wilson with meeting the AACSB accreditation standards. To meet the AACSB standards, Wilson also had to hire new faculty, reduce teaching loads to allow time for research, offer student scholarships, strengthen library resources, and collaborate with nearby high schools and colleges to develop a pipeline of interested students. In achieving AACSB accreditation at Texas Southern, Wilson executed a blueprint for success and subsequently moved to Howard University to replicate that achievement.

As dean of Howard University, he encountered many of the same challenges he had at Texas Southern. The administration was informed of the reasons and urgency for establishing an autonomous business school based on a proposal completed prior to his arrival. Gaps identified in the business training received at Howard included: their graduates were less competitive than graduates from accredited business schools; there was a need for more qualified professors; there was a need to align best practices in pedagogy with those of accredited business schools; fundraising needed improvement; and joint and exchange programs needed to be coordinated with more established business schools. Texas Southern was highlighted in the proposal as the first HBCU to achieve AACSB accreditation, and it was noted that Howard was not keeping pace with business schools of a similar size and nature, including HBCUs such as Atlanta University, which was also pursuing accreditation. Additionally, eleven other HBCUs were advancing their programs with modern or distinct physical facilities for business education.[12]

Due to his success at Texas Southern, Wilson established himself as a leader in HBCU business education and in American business school academia as well. He was well known and respected in philanthropic and corporate circles, and by the leaders of the business school at his alma mater, Indiana University. In 1966, Indiana University called upon him to participate in a conference aimed at assessing the feasibility of creating an organization to recruit more "qualified" African Americans into AACSB-accredited MBA programs. From this conference, the Consortium for Graduate Study in Management (the Consortium) was formed. The idea for the Consortium originated with Sterling Schoen, a professor at Washington University in St. Louis, Missouri, during the turbulent 1960s. In a 1979 interview with *Washington University* magazine, Schoen recalled, "In 1965, universities were in a time of turmoil and confusion; people were asking what we should do about equal education opportunities. I thought, why not do something we know how to do: train MBAs."[13]

As a sociologist and professor of organizational behavior, Schoen was well aware of the issues surrounding the exclusion of African

Americans in the corporate sector. Three years prior, he had completed several studies that highlighted what African Americans had been experiencing for almost one hundred years. His studies revealed that "Not one African American was employed in a management position at a Fortune 500 company, and only about fifty African Americans out of 12,000 students were enrolled in MBA programs across the country."[14] To implement change in this area, Schoen approached several of the nation's top business schools, hoping that at least five would participate in the Consortium. Only three signed on: Washington University, Indiana University, and the University of Wisconsin, with others expected to join later as the Consortium demonstrated its success.[15]

The Consortium indeed experienced success. In 2016, it celebrated its fiftieth anniversary, and its leaders acknowledged their pride in the organization's legacy of supporting over 10,000 men and women of color to earn graduate business degrees since 1966. During that celebration year William G. Panschar, the first chair of the Indiana University MBA program reflected, "Our thought was not to come up with a program that would send these bright young people with an MBA back to their own neighborhoods and start businesses. Nothing could be further from the truth. Our thought was that we were going to get them into the mainstream corporate America."[16]

As of 2023, 12,000 students had completed their MBAs through the Consortium, and the cooperative network of universities committed to the mission had grown to twenty-three member institutions. While the Consortium's original mission was to support black men, in 1970 it opened up to women, Hispanics, and Native Americans. In 2004 it opened up to all American citizens and permanent residents who demonstrate a commitment to the organization's mission.[17]

Quiester felt inspired by everything he learned during his conversation with Wilson, and his respect and admiration for him was further magnified as a result of this knowledge. Although he had spent his entire career in the classroom, he recognized the challenges that lay ahead for Wilson, even though he didn't fully understand the specific details involved in establishing an accredited business school. He viewed this opportunity to join Wilson's team as a way to broaden his knowledge, skills, and professional development, particularly in grasping the concept of accreditation, which had not been a focus in his previous roles. He was also attracted to the chance to work with Wilson, admiring his distinguished reputation in business school academia, the HBCU community, and the accounting profession. Quiester saw this as an opportunity to make a meaningful contribution to the field of business education and felt particularly excited about the potential to create positive change at an HBCU.

Clearly, Wilson's achievements captured the attention of HBCU presidents and chancellors. They closely followed each other and collaborated to tackle the negative impacts of segregation on black education, while also vying to be the first to implement innovative programs. Consequently, individuals with combined qualifications of MBA/CPA/PhD in accounting were appointed to lead HBCU business programs into the post-Civil Rights era. Among the eleven African American MBA/CPA/PhDs in accounting, eight rose to the deanships of HBCU business schools: Wilson at Texas Southern and Howard Universities, Harrison at Southern University, Sawyer at Morgan State, Hale at Langston University for a time, Mobley at Florida A&M University, Johnnie Clark at Atlanta University, and Quiester Craig at A&T. Watkins served as dean at A&T for one year before Quiester succeeded him. Ruth Coles Harris, a CPA and dean of the business program at Virginia Union University, was also part of the HBCU business school dean peer group, despite not holding a doctorate in accounting. She earned her doctorate in education from the College of William and Mary in Williamsburg, Virginia, as she was restricted from pursuing a doctoral program in accounting in her home state.[18]

These individuals were the first leaders of business schools at HBCUs to meet the faculty educational standards set by the AACSB. They were available when needed and equipped with their strong credentials to initiate the transformation of HBCU business school education, similar to Wilson's efforts, in order to prepare their students for professional careers in the corporate sector. Although Quiester's focus was that of a professor rather than a leader during his meeting with Wilson, he did recognize that he was in high demand. HBCU leaders likely preferred the combination of an MBA/CPA/PhD in accounting to help establish the accounting department as an integral component of their business administration programs. In 1963, just seven accounting programs existed at HBCUs, a number that increased to twenty-four by 1968 when the CPA profession was formally integrated.[19] Importantly, the credentialed individual with an MBA/CPA/PhD in accounting was also budget-efficient for HBCUs, as many of these individuals served in multiple roles as dean, chair of the accounting department, and as professors of accounting subjects.

Each of these individuals came from diverse backgrounds and overcame obstacles to obtain their credentials and earn their rightful place professionally. Campfield, Cramer, Tillman, and Hale made their mark by diversifying business school faculties at traditionally white institutions. Campfield served as a visiting professor at more than twenty colleges,[20] many during the time he could not be hired as full-time faculty because he was African American. Cramer, who studied under Wilson at Texas Southern and attended Indiana University at Wilson's recommendation, was the first tenured black faculty member at a traditionally white business school.[21]

As a woman, Hale broke numerous barriers in business school academia and the accounting profession. Professionally, she operated an accounting practice in Atlanta. At her undergraduate alma mater, Langston University, Hale chaired the business department, raised funds to increase salaries, expanded the library, supported faculty in their doctoral studies, and assisted youth in developing skills.[22] In 1971, she joined Utah State University and led the School of Accountancy for thirteen years[23] and later joined Brigham Young University. While on the faculty at Brigham Young, she became the first African American to serve a term as the national president of Beta Alpha Psi, the national honor society for the accounting profession. Hale also joined the AICPA in 1955 and the American Women's Society of CPAs, where she served as national president for one term. While in Utah, she was welcomed into the Utah Association of CPAs and joined its board of directors.[24]

Each of these individuals achieved unique and significant accomplishments, contributions, and advancements in diversifying business schools, professional organizations, and the management profession; teaching at predominantly white institutions; and taking on leadership roles within professional organizations. Regardless of the side they worked on, the achievements of the pioneering MBA/CPA/PhDs in accounting significantly shifted perceptions of people of color in business school academia, professional organizations, philanthropy, and corporate America. All eleven—Campfield, Wilson, Harrison, Sawyer, Hale, Cramer, Mobley, Tillman, Watkins, Clark, and Coles Harris—played a role in laying the groundwork that Quiester Craig benefited from in obtaining his education and in the success he experienced as his career advanced. While each of these individuals had a significant impact, Wilson stood out as a giant in the realm of HBCU business school academia for being the first to achieve AACSB accreditation for an HBCU. "Privately, we referred to him as the Chief and sometimes the Godfather because of his accomplishments," Dean Craig shared with admiration.

As Quiester's visit to Howard University came to a close, his respect for Wilson grew even more. He admired Wilson as a leader and envisioned that working under him would provide an opportunity to watch and learn from his experiences. Wilson reinforced ideas that Quiester already knew, such as, "Don't give up, be bold, and anything is possible if you work and believe." Quiester recognized that Wilson set high expectations for his faculty and students and that he had top-quality CPAs and MBAs among his faculty, credentials that were equivalent to the accounting PhD qualifications required for AACSB accreditation. With his PhD in accounting, he knew that was an even stronger credential for the job.

As a result of the meeting, Quiester gained a broader perspective on Wilson's body of work up to that point. He also acquired insights into the importance of external support in building a high-quality business program; the advantages of full membership in the AACSB, which provided access to information and deans from America's finest business schools; and how Wilson had to believe in himself, work hard, and earn his way. He had an excellent experience visiting with Wilson and was receptive to his ideas, particularly since the plans for the business school were substantial.

In the final analysis, Quiester was pleased with the opportunity that Wilson presented to him and felt that working for him would be a valuable experience; however, his decision ultimately came down to location. He simply decided that he did not want to adjust to the fast pace around Howard University's campus. Being an Alabama boy, he was not fond of a big city environment, so he returned to FAMU to finish the spring semester of 1972 with the intention of continuing his career there. However, by the summer of 1972, he had accepted a position as dean of the School of Business and Economics at A&T.

CHAPTER 11

Accreditation, the Equalizer

To be considered for the position of dean of the School of Business and Economics at A&T, the chancellor, Dr. Lewis Carnegie Dowdy invited Quiester to visit the campus in Greensboro, North Carolina, to discuss his vision for the university and his goals for the business program. During this visit, he had a humorous encounter with a familiar person from his past, which established a friendly tone for his relationship with Chancellor Dowdy—one that was "mutually respectful, highly productive, and exceedingly meaningful."

This was Quiester's second invitation to A&T. During his first year at FAMU, Dr. Ted Mahaffey, who led the business program, invited him to discuss a position in the accounting department but their negotiations stalled. Quiester knew a great deal about A&T because it was well regarded academically and athletically. He used to visit the library on Mondays while at Atlanta University to read the black newspaper out of Baltimore, Maryland, which covered the black community, black colleges, and black college sports. So, he was familiar with A&T from that perspective and viewed it as a good school. On his second visit, he remained open-minded and noticeably interested in what Dowdy was aiming to achieve, but he still wasn't fully considering the idea of leaving the classroom just yet. His meeting with Wilson, however, had been insightful.

Dowdy was a long-term employee at A&T who rose through the ranks, holding various teaching and administrative positions before being appointed chancellor of the university. He stood about six-foot-one-inch tall and consistently wore suspenders. His credentials were impressive, as was the way he carried himself, delivered his messages, moved about, and conducted himself in various actions. He was involved in many initiatives and had a clear, ambitious vision for the university that he was executing effectively. Dowdy was known as "Big Lou" around campus, but not because of his physical size. He had a lean stature. He was called "'Big Lou" because his thoughts and accomplishments were substantial.[1] He always maintained his composure and found humor in situations as well.

Dowdy's work was indeed a determining factor in shaping his identity. He received acclaim for guiding A&T through the tumultuous 1960s, enhancing the university's academic standards, and transforming it from a "black school run by a white male-dominated board of directors" into a proactive institution that demanded the same resources the predominantly white public universities (in the state) had long enjoyed.[2]

By the time Quiester visited, Dowdy had been at A&T for nearly twenty-one years. He joined the faculty in 1951 as an instructor in education and director of student teaching. Before being appointed the sixth president of A&T in 1964, Dowdy served as an assistant professor of education, dean of instruction, and acting president in 1962 and 1963 while then-President Samuel Proctor answered a call from President Kennedy to serve in the Peace Corps. Shortly after Proctor returned, he resigned, and Dowdy was officially appointed president of the university, a position he held for sixteen years before retiring in 1980.[3]

Dowdy guided A&T through significant societal changes. Both the Civil Rights Movement and the dismantling of the dual system of separate but equal higher education in the Southern States occurred during his tenure. Students at A&T were already engaged in the Civil Rights Movement before he assumed the presidency. The Greensboro Four—Joseph McNeil, Franklin McCain, Ezell Blair, Jr., and David Richmond—were A&T freshmen who sat at the "whites-only" Woolworth's lunch counter in Greensboro on February 1, 1960, to protest segregation. Their actions not only inspired the sit-in movement that ultimately spread to fifty-five cities across thirteen states but also served as a precursor to the ongoing protests and activism during Dowdy's tenure.

In 1963, over 1,000 A&T students, led by student council president Jesse Jackson, were arrested following desegregation demonstrations in downtown Greensboro. North Carolina's white political establishment directed Dowdy to secure the students' release and ensure their compliance; otherwise, A&T risked losing its state funding. The demonstrations concluded with significant integration of downtown Greensboro, and Dowdy was recognized for handling the situation without losing the students' respect or the state's financial support due to his diplomatic skills. His diplomatic abilities were tested again in May 1969 during the three-day Dudley High School disturbance that spilled over to A&T and ultimately brought the National Guard to its campus.[4]

By the time Quiester arrived for his interview in the summer of 1972, things had calmed down, and the racial issues had receded beneath the surface. He found Greensboro to be a pleasant city. It was larger and prettier than Tallahassee, quieter compared to DC, and he thought it resembled Montgomery, where he grew up.

During his visit to meet Dowdy, Quiester toured A&T's campus and noted the well-manicured and maintained grounds. The business school was located in Merrick Hall, which was air-conditioned, and the prospect of working in an air-conditioned building appealed to him. He was impressed by the city, the campus, the buildings, and the individuals Dowdy arranged for him to meet. He found these individuals impressive, perceiving them as progressive. Among those he met were Dr. Glenn Rankin from the Dowdy administration, Dr.

Alvin Blount, and Cal Irvin, A&T's head basketball coach who later became the athletic director.

Clearly, Dowdy intended to impress Quiester, and he accomplished this by introducing him to some of Greensboro's influential figures in the African American community. Dr. Alvin Blount was among those individuals. Blount, a native of North Carolina, was a distinguished graduate of A&T. He graduated magna cum laude in the class of 1939 with a degree in chemistry, serving as student body president and chairman of the student newspaper. Due to his academic achievements, he received a state tuition grant that contributed to funding his medical degree from Howard University Medical School. While at Howard, Blount had the great fortune of studying under Dr. Charles Drew, an African American renowned for developing a new understanding of blood plasma, which permitted blood to be stored for transfusion.[5]

As an adult, Blount became well known for two noteworthy achievements: After President Harry Truman desegregated the U.S. military in 1948, he was the first African American to serve in the first integrated Mobile Army Surgical Hospital (MASH) unit during the Korean War, and he was also the first African American to serve as the chief surgeon of a MASH unit. MASH units became well known when their history was chronicled first in a published novel that gave rise to an Academy Award winning film in 1970, and later, a popular long-running television series. An even greater accomplishment was his role in helping to integrate hospitals across the Southern States as part of a group of African American doctors, including George Simkins, Jr., a dentist, activist, and leader of the Greensboro Chapter of the NAACP, who served their black patients in separate but unequal medical facilities. In the 1950s, these doctors sought help from the NAACP Legal Defense Fund to challenge the city's segregated hospital system and won.[6]

Quiester felt right at home meeting Calvin "Cal" Irvin, the head basketball coach, due to his passion for sports. Irvin was a two-sport athlete who played both basketball and football at Morgan State. He also had a brief stint playing in the Negro Baseball League. As the basketball coach at A&T, he secured four basketball titles in the CIAA. Irvin made history and stunned the basketball world when he led A&T to the Final Four in the 1959 NCAA (Small) College Division Basketball Tournament, which was the predecessor to today's NCAA Divisions II and III. He also earned a reputation not only as a basketball coach but as a revered mentor to hundreds of African American men, including NBA star and coach Al Attles, who played college basketball under Irvin and was a part of the 1959 run.[7]

Dowdy was eager to close the deal with Quiester. He had touched on several of his sweet spots, introducing him to individuals involved in sports and civil rights. Being from Montgomery, Alabama, Quiester was very aware of the struggle, and he, like Dowdy, believed that it should not dictate the future. During their meeting, Dowdy discussed the past, present, and his expectations for the future regarding the business program and all academic programs at A&T. He expressed his belief that change was inevitable, and now that it had occurred, he wanted A&T to take the lead in making change. Dowdy explained that his vision for change meant that African Americans would no longer be excluded from mainstream society, and that one day they would gain access to professional white-collar jobs and management careers that would improve their socioeconomic conditions. With that day finally here, he emphasized the importance of ensuring that A&T's students were academically prepared in every field of study offered by the university, including business.

Dowdy began charting the course toward his vision as soon as he took office as president. In his inaugural address, he articulated what he considered to be the three most important characteristics of colleges at that time: to be dynamic and aggressive, to be attuned to the critical issues and aspirations of our society, and to possess a clear sense of direction along with a rigorous and ongoing evaluation program. He promptly called on the A&T family—the faculty, students, alumni, philanthropic organizations, and the Board of Trustees—to support his initiatives aimed at curriculum reform, academic reorganization, enhancing student quality, and fostering faculty development at the university.[8]

Early in his presidency, he led the university in launching an all-important Institutional Self-Analysis and Long-Range Projection study, using the findings to set goals to be achieved within five to ten years. Acknowledging the challenges presented by society and the significance of his faith in reaching his goals, Dowdy pledged "a rigorous pursuit of excellence."[9]

He wrote, "In the years ahead, if God be willing, we shall carry forward with all our strength the great work in which we are engaged, building upon the splendid foundation erected by our predecessors, striving for excellence in all we do. We shall be alert to the complex problems, the deep conflicts and the tremendous challenges in the world and keep before us the vision of bringing light to our youth, knowledge to our people, progress to our State, strength to our Nation, and hopefully, wisdom to ourselves."[10]

In that context, the Dowdy administration established a strategic goal to complete the process of national program accreditation in all subject areas with defined standards and criteria set by a national professional body. He wanted all departments and schools to accomplish this goal by 1976.[11]

Dowdy understood the significance of accredited academic programs. In his meeting with Quiester, he discussed the importance of accreditation regarding its impact on student preparation and the university's future growth. He conveyed the message that national accreditation communicates to the public and how it could reshape the negative perceptions surrounding A&T, its students, and HBCUs in general. He also stressed program quality as essential to accreditation and focused on how it would improve the competitiveness of A&T's graduates in the job market while also bolstering the university's position for growth. As historically black public colleges lagged in having accredited academic programs, Dowdy's strategy for A&T focused on overcoming the various challenges to achieve this goal. "He regarded national accreditation as an equalizer that could level the playing field for A&T and its students," Dean Craig explained.

At the time of Quiester's visit in 1972, three out of nine academic programs eligible for national accreditation had been successfully accredited. The School of Engineering, the School of Nursing, and the Department of Chemistry received national accreditation in 1969, 1971, and 1972, respectively. Committed to his goals and the established timeline, Dowdy had the process in motion for other academic programs, including the business program. He was meeting with Quiester to determine his suitability to become the dean of A&T's business school and lead the process for AACSB accreditation.

As Dowdy spoke, Quiester realized that he was asking him to take on the same role that his mentor, Wilson, was performing. He was initially concerned for two reasons. First, he admired the PhD cohort of seven and had not yet fully processed that, now that he was a PhD, he was their peer. Secondly, he had limited experience with accreditation and, at that moment, he knew only what he had learned from Wilson and what he had absorbed from listening to Dowdy. With Wilson having achieved accreditation once and pursuing it again, along with Dowdy's highlighted success at A&T, Quiester was left with the impression that national accreditation could not be that difficult to obtain. Clearly, Dowdy's aspirations for the university and the business program sparked his interest, although he was still focused on classroom teaching. He did not yet envision himself as an administrator. However, he was very impressed with Dowdy and A&T.

Staying true to his vision, Dowdy had already set the wheels in motion for the business program. The most significant progress toward national accreditation efforts for the business program was the completion of a self-study that identified the improvements needed to obtain AACSB accreditation. In 1969, deans from the Schools of

Business Administration at Wake Forest University and Georgia State College (now Georgia State University) served as consultants in completing the self-study. It addressed eleven areas: purpose and goals, organization and administration, educational programs, financial resources, faculty, library, students, physical plant, special activities, graduate program, and research. The recommendations outlined the enhancements needed to meet the AACSB standards. Only two of the recommendations did not have significant costs associated with them: changing the division status to school status and renaming the school to the School of Management and Administrative Science. By the time of Quiester's visit, the division status had been upgraded to school status; however, the suggested name change was never implemented. The Division of Business became the School of Business and Economics.[12]

All of the remaining recommendations in the 1969 Self-Study Report required substantial funding and significant change. One recommendation addressed the need to offer more specialized business subjects instead of the general program of business being offered. This meant that the accounting department would remain an autonomous entity, while the business education and office management department would separate office management into its own autonomous department. The business administration department would be restructured from a general program of study into nine departments to provide more specialized study: Management, including Office Management; Marketing; Finance; Information Systems and Data Processing; Operations Research; Risk and Insurance; International Business; Public Administration; and Transportation.[13]

To implement the program restructuring, it was advised that department chairs be promptly appointed, along with a sufficient number of faculty members with terminal degrees in accordance with the AACSB's full-time faculty standards. Terminal degrees referred to hiring faculty with PhDs in their respective specialized fields. With student enrollment projected to reach 1,000 by 1980, a total of thirty faculty members was suggested. Faculty teaching loads were to be reduced to six hours per semester to facilitate increased faculty research. The 1969 Self-Study Report also proposed the establishment of distinguished professorships with nationally recognized experts at salaries of $30,000 each and the creation of two additional faculty positions: one to develop innovative programs, materials, and methods tailored to meet the needs of "underprivileged" students, and a curriculum expert to equip faculty in utilizing more quantitative approaches and updated technologies.[14]

The 1969 Self-Study Report also recommended an increase in the budget and new facilities for implementing the new academic program. The budget was projected to rise from $30,310 to $145,000, and $2 million was required to construct a new three-story, air-conditioned building equipped with a high-speed elevator and facilities for television and computer science capabilities.[15]

The recommendations in the 1969 Self-Study Report addressed every possible issue in building a high-quality business program that would meet the AACSB accreditation standards. These were all appropriate actions. The only issue with them was that they did not consider the financial constraints faced by A&T as a public HBCU. Numerous complex problems underlying those recommendations required resolution and implementing them would require significant effort and cost. Additionally, it would take time. During Quiester's visit, Dowdy did not emphasize the complexity of the task; instead, he focused on his vision, goals, accomplishments with accreditation, and, of course, the impact he desired for A&T's students and the university.

Dowdy was a student-centered chancellor, and as it related to the business program, his ultimate goal was to provide A&T's students with opportunities for success in white-collar professional careers. He aimed to meet the demands of business and industry in placing graduates, and the 1969 Self-Study Report indicated that this was possible to some extent. Top-ranking students were noted as facing little difficulty in securing well-paying positions with nationally recognized firms across the country, with some receiving four to five lucrative offers and "rewarding promotions" within their companies. In contrast, it also pointed out that the business program, in its current state, would increasingly struggle to meet the demands of business and industry. In terms of Dowdy's goals and aspirations, this undoubtedly intensified the urgency to upgrade the business program and achieve AACSB accreditation.

The ideas Dowdy expressed to Quiester about student placement were aggressive. With HBCU students having been excluded from the management profession for so long, he wanted every job they were aware of on campus to be filled with one of his students. So, as he saw it, time was of the essence. He wanted to move fast and work hard to elevate the business program to a high-quality academic standard. He also recognized that first impressions are often lasting impressions, and he did not want to damage the university's reputation. As Dowdy discussed his dedication to achieving his goals, the significance of these goals for the university's long-term viability, and the impact he wanted to have on students' lives, Quiester became increasingly interested in the opportunity that was being presented to him.

He shared, "Dowdy impressed me. As he spoke about the impact a dean could have on students' lives, I realized I didn't have to sacrifice what I loved most about teaching. He encouraged me to consider new career possibilities for myself. As one of the younger MBA/CPA/PhDs in accounting, I hadn't thought much about becoming a leader like my mentor, Wilson, or my boss, Mobley, and the others I admired. But Dowdy presented me with that opportunity, and it forced me to contemplate the potential, in the particular area. I began to think about the outcomes if I were dean. What if I led faculty and student recruitment and secured scholarships for the students? What impact could I have on students as a leader? Looking back, what Dowdy was doing to elevate the university to a higher level of academic excellence was groundbreaking for a black public college in the South at that time. Resources were suspect at best. His vision for national accreditation of all the university's qualifying programs was groundbreaking, considering the circumstances. With his achievements in this area, he laid the foundation for what has brought A&T to where it is today."

Dowdy was implementing his vision at the university at the same time that higher education was being restructured in the state of North Carolina, following a trend that was happening across the country from the 1950s to 1970s. As the restructuring related to accreditation, the objectives that were established by the North Carolina Board of Higher Education in 1968 required that all North Carolina institutions "seek and maintain" regional accreditation and all state authorized professional programs "maintain minimum standards" of national accreditation. For programs that could not gain national accreditation, it was stated that the General Assembly would "provide additional support" for them or consider "discontinuing the program." Obviously, this raised the bar for HBCU presidents and likely concerned them since some of their academic programs, such as business education, were underdeveloped. To Dowdy's good fortune, he already had the wheels in motion for obtaining national accreditation for academic programs at A&T as a part of the vision he established for the university upon assuming the presidency in 1964.[16]

As the restructuring related to the state's five historically black universities—Elizabeth City State, Fayetteville State, North Carolina Agricultural and Technical State, North Carolina Central, and Winston-Salem State—these universities were brought under the umbrella of the Consolidated University. At the same time, five other institutions—the state's Native American school, Pembroke State College for Indians (now UNC Pembroke); and three traditionally white institutions, Appalachian State University, East Carolina University, and Western Carolina University—and the North

Carolina School of the Arts, which offered high school programs for performing artists as well as a college curriculum, were also brought under the Consolidated University.[17] Prior to the restructuring, the Consolidated University included UNC-Chapel Hill; North Carolina State University, a land-grant institution; UNC Greensboro; UNC Wilmington; UNC Charlotte; and UNC Asheville. Essentially, the restructuring brought all of the sixteen institutions under the UNC System. Under this new structure, President Dowdy became Chancellor Dowdy, and governance, which had been solely in the hands of the local A&T Board of Trustees, was now shared with the North Carolina Board of Governors.[18]

During this same period, the federal government faced pressure from the NAACP Legal Defense Fund to dismantle the dual system of separate but equal higher education, as mandated by the *Brown* decision. The initial impact of *Brown* focused on the desegregation of primary and secondary education, with little attention given to the desegregation of higher educational institutions. Consequently, North Carolina and nine other states failed to provide adequate or timely restructuring plans for desegregation as required by the federal government, resulting in a lawsuit filed by the NAACP known as *Adams v. Richardson*. This lawsuit claimed that the Department of Health, Education, and Welfare (HEW) had defaulted in the administration of Title VI of the Civil Rights Act of 1964 by continuing to provide federal funding to these states, since little had been done toward desegregating their public colleges and universities.[19]

Unlike the numerous lawsuits leading up to the *Brown* decision, during which the NAACP and the African American community collaborated to gain equal educational opportunities for black youth, black college presidents did not support the *Adams v. Richardson* lawsuit. They feared that their institutions would be closed under a strict interpretation of separate but equal facilities.[20] They also recalled the experiences of Lincoln University in Missouri and others whose desegregation in the early 1960s and 1970s resulted in a majority white student enrollment; Lincoln University was nearly 50 percent white and two HBCUs in West Virginia were 80 percent white, while Kentucky State stood at about 40 percent white.[21]

To express their concerns about the NAACP's lawsuit, 107 black college presidents, through their professional organization, the National Association for Equal Opportunity in Higher Education (NAFEO), filed an amicus brief arguing that "black institutions had not promoted segregation and therefore should not be punished for having served the black community at a time when no one else would."[22] They advocated for the special mission and needs of black colleges and recommended that the unequal status be recognized when establishing criteria for the desegregation plans. They also noted that the real danger in desegregating was the reality of diminishing higher educational opportunities for African Americans.[23]

While the ultimate outcomes of the restructuring positively impacted all the institutions within the UNC System, central to the prolonged discussions, disputes, perceptions, and politics were many unanswered questions about the future of HBCUs. One primary question that remained unanswered was: What role would HBCUs play in the larger system? As the state reorganized while negotiating the mandated desegregation, HBCU presidents questioned whether the restructuring was merely "a smokescreen" for closing their institutions or if they would gain or lose under the new system. When the conversation shifted to perceived unnecessary duplication within the system, the underlying causes were not explicitly tackled.[24] This raised concerns for HBCU leaders because, at the state's five HBCUs, program duplication was a direct legacy of segregation—an issue created by the state itself. With A&T located near UNC Greensboro, it faced particular vulnerability. In North Carolina, these issues dominated the news headlines and preoccupied the UNC System, HBCU presidents, HBCU students, and the HBCU community for nearly a decade until they were ultimately resolved in a consent decree in July 1981.[25] This was the environment in which Dowdy pursued his vision to upgrade A&T's academic programs to national accreditation. Throughout this process, he relied on his faith to create an academically competitive institution while at the same time fighting to keep it.

During Quiester's visit with Dowdy, there was no discussion of the dismantling. Dowdy was laser-focused on his vision of national accreditation for A&T's programs of study, particularly regarding what he envisioned for the business school. Fortunately, he came to the decision that Quiester Craig was the right person to lead the initiative.

Quiester never inquired how Dowdy became aware of him. He always assumed it was due to Mahaffey. However, quite surprisingly, he received an endorsement from an acquaintance he didn't know they had in common. Quiester's visit to A&T concluded with dinner at The Oak, Dowdy's campus residence. Dowdy's wife, Mrs. Elizabeth Dowdy, was present, and later, another gentleman joined them at the table. As they conversed, the gentleman leaned over to Dowdy and remarked, "I don't know what kind of dean he'll be, but whatever you ask him to do, be prepared for him to do it."

As Quiester recognized the voice of the person speaking, he looked over more closely and immediately dropped his head. Dowdy glanced at him and smirked as Mrs. Dowdy politely left the table to avoid bursting into laughter. "I recognized the gentleman who spoke as the Dr. Dowdy whose car I had towed while fulfilling my duties on the parking committee during my early days at Lincoln University," Quiester stated. "I was called to the president's office about that, and my colleagues explained that there are some things you just don't do. I had never connected the Dowdy name and learned at that dinner that they were brothers. We all had a good laugh about that encounter," he shared, laughing.

All laughs aside, Dowdy's offer came with a clear mandate. He wanted the business program accredited by the AACSB, pure and simple. So, as the opportunity presented itself, Quiester Craig decided to give it a try. When he accepted the position he was just thirty-six years old and he had no idea of the complexity of the job he had signed up for, nor that he would stay with it for the length of time he did. But nothing pleased him more than to be a part of accomplishing Dowdy's vision to get all of A&T's qualifying academic programs nationally accredited. The business program was the last one. Of the challenges Dowdy faced as chancellor, years later Dean Craig was quoted in a newspaper article saying, "He had to be a magician. He was given a lot of chairs without seats in them."[26]

CHAPTER 12

The Craig Era Begins

As a new leader, Dean Craig had to develop his plan to fulfill Dowdy's vision of establishing an AACSB-accredited business school. When accomplished in 1979, it became the fourth business school in North Carolina and the UNC System to receive the AACSB designation, joining UNC-Chapel Hill, East Carolina University, and Appalachian State University. At that time, only four HBCU business schools had been accredited: Texas Southern University, Atlanta University, Howard University, and North Carolina Agricultural and Technical State University. As predicted, Atlanta University outpaced Howard University when Johnnie Clark earned AACSB accreditation for the Atlanta University Graduate School of Business Administration in 1974, making it the second HBCU to reach that status. Wilson secured AACSB accreditation in 1976 for Howard University's undergraduate business program, making it the second undergraduate HBCU business program to be accredited, and A&T became the third. Wilson earned AACSB accreditation twice, at two different schools—Texas Southern University and Howard University—marking a significant achievement for him as a business school dean. Upon accreditation in 1979, like Wilson and Clark, Dean Craig became one of only a few African American AACSB deans from HBCUs.

Accreditation represented a significant achievement for all HBCUs, considering their history. A&T, a small public black college in the South, took particular pride in its status as a business school with a designation that indicated program quality on a national level. With the attainment of accreditation, business education at A&T had advanced considerably from its modest beginnings. The School of Business and Economics at A&T was officially established as the Commercial Department during the 1924–25 school year, but this was not the beginning of business education at the institution. As early as 1898, a limited selection of relevant courses was available to students aimed at developing the knowledge and skills necessary to start their own businesses in the pursuit of economic security in segregated America. Early students earning degrees in agriculture and the mechanical arts, as well as certificates in various trades, were instructed in basic business principles to prepare them for operating their own farms, service establishments, and small retail stores as a means of achieving economic survival in the prevailing social climate.

From the beginning, the college offered courses that taught skills useful for doing business in agricultural-related areas, including farm and poultry farm management, farm accounting, agricultural economics, commercial beekeeping, manufacturing of dairy products, marketing, and financing vegetable gardens. In addition to agricultural studies, students were also taught trades so they could start businesses in fields such as hotel and lunchroom management, mattress and cabinet making, blacksmithing, woodturning, wheelwrighting, contracting and building, electrical work, automobile mechanics and photography.[1]

Whether pursuing a degree in agriculture, mechanical arts, or obtaining a certificate from the trade school, the curriculum provided essential knowledge to help manage the financial and legal aspects of one's business. In those early years, students were required to complete a specified number of hours studying a combination of courses in bookkeeping, accounting, business writing, business math, and business law and contracts.[2] During this period, professional careers in business available to A&T's students were offered by prominent African American businessmen John Merrick and Charles C. Spaulding. Together, they founded the Mechanics and Farmers Bank, North Carolina's oldest black-owned bank, along with the North Carolina Mutual Life Insurance Company, both of which served as anchor businesses for Durham's Black Wall Street. As early as 1903, A&T's graduates found employment at the bank and worked as insurance agents, selling life insurance to African Americans across the state.[3]

In the school's early days, the focus of business training was quite different from what Dean Craig was hired to do in 1972. His role was to develop an AACSB-accredited business program at the business school to prepare students for competitive management positions in corporate America, since African Americans had gained access to those career opportunities with the passage of Title VII of the Civil Rights Act of 1964, which prohibited employment discrimination based on race, color, religion, sex, and national origin. To achieve his goals, he needed to lay a solid foundation to ensure the success of his students as they entered the long-established management profession, which expanded during the post-Civil War economy due to the introduction of the new technologies of that time: manufacturing, rail, and transportation, as well as the new laws that facilitated the rise and growth of the corporate entity.

As the management profession solidified in the American economy, business training at the collegiate level followed, when in 1881, Joseph Wharton—a prominent mining and manufacturing industrialist and founder of Bethlehem Steel—endowed the Wharton School of Finance and Economy at the University of Pennsylvania.[4] After a seventeen-year gap, the University of Chicago and the University of California, Berkeley, were the next to establish their colleges of business, and by the 1920s, business education at the collegiate level had taken root. During this period, the nation's economic landscape experienced tremendous growth in managerial jobs, and in response, both undergraduate and graduate business studies became the fastest-growing degree programs in American higher education, with over 400 colleges and universities offering some form of the business curriculum and 132 of these schools offering business as a major.[5] As business schools rapidly grew, the AACSB, established in 1916, was the main organization through which business school deans addressed educational standards for business education.

HBCUs were a part of the business school growth in the 1920s. In 1929, there were twelve HBCUs offering four-year curriculums leading to a bachelor's degree in business,[6] with Howard University being the first. That number increased to seventeen by the 1935–36 school year,[7] and by 1940, there were twenty-eight. Only six of the total business programs were started prior to 1926.[8] Wilberforce University was the first HBCU to offer business courses in 1865 followed by Fisk University in 1916 to assist African Americans with gaining some fundamental knowledge of economic and business principles.[9] Leaders in the black community recognized the importance of business education as far back as the mid-1800s. Entrepreneur and abolitionist Martin Delany said in 1852: "Let our young men and women prepare themselves for usefulness and business; that the men may enter into merchandising, trading, and other things of importance. . . Educate them for the store and the Counting House to do every day practical business. . . What we need most then, is a good practical business education."[10]

With A&T's business program having officially started in the 1924–25 school year, Dean Craig had a foundation to build on in his new role. In the fall of 1928, Mr. Llewellyn A. Wise was hired as the first instructor with college-level business school credentials. He held a Bachelor of Science degree from New York University and a Master of Arts from Atlanta University. Wise restructured the curriculum to include business administration and secretarial science. The business administration curriculum included Principles of Management,

Money and Banking, Salesmanship, Office Management, Business Law, and Real Estate. Over the years, he continued to develop the program by adding additional courses, including Accounting, Principles of Insurance, Advertising, and Retailing. The Secretarial Science curriculum encompassed typing, shorthand, stenography, operation of business machines, and office management. Starting in the 1929–30 school year, students earned certificates in secretarial science.[11]

Wise complemented the academic program with student enrichment activities to promote personal and leadership development. Students had opportunities to meet successful African American entrepreneurs. Notably, a student trip to Atlanta's Auburn Avenue business district in 1947 included visits to some of the city's largest and most successful black-owned businesses, such as Atlanta Life Insurance Company, the *Atlanta Daily World* Negro newspaper, and Citizens Trust Company, among others. On the way to Atlanta, they stopped in Anderson, South Carolina, to meet Mr. Peek, a restaurateur, funeral director, and realtor. During lunch at his restaurant, Peek spoke of his success, attributing it to the segregated black market in a non-competitive city. The students also toured a dry-cleaning company owned by Mr. Thomas, who credited his success to a "'stick-to-it-ness' attitude and determination."[12] These experiences provided students with insights into the employment and entrepreneurial opportunities available to them during that era.

A&T was visited by many speakers, such as W.J. Kennedy, the president of the North Carolina Mutual Life Insurance Company. In 1953, Kennedy delivered an inspiring and realistic message that highlighted the achievements African Americans had made in business up to that time. He discussed the history of the roughly one hundred black-owned corporations in insurance, banking, and building and loan associations, which had combined assets exceeding $227 million. He acknowledged that although these businesses were small compared to the national landscape, their success demonstrated the

African American community's capacity to organize, develop, and manage corporate enterprises. He advocated for the development of stronger group achievement programs so that those businesses could grow on an even larger scale.[13]

Under Llewellyn Wise's leadership, the accounting department was first established in 1950 by Mr. Harvey Alexander. Alexander joined A&T's Department of Business after a stint as an accounting professor at Southern University.[14] He was the sole accounting faculty member in the department for six years, with one faculty member joining him in his seventh year. During this time, the school's Annual Bulletin listed a wide range of accounting courses, including Principles, Intermediate, Advanced, Cost, Federal Taxation, Accounting Systems, Auditing, Governmental, and several others.[15] Like Dean Craig did at Lincoln University, Alexander likely taught a broad range of accounting subjects in alternating semesters during his seven years at A&T.

In addition to being an accounting professor, Alexander was also a Tuskegee Airman, and the first African American student admitted to the School of Commerce at the University of Illinois. He transferred there after spending two years at Fisk University in pursuit of an accounting degree. He left the University of Illinois for the University of Michigan in 1942 after encountering discrimination from his professors and fellow students. Two weeks after his arrival at the University of Michigan, he was drafted into World War II, where he trained as a pilot and became a Tuskegee Airman. Although he never saw combat, he took pride in achieving what so few had accomplished by qualifying as a pilot.[16]

Like all Tuskegee Airmen, Alexander was denied the opportunity to become a commercial pilot after completing his service in the U.S. Army due to segregation. In 1945, he returned to the University of Illinois on the GI Bill, where he earned a BS in Industrial Management. Unable to find a local accounting job with that degree, he later earned a master's degree in accounting from

Duquesne University and pursued a career teaching accounting at the collegiate level.[17]

Wise led the business program for twenty-five years, until the 1952–53 school year. By that time, the department had seven faculty members and offered majors in Business Administration, Business Education, and Secretarial Science. The focus of the program was on business education, secretarial training, and office management, with thirty-four degrees granted in this area during the 1952–53 school year. In the same year, thirteen degrees were granted in business administration.[18] During Wise's tenure, more than 150 students completed the department's curriculum and secured employment. Wise remained on the faculty until the 1969–70 school year and was named chairman emeritus for his contributions to establishing, growing, and sustaining the business program for over two decades.[19]

Dr. James L. Stuart succeeded Wise in the 1953–54 school year. He specialized in business education and office management, which remained the focus of the business program during his tenure. Stuart earned his undergraduate degree from Hampton Institute, his graduate degree from Boston University, and his PhD from Ohio State University.[20] He continued with student enrichment activities, including the organization of the Gamma Phi chapter of Pi Omega Pi, a national honor society for business teachers, in 1954.[21]

In 1957, Alexander left A&T to serve as the business manager at Shaw University, an HBCU in Raleigh, North Carolina.[22] After his departure, the accounting department experienced challenges in retaining faculty and maintaining continuity in its course offerings. It had one professor during the 1957–58 school year; however, there were none listed in the Annual School Bulletin for the following ten-year period. Only Natwar Ghandi, an instructor in business administration, was listed as an accounting instructor in the 1968–69 school year.[23]

After gaining experience at Shaw University, Alexander returned to A&T in the role of business manager in 1961. Due to the shortage of African American accountants at the time, professors often transitioned from the classroom to administrative roles within the college. Dean Craig was no exception. Soon after the business program was accredited in 1979, he assumed the role of Acting Vice Chancellor of Fiscal Affairs in Dowdy's administration for one year, from May 1980 to June 1981.

Stuart left the business department in the 1957–58 school year. At that time, the total enrollment in the business program reached sixty-four.[24] Following Stuart, Dr. Ted Mahaffey became the chair of the Department of Business in the 1961–62 school year. At that time, the Department of Business was a part of the School of Engineering. In keeping with Dowdy's accreditation plans, on July 1, 1967, the Department of Business was made an autonomous unit called the Division of Business Administration with four departments: Accounting, Business Administration, Business Education and Office Administration, and Economics. In 1968, the Department of Economics was moved to the Division of Social Studies in the School of Arts and Sciences and returned to the Division of Business in 1972, causing several name changes of the business program over that period. When the economics department was reunited with the business program in 1972, the Division of Business became the School of Business and Economics.[25]

Under Mahaffey, student enrollment showed steady increases, which was an indication of the changing employment trends for African Americans. Enrollment grew from sixty-four in the late 1950s to 645 in 1966, and by 1968 it had increased by 13 percent to 725.[26] Like Lincoln University and FAMU, where Dean Craig had taught, A&T students also shifted their focus away from business education, office management, and secretarial training to require more courses in business administration and accounting. While the courses for the business program were maintained at the status quo, Mahesh C. Jain, a professor in the business administration department, added accounting courses to his teaching load. Jain had an undergraduate degree from Delhi Polytechnic, an MBA from Atlanta University, and a Bachelor of Law degree from the Commercial University of India. For the 1968–69 to 1971–72 school years, Jain was joined by another accounting faculty member. In pursuit of Dowdy's goals, Dr. Herbert Watkins, one of the eleven African Americans with the MBA/CPA/PhD in accounting credentials, was hired to lead the accounting program.[27]

Additionally, aligning with Dowdy's goals, Mahaffey's signature initiative was the completion of the 1969 Self-Study Report for the business program. Under his leadership, student enrichment activities in business education remained a vital part of the department's focus. Students joined organizations such as the American Business Education Association and the Future Business Leaders of America; subscribed to *Business Education World*, a monthly magazine for aspiring business teachers; and participated in typing contests.[28] Student activities evolved with the times, and by 1970, students participated in an intercollegiate business school competition at Emory University in Atlanta, utilizing computer technology to analyze and report their findings on their project.[29]

One significant enrichment activity that Mahaffey introduced was student internships. In the fall of 1961, thirteen business administration majors worked as interns with local insurance companies, banks, retail stores, dry cleaners, and supermarkets.[30] While Mahaffey was likely applauded for these efforts, they were not the types of internships Dowdy envisioned for A&T's students. He asked rhetorically, "How can a kid who spends his accounting internship in a corner grocery store making change from a cigar box compete with a white kid working at a large eastern bank?"[31] Dowdy's vision was clear: He aimed to develop a business program that would prepare students for leadership roles in white-collar professional careers within corporate America. Mahaffey soon left and joined the Dowdy administration, and Watkins was appointed dean of the business school; however, he left the position after just one year. It was now Dean Craig's responsibility to create a roadmap to reposition the business school as an AACSB-accredited business program, signifying quality at a national level.

Dean Craig felt a mix of excitement and nervousness about his new leadership role. He was now responsible for overall program development at A&T's business school rather than just teaching in a classroom. However, he was confident that his classroom skills would help him in creating a roadmap for both program and student success.

With a strong foundation in program development from his time at Lincoln University, his training and observations at the University of Missouri and FAMU, and the roadmap in the 1969 Self-Study Report, Dean Craig should have hit the ground running. However, Dowdy concealed the report from him after he was hired. No one truly knows why, but my theory is that he may have feared sharing it might have diminished his chances of persuading Dean Craig to accept the challenge, particularly since funding for the initiative had not yet been secured. After all, the report had been available for several years, and little progress had been made with implementation. Dowdy had also lost two deans in consecutive years, both holding doctorates from leading universities, one with the same credentials as Dean Craig. So, even as Dean Craig moved forward without the benefit of the 1969 Self-Study Report as a roadmap, it didn't take him long to uncover the critical information that Dowdy chose not to share.

One of the first things Dean Craig did was familiarize himself with his administrative staff, the faculty, the students, and the environment at the business school. He felt that he needed to gain everyone's confidence and encourage them to participate in the process of implementing change. Getting to know the people, the university, the culture, and the details of accreditation was a significant part of his first year.

One of the first people Dean Craig consulted was Jannette Suggs. She earned an undergraduate degree from North Carolina

Central University and began working at A&T in January 1970 for Mahaffey. She served as his administrative assistant during the spring semester of 1970, and after he left, she worked with Watkins during the 1971–72 academic year. Jannette first met Dean Craig when he came to meet with Mahaffey in the spring of 1971. Upon his arrival as dean, her first thought was, "Who is this towering man? His presence stood out. I am short, and Dean Craig is a tall man. I wondered about his personality, what he would do, and if he would keep me. I thought I would have to find another job."[32]

Jannette's worries were short-lived. She immediately became Dean Craig's go-to person and remained so for his entire forty-one-year tenure. She stepped up right away and became a major influence and force for him. She helped him learn his way around A&T, knowing the people and being familiar with the university's processes while understanding what was expected. His learning curve was significantly shortened from the beginning due to her knowledge and skills. She was a tremendous asset to him, and in addition to her role in the office, she also became a wonderful long-term friend. Dean Craig described Jannette as "super-talented, super organized," and a source of strength for him. "Jannette was the boss of the office and the gatekeeper. Jannette hired me," he shared with a laugh.

Over the years, Jannette managed Dean Craig's office and his schedule. No one could reach him without going through her. She screened phone calls and office visits alike. One incident occurred when one of his Lab High friends called the office multiple times, and because she was using her married name, he didn't recognize it and declined the calls. He stated, "She called back so many times that Jannette asked, 'Who is this sister?'" Dean Craig's friend finally caught on and used her maiden name, which he recognized. It was only then that she connected her to Dean Craig. "That's how Jannette ran the office. Over the years, they became close friends," Dean Craig recalled.

Jannette subjected in-person visitors to the same level of scrutiny. Dean Craig was known for cold-calling students and inviting them to visit his office. At the beginning of her second year in 2001, Akilah Thompson received such an invitation. He wanted to reward her with a scholarship for her outstanding academic performance after her freshman year. Akilah recounted her visit: "At first, I was nervous. I had never been called to the dean's office for anything good in high school. I attended a predominantly white high school and always felt different. So, I rebelled to fit in. Based on my past experience, I was trying to figure out if I had done something wrong. I remember that day. I arrived at the office as a typically stylish and arrogant New Yorker. I was wearing a red Kangol hat, a revealing red halter top, skintight jeans, and Chanel sunglasses. I acted like I owned the place and probably, with an attitude, asked to see the dean. I remember Mrs. Suggs saying to me, 'Young lady, you will not see Dean Craig looking like that.' I scrunched my face in disbelief and said, 'Excuse me?' She replied, 'You do not come to anyone's office with your boobs out, a hat on, and sunglasses on.' I am sure I rolled my eyes, sucked my teeth, breathed extra hard, and did everything else to let her know how frustrated I was that she was trying to check me. I left the office embarrassed, my ego crushed, but a major shift happened. I returned the next day and asked to see Dean Craig. Mrs. Suggs recognized me from the day before and smiled. She said, 'Take a seat, and I will call you when he is available.'"[33]

Jannette was the boss of the office, ensuring that everything operated smoothly and was completed on time. She cared deeply for the students, just like the rest of the team. She played a key role in establishing and upholding the standards set by Dean Craig for the program, faculty, and students. She recognized that the mission was to elevate students to a higher level, and she understood the importance of their demeanor.

During Dean Craig's first year, it seemed like every day he was surprised with something new. As a new leader, he looked into everything—the people, the environment, and all the issues that needed addressing at the business school. Fortunately, most of the troubleshooting he undertook involved short-lived problems, but some alerted him to the need for change. He quickly learned that change would take time and was highly dependent on involving everyone in the process. This was especially true for issues affecting the faculty, as they were sometimes slow to accept change, regardless of how many discussions and interactions were held on a topic.

To make change easier, Dean Craig developed a habit of seeking input first, often working behind the scenes to gather support on various issues. He secured backing from anyone he could as he continued to persuade the larger group toward necessary changes. When he struggled to obtain support for issues he deemed critical to the mission, he encouraged the faculty by saying, "let's try it anyway." This strategy allowed him to concentrate on immediate concerns while also familiarizing himself with long-term challenges that needed addressing. One such urgent matter he identified was class schedules.

Dean Craig had a different perspective on the current structure of his faculty teaching back-to-back classes. Drawing from his years of experience with heavy teaching loads, he believed that faculty members needed a chance to refresh themselves and allow their minds to adjust between classes by taking a break. This new idea sparked considerable discussion, particularly since other deans on campus permitted back-to-back classes, and professors favored them because it allowed them to finish their days early. This was one of those instances where Dean Craig advocated for his "let's try it anyway" approach.

One of Dean Craig's greatest challenges in his new role was implementing change, even when there was agreement. Change occurred at a slow pace, something he had to adapt to as a leader. He needed to learn how to effectively manage change with patience as he presented new ideas to the administration, faculty, his administrative staff, students, and some of his colleagues at other colleges and schools. Over time, he had to foster a shared belief among the various stakeholders within the business school about the mission: that A&T could develop an outstanding business program with national accreditation by the AACSB. This was particularly difficult for him, especially since there was only one black undergraduate business program to reference at the time: Texas Southern University. When he began this process, accreditation for programs at HBCUs was not a front-page issue. So, he recognized early on that he needed to build a team filled with hope, belief, commitment, and a "willingness to do and to do better."

Dean Craig faced a significant challenge in creating a culture of change, motivating both faculty and students, hiring new staff, fostering the belief that the mission could be accomplished, and adapting to his role as a leader. Simultaneously, he was learning about the operations of the business school, A&T, the UNC System, and what was required to achieve accreditation. He also chaired the accounting department and taught accounting courses. To manage his responsibilities, he simply encouraged people to do their best while he acclimated. During his first year, he discovered the importance of reaching out for support and perspectives from his administrative staff, faculty, the university's administrative office, and other colleagues he befriended at the university. He even contacted his colleagues leading business programs within the UNC System to gather their insights on the mission he was undertaking. To his surprise, most of them were skeptical that A&T's business school could achieve accreditation. This sentiment was shared among the leaders of business programs at both the HBCUs and predominantly white institutions. While everyone had varying opinions, the consensus from both groups was that A&T was perhaps biting off a bit more than it could chew.

Dean Craig felt disappointed to hear their opinions, but he understood their perspective. For the traditionally white institutions, it was partly about the environment. While things were changing, perceptions were often difficult and slow to change. Also, most of them were not accredited, so they did not think A&T could achieve what they had not. As for the leaders of business programs at black colleges in the state, only a few were beginning to think along those lines. They all recognized the challenges of being a state institution of higher learning in the South, particularly as it related to the lack of financial resources.

As a new administrator, Dean Craig received firsthand experience with financial constraints when he reviewed his budget for the first time. At the time of the 1969 self-study, the total budget for the business program was $30,310. This amount did not include payroll, which was managed at the state level. The budget was divided among the four departments: Accounting received $7,100; Business Administration, $11,110; Business Education and Office Administration, $9,000; and the dean's office received $3,100.[34]

A little less than 70 percent of the total budget was allocated to library books ($21,360), and the remainder was divided among supplies ($3,500), equipment ($5,000), and travel ($450). The share allocated to Dean Craig's office was $1,500 for supplies, $1,500 for equipment, and $100 for travel. Although the budget had increased slightly when he arrived, the proportionate share of spending among the departments and the line-item expenses were just as deficient as they were in 1969. Also, the total budget for the business school was significantly below the recommended budget of $145,000 in the 1969 Self-Study Report, something Dean Craig was not yet aware of, having not received the report from Dowdy.[35]

As he began planning for his first AACSB meeting, scheduled for spring 1973 in Honolulu, he became aware of the limitations of his budget. He was able to attend the meeting because the AACSB permitted business schools that were not accredited to become dues-paying members and participate in meetings. This allowed deans to learn about quality programming and business school trends, and gain access to important information and deans from accredited business schools, even if their business program was not yet accredited. As he began making travel arrangements, he realized that the travel budget for his office was so limited that it could not even fund a trip across town.

As he contemplated his budget, Dean Craig began to have second thoughts about the ambitious vision Dowdy had presented, questioning, "How can this car run without gas?" Without the funds to travel to the AACSB meeting, he was uncertain when and how he would get started. He believed that attending the meeting was essential to understanding the accreditation process, the standards, and what he needed to do. While he appreciated Dowdy's vision, the budget did not align with that vision or the responsibilities Dowdy had hired him to fulfill. Dean Craig felt both confused and doubtful about his commitment. To alleviate the anxiety he was experiencing about accepting the position, he decided to have a conversation with Dowdy. However, to address the issue, he had to meet with Dr. Glenn F. Rankin.

Like Dowdy, Rankin rose through the ranks at A&T. He was an alumnus of the university who, after serving in WWII, continued his education and earned both a Master of Science and a PhD from Pennsylvania State University. He joined A&T in 1950 as a professor and took on additional roles, including acting dean of the School of Agriculture, assistant to the president, and dean of students. When Dowdy became president in 1964, Rankin succeeded him as dean of instruction.[36] Following the restructuring of A&T into the UNC System in 1972, Rankin's title changed to Vice Chancellor of Academic Affairs.

Rankin was second in command in the Dowdy administration, and all the deans of the academic programs, including Dean Craig, reported to him. To his surprise, Rankin acted as a buffer to Dowdy, and Dean Craig had to get used to working with him when he wanted answers to his many questions so he could move forward with his responsibilities. Understanding that the accreditation initiative lacked funding, Dean Craig had to approach Rankin to request the necessary funds to advance the project. Often, he would approach him, expressing a sense of urgency for his needs, and Rankin would slow him down, asking for time to sort things out.

For the funds Dean Craig required to attend his first AACSB meeting, Rankin requested he submit a budget and ultimately secured the funds to cover his travel. This not only alleviated Dean Craig's anxiety regarding his ability to achieve the goals but also marked the beginning of a long and fruitful relationship between the two. It was the first of many issues he would resolve over the years with Rankin and others who succeeded him in that role.

Dean Craig's first recruitment success occurred in the fall of 1972 during his initial year. He was looking to hire a PhD candidate for the business administration department, as required by AACSB standards. A friend at an HBCU, not to be named, made him aware of Danny Pogue, who had interviewed for a position at their institution. They spoke and a relationship developed. Pogue had completed his doctoral studies at Ohio State University and was in the process of finishing his dissertation.

Pogue graduated from Texas College, a private Christian HBCU in Tyler, Texas, and Texas Southern University, where he earned his MS degree. Moving forward toward accomplishing his mission, Dean Craig invited Pogue to A&T for an interview. "During one of our calls, Danny decided to visit A&T," he recalled. "We showed him around campus, introduced him to some of the faculty, and discussed our accreditation goals and aspirations to elevate our students. Danny shared several great ideas for working with students and I was impressed. He was cordial and had a pleasant personality, which was further enhanced by the fact that he was nearing completion of his PhD."

Despite being heavily recruited and having several opportunities at various HBCUs, Pogue, much to Dean Craig's delight, joined A&T in January for the spring semester of the 1972–73 academic year. Dean Craig described him as "talented with an obvious gift for networking and utilizing his interpersonal skills." After spending a brief time on campus, he got to know everyone in the administration, as well as faculty and staff from other departments and schools. His extensive connections made him incredibly resourceful. He demonstrated high dependability, remarkable productivity, and was an excellent writer and typist. Dean Craig admired his typing skills, something he never could do. With his personality, social skills, and resourcefulness, Pogue quickly secured his position on the core team, and following the 1979 accreditation, he became Assistant Dean, marking the first such role on A&T's campus.

Dean Craig completed his administrative team by hiring Ms. Evelyn McKeathen. An A&T graduate in business education, Evelyn joined Dean Craig's office during his second year. He hired her to manage the budget after noticing that Jannette was being "pushed too hard" with all that had to be done. Dean Craig described Evelyn as "dedicated to the organization, clear on the mission, and deeply committed to her duties as well as the students."

With Jannette and Evelyn, Dean Craig had an exceptional administrative team, and their key strength was their reliability and dedication. They managed nearly everything, including correspondence, scheduling, facilitating student visits to his office, coordinating his external relationships, and much more. He consistently involved them in planning and strategy discussions for the business school, allowing them to contribute to the decisions made. While doing his work-study in Dean Craig's office, Kenneth Burton, a business economics major in the class of 1991, gained firsthand insights into Dean Craig's interactions with his staff. Kenneth noted how Dean Craig always established clear expectations and how he motivated his team to emulate excellence by leading through his impressive example. He recalled how Dean Craig empowered Jannette and Evelyn to excel in their roles by entrusting them with responsibilities and allowing them the freedom to manage their tasks. One of Dean Craig's early successes was assembling his core team. With J. Suggs, E. McKeathen, and D. Pogue—whom he called the JED Principle—

as his first line of defense, he felt even more assured that he could achieve Dowdy's objectives and timeline to earn accreditation of the business program.

When it was time for Dean Craig to travel to his first AACSB meeting, he felt excited about the trip. The AACSB meeting, together with the Pacific environment and Honolulu, offered him a new and different experience. It was the first time he had flown for such a long duration across so much water. Once the sessions started, he observed that deans from well-established business schools, including the elite universities, were in attendance. Dean Craig was happy to see deans from several HBCUs; some, like him, were attending for the first time, while others had been there before. He saw this as a sign that they recognized the importance of AACSB accreditation for the growth of business schools at HBCUs and for preparing HBCU students to compete in corporate America. Milton Wilson was present, and as always, he provided valuable information and encouraged the HBCU business school leaders in following his example. Dean Craig took this opportunity to connect with deans and begin building a network, allowing him to utilize them as resources or seek assistance as he learned the ropes. The business school at the University of Missouri, where he earned his PhD, was one institution he included in his network, as it was among one of the early business schools to achieve accreditation.

Dean Craig was impressed by the quality of the meetings. All the sessions were well attended. Deans from accredited business schools delivered presentations on program and faculty standards, elements of program quality, processes, and continuous improvement requirements, among other topics. As he absorbed the presentations, he initially felt frightened as he began comparing the accreditation standards to the state of the business school back at A&T. From those meetings, it became evident to him how much work was needed to align A&T's business program with the AACSB standards. The most startling revelation was the number of doctorates required on the faculty to meet the standards. "That realization made me quiver," he recalled. Aware of the low number of African American PhDs in the nation, Dean Craig knew that satisfying the faculty standard would be a significant challenge.

He left Honolulu better informed as to the details of the job he had signed on to do. He also came to understand why there were not a lot of business schools accredited back then. In his role as dean, he recognized that he was in a complex job—something he had not thoroughly explored in any level of detail with either Dowdy or Wilson. As he reviewed the standards, which were both intensive and extensive, and deepened his understanding, it became clear that Dean Craig needed the support of everyone—the administration, faculty, students, and alumni—with each making their unique contributions. He also realized that everyone would need to stretch, himself included.

Despite this newfound knowledge, Dean Craig remained optimistic about the timeline, aiming to align with Dowdy's vision of obtaining accreditation for the business program by 1976. However, as he delved deeper into his new role, the challenges he faced became more significant than they initially seemed, causing the timeline to slip. Nevertheless, he did what he was trained to do as a Morehouse Man. He rolled up his sleeves and got to work addressing those challenges as he led the initiative to develop an AACSB-accredited business school at A&T.

PART V

MAMA, LOOK AT YOUR BABY SON NOW

From left to right: Dean Quiester Craig; Sharon Donahue, Director of the AICPA's Committee on Recruitment from Minority Groups; and Dr. Mark Kiel, Accounting Department Chair, circa 1980s.

From left to right: Assistant Dean Dr. Danny Pogue, two unidentified corporate representatives, and Dean Quiester Craig discussing matters of the business school, circa 1970s.

From left to right: Dr. Milton Wilson, Dean Quiester Craig, and Reverend Jesse Jackson, Sr. at the AACSB's Annual Meeting, 1993.

CHAPTER 13

Tackling the Challenges of the Business Program

In 1972, the programs offered at the business school were outlined in the Annual Bulletin as follows: "divided into three parts: general education, business and economics core, and selected areas of specialization (accounting, business administration, business education, office administration, or economics)." About 40 percent of the total credit hours for a degree was dedicated to general studies so that students, as freshmen and sophomores, could establish a broad foundation in general education. Another 40 percent consisted of courses designed to provide students, as juniors and seniors, with a comprehensive background in essential areas of business and economics, while the remaining 20 percent was allocated to their specialization.[1]

The 1969 Self-Study Report recommended offering more choices in specialization at the business school in Marketing, Finance, Information Systems and Data Processing, Operations Research, Risk and Insurance, International Business, Public Administration, Business Economics, and Transportation.[2] To achieve specialization and comply with the AACSB standards for curriculum and faculty, Dean Craig needed to enhance the curriculum and recruit faculty with PhDs in their specialized fields to teach the subject matter.

He inherited twenty-four faculty members. The economics department employed eight faculty, while seven were in the business education and office administration department, six worked in business administration, and the remaining three were in the accounting department. The minimum educational qualification for his initial faculty was a graduate degree. There were seven PhDs: four in the economics department, two in the business administration department, and one in the business education and office administration department. With his PhD, Dean Craig raised the total to eight.[3]

"The AACSB standards required that academically qualified faculty teach 60 percent of the business school student population," Dean Craig shared. To be considered academically qualified, a faculty member needed a terminal degree, specifically a PhD. They also had to meet additional requirements beyond teaching. After two to three years of employment, PhD faculty were expected to engage in research to contribute to and/or expand the professional knowledge in their academic field. Their research needed to be published and presented at professional organizations, and they had to participate in continued learning and community involvement.

Initially, Dean Craig felt conflicted about making time in the business program for research, as it would significantly reduce the faculty's teaching and student development time. Having devoted himself to his teaching career thus far, his main priority was to emphasize actual instruction and the development of his students, understanding that this support was essential for their success in their chosen fields. However, now that he was a dean, he faced additional responsibilities—most notably, pursuing AACSB accreditation, which required a different approach than he was accustomed to. So, he concluded that he needed faculty who excelled in teaching and developing students while also being able to conduct research recognized for its competitiveness.

Dean Craig estimated that he would need between twenty-four and twenty-six PhDs based on his assessment of how the curriculum would be restructured. He was starting at a significant deficit. That deficit increased the day before school started in his first semester when Dr. Albert Smart, who chaired the business administration department and taught marketing, resigned to become the first black faculty member at the College of Business at Northern Illinois University.[4] Dean Craig knew Smart from his days at Atlanta University and encouraged him to stay, but he was unsuccessful in his efforts.

After Smart's departure, Dr. Katie White was the only PhD in the business administration department, which was why Dean Craig's first hire was Pogue, to fill this gap. A management professor, White held a BS and MS from North Carolina Central University and earned her PhD from the University of Illinois.[5] Dean Craig described her as "highly dependable and extremely patient with her students, who respected her greatly for the support she provided." Committed to the university, White remained on the faculty until her retirement. Her commitment was advantageous for Dean Craig, as there were very few African Americans with doctorate degrees in the business disciplines.

The business administration department was the primary focus of accreditation, while all other departments played a supporting role in the process. To complete a degree in business administration, students took required courses from all departments within the business school. This interdisciplinary approach allowed Dean Craig, as he pursued accreditation, to develop all the departments according to the AACSB standards. This included the economics and business education and office management departments, even though these areas were generally not included in the business school at most institutions of higher learning, and also the accounting department.

These departments positively reflected on the university because of the individuals who led and worked in them, their educational backgrounds, and the way they supported Dean Craig's mission. When Dean Craig joined the department, Dr. Florentine Sowell chaired the

Department of Business Education and Office Administration. She earned her BS from the University of Omaha, her MBA from the University of Chicago, and her PhD from the University of North Dakota.[6] In the mid-1970s, she left the department before accreditation, and Dr. Meada Gibbs replaced her in the 1973–74 school year when Dean Craig hired her away from Winston-Salem State University, an HBCU located thirty minutes west of Greensboro. To address a gap that Dean Craig identified in some students' communication skills, Gibbs established a Toastmasters chapter at the business school to offer students an opportunity to enhance their public speaking, networking, and leadership abilities. As the chapter took root at the university, students from other schools began to participate in the program.

Gibbs prepared her students in numerous ways. Cynthia McMurray Washington, class of 1979, remembered her as a role model. "I was in awe of Dr. Gibbs and the other young black men and women who dominated the learning environment in Merrick Hall. She was a stunning woman, nearly six feet tall, always impeccably dressed, and extremely professional in her leadership role. She was a well-put-together young black woman and an excellent mentor. Although I did not achieve academic honors at the university, Dr. Gibbs recognized my personality, acumen, skill sets, and unique communication abilities. In my senior year, she invited me to her office to inform me that she had personally arranged for me to meet with a recruiter from Dow Chemical Company in Midland, Michigan. She coached me and spoke to me as a mother would, guiding me on how to present myself and describe my college experiences. I was offered a position, and that opportunity was instrumental in launching my professional marketing career. I modeled myself after her in shaping my executive presence."[7]

The 1969 Self-Study Report recommended hiring faculty to address the special needs of "disadvantaged" students. While Dean Craig viewed none of his students as disadvantaged, he recognized their areas for growth and supported them in closing the gaps. Similar to Gibbs, he held all his faculty accountable for identifying and implementing student development activities, and such a position was never filled.

When Dean Craig joined the business school, the economics department had four PhDs and was the most advanced department due to its early achievements in research. The department offered nine hours of required courses for a business administration degree, including Money and Banking, Microeconomics, and Macroeconomics. Dr. Sidney Evans served as the department chair. He earned his BS in economics from Virginia State University, his MS from Iowa State University, and his PhD from Ohio State University.[8]

Before Dean Craig arrived, Evans had carried out several recommendations from the 1969 Self-Study Report. His efforts established the Learning Research Laboratory in Merrick Hall, providing a space for students to receive tutoring services and access resource materials to support their academic studies in the business school. He also launched the Transportation Institute in 1970 to promote transportation-related research. Dr. Basil Coley, who earned his BS degree from A&T, his MS from Pennsylvania State University, and his PhD from the University of Illinois, succeeded Evans as department chair in the 1973–74 school year. He was another longtime faculty member who retired from A&T.

Completing Dean Craig's inherited faculty with PhDs in the economics department were Drs. Alice Kidder and David Chen. Kidder completed her undergraduate degree at Swarthmore College and earned her PhD from the Massachusetts Institute of Technology. Chen received his BS from National Taiwan University, his MS from New Mexico State University, and his PhD from the University of Wisconsin.[9] To Dean Craig's delight, Chen was also a long-term faculty member who remained at A&T until his retirement.

Kidder came to teach at A&T through the Woodrow Wilson National Fellowship Foundation, an organization that, in the late

1960s, provided opportunities for white educators to teach at black colleges to assist with building capacity. She taught at Spelman College and Atlanta University prior to joining A&T in 1969. She left for Syracuse University after eleven years. Kidder's grandfather influenced her in the area of social justice, which was why she taught at HBCUs as a young professor.[10]

She remembered Dean Craig as upright, forward-looking, strict yet approachable, and very focused on accreditation during their overlap at A&T. "He took a lot of measures to increase faculty competence," Kidder recalled. "I was aware of the underfunding that existed at A&T, and I assisted with writing proposals to upgrade equipment and make other improvements at the business school. I also did research and helped write the proposal to secure funding for the Transportation Institute."

Kidder described her experience at A&T as "very moving." She explained, "As a white person at a predominantly black college, I initially thought people would be resentful of me. It was quite the opposite. People were helpful and kind, and the faculty was dedicated to assisting the students in getting the education they needed. They were focused on the mission. Later in life, I came to understand these experiences as part of my education. I had the opportunity to interact with black faculty and students, and I learned that it is not appropriate to generalize about people based on their appearance or differing interests. I learned a lot about the diversity within the black community, and I came to understand the unfairness of the privileges that come with being white."

Kidder felt honored to take part in Civil Rights history during her time at A&T. When social unrest led to the abrupt end of the spring 1969 semester and brought the National Guard to A&T's campus, seniors were sent home. Upon their return in the fall, Kidder assisted with administering their final exams. She also shared an office with Dr. Juanita Tate, who mentored Reverend Jesse Jackson, Sr., when he was a student. She observed Tate's pivotal influence in inspiring him to launch Operation PUSH and to incorporate economic empowerment into his activism.[11]

The faculty composition at the business school was predominantly African Americans, along with several international faculty and several white Americans. "All faculty were welcomed at the business school if they could and would help our students," Dean Craig stated. "Regarding African American faculty, I believed having them on the team was crucial to inspire our kids further. I wanted the students to feel proud and motivated by seeing individuals like them in front of the classroom."

The faculty that Dean Craig inherited immediately began working on restructuring the curriculum to better reflect specialization and meet employers' needs. In 1972, the business administration curriculum offered twenty-seven courses: seven in business principles, five related to insurance topics, two in office and personnel management, and several others in electronic data processing, corporate finance, money, credit and banking, business law I and II, business statistics, and business communications.[12] By 1979, the curriculum had been restructured to offer three areas of specialization: Banking and Finance, Management, and Marketing, with specified credit hours for each.[13]

Before Dean Craig could implement any significant changes to the curriculum, he first needed to gain the support of the faculty. Negotiations were essential because, while some faculty members supported the changes, others wanted to maintain the status quo. With input from the faculty, Dean Craig developed what he called a "diplomatic process" to determine the curriculum changes. This process involved educating, selling, negotiating, and reaching a majority agreement by vote.

His primary concern was to provide faculty with enough time to familiarize themselves with the changes and conduct their own research. On his part, Pogue conducted the research, Jannette and Evelyn prepared the presentation, and he facilitated the discussion.

During the meetings, faculty shared their perspectives and concerns. He showed understanding toward their worries, especially since faculty members were anxious about the potential impact on their positions if the courses they taught were removed from the curriculum.

While discussions unfolded in the meetings, Dean Craig quietly lobbied individual faculty members to garner support for the necessary changes. The vote took place only after he secured enough backing to succeed, and ultimately, the majority prevailed. Although the process moved slower than he desired, many viewed it as fair. After the business school reached consensus, the university's curriculum committee needed to approve the changes. This step also required negotiation and persuasion, especially when revisions affected students across the university.

As curriculum and faculty go hand in hand, changes to the curriculum sometimes necessitated the hiring of new faculty members. This was particularly true as the curriculum became more specialized. Two new professors, Dr. Robert "Bill" Howard and Dr. Betty Brewer, were hired in the mid 1970s to teach finance. Brewer earned her BS degree from East Carolina University and both her MBA and DBA degrees from Kent State University.[14] Howard received his PhD from Ohio State University, his MBA from the University of Chicago, and his BA from Williams College.[15]

While curriculum changes were not always easy for faculty members to absorb, they were often just as challenging for students. Both Brewer and Howard became long-term faculty members at the business school, and throughout their years there, they were demanding, with no easy way through finance or any of the other courses they taught. Students referred to Dr. Howard as "Dr. Death" and Dr. Brewer as "Vanilla Killer," being that she was one of the white faculty members. Student participation was essential to Dean Craig's accreditation efforts, and he needed to ensure they understood their role.

This was the case for Howard's managerial finance class early in his tenure in the fall of 1975. As a newly minted PhD from Ohio

State University, and with buy-in to Dean Craig's mission, Dr. Howard challenged the students, holding nothing back in the complexity of the coursework. The assignments for the course included "hours of reading, constant homework, pop quizzes, and tests that were harder than Russian physics," according to Willie A. Deese, a business administration major in the class of 1977. Student complaints about the workload and its impact on other classes fell on deaf ears and were met with dismissive responses. Dr. Howard was not hearing it. About seven weeks into the class, the students decided they had suffered enough and needed to do something about it.[16]

Deese recalled, "I'm not really sure who started the discussion; I just know it was a Wednesday in mid-October, a few days before the deadline to drop classes. We were sitting in the Merrick Hall Auditorium, waiting to take a test, when someone muttered that they were tired of this class, the way it was being taught, the mountains of work, and the impact it was having on our lives. It was a kinetic moment as more students began to join in the conversation. Maybe it was the stress of the impending test and the fact that most, if not all of us, knew we weren't ready for it that led us to decide we wouldn't take it that day. Believe it or not, we agreed to boycott the test!"[17]

The students not only boycotted the test, but they also felt they wanted a meeting with Dean Craig about how this class would be taught moving forward. They were all in agreement, so when Dr. Howard entered the auditorium that day, he was caught off guard.[18]

"As he began handing out the test, we informed him that we weren't going to take it," Deese recalled. "He tried to reason with us, but by that point, the whole class felt emboldened. Our response was that we also wanted to have a say in how the course would be taught moving forward. A bit more discussion followed. Dr. Howard then told us that he would speak with Dean Craig to share our concerns. As he left for Dean Craig's office, which was just a ten-second walk from the auditorium, I'm sure he heard a few of us saying, 'Get Dean Craig; we want him to know how we feel.'"[19]

Ten minutes later, Dr. Howard and Dean Craig entered the auditorium. Dean Craig addressed the students, saying, "I understand that you all have decided to boycott today's test and that you believe the course should be taught differently. Well, I agree that you don't have to take the test today since most of your class time has been wasted. But let me be clear: He is teaching this class exactly as I expect him to and will continue to do so. Furthermore, the test will be given on Friday. Anyone who is not here on Friday to take the test will receive an F unless, of course, you choose to drop the class."[20]

Dean Craig then took a long walk down the auditorium corridor and left the room. "For the record, that was not an inclusive moment. The discussion was brief, blunt, and one-sided," Deese recalled.[21] Dean Craig had spoken. To reiterate his point, he stood in the doorway of his office with his arms folded as the students exited the auditorium.[22]

Dr. Howard was back in charge, and the message was clear: The business school was on a mission to become AACSB-accredited, and the students better get on board. "We all took the test that Friday. As you might imagine, there was a fair amount of studying between Wednesday afternoon and Friday afternoon. Most of us stayed in Dr. Howard's class that semester, and most of us passed the course. That event became part of the business school folklore as a short, non-violent protest that was intense but ultimately futile, and we named it the Merrick Hall Auditorium Insurrection," Deese concluded.[23] As for business school folklore, Dean Craig distinctively remembers the students singing "We Shall Overcome" as they left the auditorium, something he says they always forget when telling this story.

Brewer, aka Vanilla Killer, instilled fear in students much like Howard, aka Dr. Death. Dean Craig attributed a quickened pace toward accreditation to both Brewer and Howard. They both contributed significantly to program improvements in finance and, as long-serving faculty members, brought stability to the business administration department. Brewer was a faculty member for most of Dean Craig's tenure, while Howard retired from the business school.

Changing the curriculum was a piece of cake compared to finding qualified faculty who met AACSB standards. Dean Craig's criteria for the faculty he wanted on staff extended beyond simply meeting the AACSB requirements. He made it a point to hire faculty who understood his vision for the business school and his students. "Just as our business program was lagging behind, our students were held back due to a long-standing lack of opportunity and exposure for people of color," Dean Craig explained. "Therefore, I tried to build a culture that would help students recognize the new career opportunities available and to help them realize their potential for success within these opportunities. I considered student development essential to the roles of the faculty, the administrative staff, and myself at the business school."

To achieve that intangible quality he sought in his faculty, Dean Craig established care and consideration as essential qualifications for faculty hired. Therefore, in addition to possessing a PhD and meeting the criteria for being academically qualified as it related to the AACSB standards, he aimed to evaluate the sincerity of candidates in helping fulfill the mission of the business school. He also sought to determine whether candidates showed, in any way, that they would have a "heart for his students." In his view, caring was essential to inspiring students and fostering a culture of excellence at the business school. During interviews, he arranged for faculty members, students, and the chair of the department to meet with candidates first. He always interviewed candidates for faculty positions last. Once the interview process concluded, he gathered the interviewers to share their insights and experiences regarding the faculty candidates.

"In making the final determination, I often relied on my gut feeling," Dean Craig shared. "We missed at times, but for the most part, we did okay. Over time, we did not have high turnover; our faculty stayed for a long while and often retired from their positions.

Continuity was important in building and maintaining the culture I believed we needed at the business school."

The culture that Dean Craig fostered was one where everyone strived for excellence and inspired each other to do the same. This included faculty, students, his administrative staff, and himself, as he believed he needed to set the example. The team aimed to do what was necessary to uplift students and help them improve. He believed that the key to their improvement was building their confidence. He wanted every student to graduate from the business school feeling confident in their skills, knowledge, and personal selves, much like what had been emphasized by his teachers at Lab High and by Dr. Mays at Morehouse College.

Since there was a shortage of available business school faculty for hire at HBCUs, Dean Craig addressed his staffing needs through various means as enrollment increased. He recruited practitioners for both full-time and part-time positions in courses such as Real Estate, Banking, and Law. One strategy involved utilizing Vance Gray, a member of the university's administrative staff, as a part-time instructor. Another option was Mr. Andrew Yarborough IV, a local attorney who taught business law part time. Taking a cue from FAMU's Mobley, Dean Craig engaged professionals as visiting professors, some he met at FAMU and some through an innovative program the university participated in during his early years, known as the Cluster Concept. Launched in 1969, this program included voluntary participation from over forty corporations, many which were not involved in government contracting. This initiative, led by American business leaders, aimed at addressing critical challenges faced by HBCUs. The Cluster Concept provided the business program with specialized equipment, along with fellowships and scholarships to support the development of both teachers and students, and ultimately provided job opportunities for students. The Cluster Concept was initiated by the John F. Kennedy administration and continued under the Lyndon B. Johnson administration.[24]

The hiring of practitioners was balanced with other strategies and approaches to build quality instruction and permanently increase the number of PhDs on the faculty. Demand was high and supply low for PhDs in business schools in general, exacerbating this issue for HBCUs. One approach Dean Craig took to increase the number of faculty with doctorate degrees was to develop faculty on staff. As things were changing at the business school, faculty were asked to change, too. It became known that continued learning was the new norm under Dean Craig, who provided financial support from foundation grants and the state to assist the existing faculty with completing their PhDs. There was a downside to that approach, as faculty members sometimes opted to leave the business school after they earned their PhDs. One example of this was Alexander Okrah, a marketing professor who listened to the call to get his doctorate. As soon as he got it, Howard University stole him away. Wilson called Dean Craig to let him know, asking, "Do you know Alexander Okrah, who used to be one of yours?"

It was a competitive environment, and Dean Craig recognized that to achieve AACSB accreditation, he would need to rely on all his faculty members. He established one set of rules for them all, including departments not covered by the AACSB accreditation standards. He expected the same level of quality, as emphasized by Dr. Michael Simmons, who continued in the economics department until his retirement.

"When Dean Craig joined in 1972 and the economics department moved over to the business school, it was clear he was on a mission. He was always in the building, which was something new for me. One evening, while I was teaching my class from 6:00–9:00 p.m., I saw him walk by. A half hour later, he walked by again. An hour passed, and he walked by once more. He was ensuring I did not let my class out early. I assume he gained confidence in me because one day I was walking down the hall when he approached, put his arm around my shoulder, and said, 'Mike, we need to talk. If you're going to stay, you're going to have to get a PhD.' By 1980, I had earned my PhD from Washington State University."[25]

Dr. Japhet Nkonge was another faculty member motivated to obtain his PhD. He served as a marketing professor in the business administration department. He completed his undergraduate studies at A&T and earned an MBA from Rutgers University. Dean Craig described him as "great with students" and noted that students considered him one of their favorites. He preferred his classes scheduled at 8:00 a.m., and Dean Craig was pleased to give him that time slot because not many other faculty members wanted it. He recalled something Nkonge mentioned to him after a faculty meeting as progress was being made toward accreditation. Nkonge said, "Dean, when you first came and started discussing the need for PhDs, I looked around the faculty meeting and noticed only a couple of faculty members who had a doctorate. Years later, in a faculty meeting, I looked around the room and realized I was the only one without a doctorate." A few years later, Nkonge completed his PhD in marketing at UNC-Chapel Hill.

The first student that Dean Craig encouraged to pursue a PhD was Dr. Gwendolyn Highsmith-Quick, nicknamed "Dr. HQ" by Evelyn for efficiency after she married and completed her doctorate. She became the first business school alumna to earn a PhD in accounting to complement her MBA and CPA license. Having spent most of her career at A&T, she viewed her work not merely as a job but as her "dream come true," an achievement she attributes to Dean Craig's support. As she explained, "I grew up in Wallace, North Carolina, with very modest financial means and am a first-generation college graduate. I was always studious. When I was a young girl, one of my most treasured Christmas gifts was a large dictionary from my father. As a youth, I often tutored others, including my cousin, who took a bricklaying course. I read the book and tutored him in bricklaying. So, I always knew I wanted to attend college and become a teacher. I initially wanted to attend UNC-Chapel Hill because I was influenced by watching their team play basketball on television. In my senior year of high school, I received a letter from Chancellor Dowdy congratulating me on my SAT scores. I was offered a full-ride presidential scholarship, which was a much better offer than the mixed funding of work-study, grants, and loans from UNC-Chapel Hill, so I chose A&T. That was one of the best decisions I ever made."[26]

Dr. HQ found herself in the business school studying accounting, where Dean Craig spoke to her about pursuing a PhD in accounting. He discussed the significant shortage of African Americans in the field and explained what it meant to hold an advanced degree, much like Dr. Westerfield of Atlanta University did for him. One day, the professor who taught the accounting principles course was unable to attend class, so he asked Gwendolyn to teach in his place. "I still remember the topics I taught that day, and I was hooked after that experience," she recalled. "Dean Craig outlined my plan, and we made it happen."[27]

Through the Consortium, Gwendolyn earned her MBA from the University of Wisconsin and later joined the faculty at FAMU as an accounting instructor. The plan was for her to work for two years and then pursue her PhD. True to form, while at FAMU, Dean Craig assisted her in applying for a fellowship from the AICPA to study for her PhD. He coordinated with his former classmate from the University of Missouri, who was on the business school faculty at the University of Tennessee, and she was accepted. Two weeks before she was to report to school, Sharon Donahue from the AICPA Minority Initiative called to inform her that, while the fellowship was still available, the U.S. Department of Health, Education, and Welfare (now the U.S. Department of Education) had withdrawn funding for the AICPA's program to increase the number of African American PhDs in accounting.[28]

"In tears, with no place to go, I called Dean Craig," Dr. HQ said. "He hired me to teach at A&T, secured funding for my PhD from Deloitte Haskins & Sells, and I was off to the University of Tennessee. I transferred and completed my PhD in accounting at the University of Houston, obtained my CPA, and later returned to A&T's business school, remaining on the accounting faculty until my retirement."[29]

Dean Craig inspired many students to pursue academia throughout his tenure. However, after meeting him for the first time, Kecia Williams decided she wanted to emulate him. When Dean Craig spoke at her freshman orientation, she was immediately influenced by him. After a twenty-year career in the corporate world, she joined the ranks of academia, earning her PhD in accounting from Texas A&M University. "In my dissertation acknowledgments, I wrote: 'I am grateful for the leadership of Dean Emeritus Quiester Craig and the accounting faculty at North Carolina A&T State University for providing the initial spark of intellectual curiosity that led me to pursue my doctorate in accounting.' My goal in my academic career is to have an impact on others, just as Dean Craig and his faculty had on me," Dr. Kecia Williams Smith, CPA, class of 1995, concluded.[30] Smith is currently paying it forward as an Assistant Professor and Director of the Master of Accountancy Program in the Department of Accounting and Finance at A&T. Dr. Lisa Owens-Jackson, CPA, affectionately known as Dr. OJ throughout A&T's business school community thanks to Evelyn, is another of Dean Craig's students whom he inspired to enter academia. She currently chairs the accounting department.

In addition to developing business school faculty from his existing staff and student body, Dean Craig also aimed to recruit externally. This was a lengthy and challenging process, but he successfully navigated it as well. To recruit faculty, he first needed to persuade the Vice Chancellor of Academic Affairs to allocate funding for the new positions. This was challenging because he had to compete with the salaries offered by more established, well-funded institutions to attract candidates with PhDs in the various business disciplines. At that time, business school faculty with PhDs were in high demand and earned 15 to 20 percent more than their peers in other university colleges and schools. To complicate matters further, every dean and department chair at A&T was striving to upgrade their faculty in line with Dowdy's plans to achieve national accreditations for all qualifying academic programs, putting Dean Craig in competition with other deans at the university.

As he built the business program, he sometimes needed to fill three or four positions, and at times, as many as nine. He had prospects with exceptional credentials whom he could call upon and needed to act quickly. Time was of the essence; however, there were protocols and processes he had to follow. He understood the Vice Chancellor's challenges in managing the needs of the whole university, but he consistently advocated for what he required anyway.

To create a path to success for his hiring needs, he first had to meet with the Vice Chancellor of Academic Affairs about two issues: business school faculty costing more than faculty in most other fields, and the business school's inability to continue pursuing a generalist route. Dean Craig needed PhDs in various specialized fields, including marketing, management, accounting, and finance. "To make my point, I sometimes came across as a bit of a smart aleck," Dean Craig shared. "I once asked Vice Chancellor Rankin: 'Who would you prefer to handle your bypass surgery, a general practitioner or a cardiologist? Both are doctors, but they have different competencies.'"

Rankin responded with a laugh: "Craig, get out of my office."

Because the state budget covered only a limited portion of faculty salaries, when positions were approved, Dean Craig was awarded a specific number of positions and salaries at any given time. The salaries were never sufficient to meet his needs, prompting him to continually seek supplemental funding to hire the necessary staff. To gain a competitive edge in recruitment, he made it a practice to seek individuals nearing the completion of their doctorate and offer them financial support to finish it. Therefore, he required supplemental funding to make competitive salary offers and to assist candidates with completing their PhDs. Supplemental funding was essential for him to compete with larger, well-established, and better-funded schools and attract the talent necessary to develop a quality business program that met the AACSB standards. His mentor, Wilson, had alerted Dean Craig to the need for external support, but for the first couple of years, Rankin worked through his issues as needed until a major breakthrough in funding for the initiative came through.

In February 1974, about two years into Dean Craig's tenure, the W.K. Kellogg Foundation of Battle Creek, Michigan, presented the school of business with a $195,000 grant to enhance its program. It was the largest grant the business school had ever received. Five years earlier, Kellogg had provided similar grants that significantly assisted the university in achieving national accreditation for its Schools of Engineering, Nursing, and Chemistry.[31]

Initially, Dowdy managed all the fundraising, and his efforts were crucial in securing external funding. Early in his presidency he reactivated the A&T University Foundation to secure external support from friends of the university and dedicated alumni. He understood that state funding, which had always been insufficient, needed to be supplemented to achieve his goals. Following the passage of the Civil Rights Act of 1964, external support from foundations and corporations emerged as a new funding source for black public colleges. Dowdy recognized its importance in supporting student scholarships and faculty development and enhancing faculty salaries. He later reflected on the foundation's significance to his vision, stating, "Through the vital A&T University Foundation, many achievements have been made possible, which otherwise would have been left in the realm of a dream."[32]

"Funding was a salesmanship job, and Dr. Dowdy sold the university," Dean Craig stated. After observing that he was ready for the challenge, Dowdy delegated some of that responsibility to Dean Craig. Representatives from foundations and corporations visited the university in support of other accredited programs, leading him to invite Dean Craig to lunch meetings and receptions with deans from other schools. During these meetings, deans had to promote their programs. As Dean Craig attended these gatherings, he didn't initially sense that the external representatives were particularly interested in the business school. However, when the opportunity arose, he shared the goals and objectives of the business school, just enough to spark their curiosity. As relationships grew, he invited them to visit the business school, explore the curriculum, and meet the faculty. He believed that seeing the business school firsthand would enhance his chances of convincing them it was worth investing in. From these meetings, the representatives were impressed, relationships deepened, and funding began to flow into the business school slowly at first, but it eventually picked up.

"The external funding we received gave us a fighting chance," Dean Craig recalled. "Without outside support to fill the gaps, we couldn't have secured the faculty we needed, and accreditation wouldn't have been possible. The impact of the dual system of higher education in the South was long-lasting, systemic, and predictable, although unfair. For a time, state authorities were not very generous to HBCUs, providing just enough funding to keep the schools operating. Desegregation and societal changes related to civil rights created a period of opportunity and hope, which unfolded gradually. However, after so many years of exclusion, catching up is nearly impossible, so public HBCUs always had to be the best we could be under the circumstances," he noted.

Once external funding began, it kept flowing in. One grant attracted another, and then another. The awards came in various sizes from multiple foundations, corporations, and individuals. Dean Craig appreciated the funding, regardless of the amount. By his account, every little bit of money that came in made a significant difference.

Dean Craig had the good fortune to learn a bit about fundraising from his mentor, Wilson. The first lesson was that fundraising was "friendraising," meaning relationships are of utmost importance. Secondly, he needed to have a strategy with well-thought-out plans because potential donors coming in have a preconceived view of the university and its activities. When he finally got a meeting, Dean Craig was advised to convince the potential donor of his success by highlighting the improvements that had been or would be made at the business school and the university. Lastly, he was to do everything he could to show commitment to the program and convey its promise. To convey promise, Dean Craig demonstrated how the programming would change the lives of his students. His bottom line was to build trust that his team could deliver. As the business program developed over time, he was so confident in what he could deliver that he would say to funders, "If you support me, I will give you a hunting license and tell you where to find highly qualified students."

Dean Craig also learned from both Wilson and Mobley how to be bold. During one meeting, he asked the funders which HBCU business school they thought would be the next to achieve AACSB accreditation. The funders named three HBCUs, excluding A&T, because they were more familiar with those programs. He suggested they keep an eye on A&T, especially since other programs at A&T had received accreditation. Fearing that Dean Craig might have insulted the funders, Pogue, who was with him at the meeting, dropped his head and looked out the window. "We all laughed," Dean Craig recalled. By Dean Craig's reasoning, since A&T had other accredited programs, it showed that the university was serious.

Kenneth Burton not only observed Dean Craig's management style while working in his office, but he also got an up-close and personal look at how he built relationships with external representatives from foundations, corporations, and other institutions. He shared that Dean Craig was "masterful" in how he connected with people. "He went beyond the transactional level and built relationships," Kenneth recalled. "He took a genuine interest in people and truly got to know them. He did this for nearly everyone he encountered, whether a corporate executive, a faculty member, a student, a custodian, or a cafeteria worker. He met people where they were and then guided them to where he needed them to be. He negotiated and struck deals that were mutually beneficial to all parties involved." Burton also observed how Dean Craig utilized his students to promote the business school. When representatives from a corporation or foundation were in his office, he would often invite a few students for a roundtable discussion, asking them to share their grade point averages or what projects they were working on. Burton concluded, "Dean Craig wielded a lot of power and influence with those who passed through his office."[33]

Dean Craig was also proud of the contributions that graduates of the business school made toward fundraising efforts. As they entered the workforce as interns and full-time employees, achieving success in their careers made fundraising easier for him. He said that the graduates "rang bells for A&T" by being competitive in the marketplace. Their performance as interns and in full-time positions facilitated the growth and sustainment of external support for the business school. Additionally, as alumni enjoyed the economic benefits of their education, many became consistent contributors.

While external funding helped address budget issues, Dean Craig still had to overcome the negative perceptions associated with being an HBCU. These perceptions continued to pose challenges for fundraising and student placement; however, they were most acute in faculty hiring.

It was well known that most faculty at HBCUs carried heavy teaching loads, and A&T was no exception. These heavy teaching loads stemmed from limited financial resources that hindered departments from being adequately staffed. Underfunding and the lasting effects of the dual system of separate but equal higher education had impeded the growth of business schools at HBCUs. Consequently, this created a deficit in the number of African American PhDs across all business disciplines. At most black colleges during that time, teaching consumed the majority of faculty members' time, leaving little to no opportunity for engaging in research. Further complicating the situation was the reality that most research funding was generally awarded to larger, more recognized institutions. In fact, faculty research was relatively new at A&T when Dean Craig arrived, growing from $36,000 in 1968 to just $4 million in 1972.[34] Research at the university increased because Dowdy established early in his presidency, as one of his strategic initiatives, that A&T would become a research institution, consistent with its land-grant designation. To secure funding for research, he testified before congressional committees three times to persuade them of the necessity of university research at HBCUs. His plea was reportedly partially answered with an award of $12.5 million to be shared by sixteen public land-grant HBCUs.[35]

Since negative perceptions prevailed in the court of public opinion regarding HBCUs, many PhDs seeking faculty positions chose not to apply at these schools. They didn't view HBCUs as competitive or as research institutions. To make matters worse, PhD candidates were sometimes discouraged from joining HBCUs by their colleagues, advisors, and other PhDs, because of their likelihood of receiving better offers and opportunities from major universities. Dean Craig faced this very issue after receiving his PhD from the University of Missouri.

In the world of academia, the issue of having time for research weighs heavily in a candidate's choice of career path. Research is how professors become known and make their mark. So, PhD candidates then and now are often advised to go to a research institution to take advantage of their degree. When conducting research, PhDs have an opportunity to create new thinking in their field, and it keeps them up to date as business dynamics change. Research provides professional development, and it is a part of continued learning. There is also prestige in where PhD candidates are placed, and being placed at an HBCU, at that time, offered little prestige compared to larger, established institutions. So, there was an assumption that if PhD candidates accepted a position at an HBCU, they would "waste" their degrees because they would only be teaching and would have little time for research.

"In contrast to HBCUs, traditionally white institutions had a huge running start," Dean Craig shared. "They had more recognition, more finances, better facilities, and more reputation. They could pay higher salaries, accommodate lower teaching loads to provide more time for faculty research, and finance the faculty's professional development activities required by the accreditation standards. After the desegregation of higher education, traditionally white institutions began hiring African American PhDs, which diluted the already small pool from which HBCUs had exclusively hired."

Collectively, all these issues created monumental hurdles for Dean Craig and other HBCU deans in hiring PhD candidates. In fact, hiring PhDs in the business disciplines was the "monster issue" that Dean Craig had to tackle in the pursuit of program quality improvement and accreditation for A&T's business school. To address these challenges, he did not wait for a PhD candidate to apply for a faculty position at A&T. Instead, he took another cue from Mobley, and he found candidates as she had found him, and expressed his interest in hiring them. Essentially, he stayed informed about who was available and promoted the idea that working at an HBCU would benefit their careers. To recruit doctoral candidates, Dean Craig positioned A&T's business school as "worthy of consideration" by PhD candidates. He had to convince them they would receive the same professional development opportunities at A&T as at traditionally white institutions. "We worked especially hard to recruit high-quality faculty with PhDs," Dean Craig stated.

To change the paradigm and facilitate research, Dean Craig implemented strategies over time to transition faculty from heavy teaching loads to more time for research. Initially, professors began with heavy teaching loads of sometimes fifteen hours and five courses due to limited faculty availability. As more faculty were hired, they were able to reduce their loads to twelve, then nine, or even six hours, which is the norm for faculty members who conduct research. As the faculty expanded in size and competence, teaching loads decreased, allowing for more time dedicated to research. This shift was a direct result of the support and cooperation received from the administration, the faculty, and external funding that supplemented the state budget. To help secure more hours for research, Dean Craig also discovered creative strategies for better managing faculty time by consulting with deans at AACSB meetings, including Milton Wilson.

As Dean Craig became familiar with these creative strategies, he put them into practice. They served as temporary solutions that he employed as needed to balance the priorities of reducing teaching loads while increasing time for faculty research. One strategy he implemented included restructuring class schedules to improve the efficiency of faculty time. He decreased the frequency of courses offered over a two-year term, created larger classes, and prioritized required courses over electives in the schedule. Under this model, elective courses were available only once a year instead of each semester. This allowed for twenty-four students in a single class once a year rather than twelve students in two classes each semester, thereby reducing teaching loads.

Another strategy involved shifting faculty to leverage changes in the schedule and help meet the standard of having academically qualified faculty teaching 60 percent of the students. Departing from academic norms, the PhDs instructed larger classes, typically the principles courses, while the remaining faculty handled the smaller classes. To meet the standards, the PhDs taught the principles courses because there were more students in them. For a time, these types of accommodations were made to satisfy AACSB accreditation standards.

"Communication was key to making all this work," Dean Craig explained. "The students needed to understand the changes to avoid missing any of their required or elective subjects. Once the structure was set up and included in the school catalogue, it was communicated to the student advisors to ensure they informed the students when the courses were offered. Some of the changes impacted areas beyond the business school." When these issues arose in the deans' meetings, Dean Craig had already worked out the specifics with the Vice Chancellor of Academic Affairs to avoid any delays in implementation.

As difficult as it was, by the end of the 1970s, Dean Craig and his team, with help from the administration and external funders, had made significant progress toward meeting the AACSB accreditation standards for the Business Administration program as well as all the other departments—Accounting, Economics, and Business Education and Office Administration. Of all the departments, the accounting program was by far the most difficult one to develop.

CHAPTER 14

Tackling the Challenges of the Accounting Program

Similar to his predecessor, Dr. Herbert Watkins, Dean Craig not only served as dean of the School of Business and Economics but also chaired the accounting department. During Watkins's brief tenure, he made some efforts to advance the accounting department, including being responsive to the AICPA's efforts to diversify the accounting profession. In 1970, he launched a program sponsored by the National Urban League and the AICPA to encourage more business school students to enter the field of accounting by exposing them to African American CPAs in the industry. These practitioners visited the accounting department as guest professors, where they taught and shared their corporate work experiences to inspire more students to major in accounting.

An article in The *A&T Register*, the student newspaper, highlighted the experience of visiting professor James Polk, a young African American CPA from Levi Strauss & Company in California. Polk expressed his gratitude for the teaching opportunity, noting it as one small way to help black students understand that success was within their reach. He observed that the students were eager and engaged in his presentation. "There seems to be almost a hungry desire for knowledge about opportunities in the industry. [Students] also want to know what is necessary to acquire these opportunities."[1] Polk also spoke of his own goals, noting that he never allowed the possible lack of opportunities to stop him from wanting to become a CPA. His advice to the students was that the field was wide open, and all they needed was the desire and willingness to put forth effort.[2]

Concerning the shortage of black CPAs, the same article in *The A&T Register* discussed the changes occurring in the profession. It stated, "The black certified public accountant, once as hard to find as a snowball in Hades, is becoming more visible in business and industry. Don't get me wrong. There is still no surplus of black CPAs, but the 150 out of 100,000 available in the United States today is a far cry from the forty-seven black CPAs in 1962."[3] According to Dr. Theresa A. Hammond, who authored the first scholarly book providing a history of blacks in the accounting profession, *A White-Collar Profession: African American Certified Public Accountants Since 1921*, there were actually seventy-nine African American CPAs in 1962. As Dean Craig's colleague and friend, she featured him in her book as one of the pioneering African American MBA/CPAs with a PhD in accounting, dedicated to improving business education at HBCUs and diversifying business school education, the accounting profession, and corporate America.

As a new dean working to establish an accredited business program while chairing the accounting department, Dean Craig had his hands full with those responsibilities alone. Yet, he chose to teach accounting courses himself instead of hiring part-time faculty, as he valued the importance of faculty being available to their students.

Juggling all three roles was taxing for Dean Craig, yet he managed it for his first four years. He acknowledged it was a strain, but his core team, the JED Principle, was there to support him. "I could not have made it without them," he stated. To lighten the load, he spent time with his family and watched wild western television shows in his spare time. Recognizing his love for sports, Dowdy assigned him to the athletic committee, where he collaborated with the athletic director and mingled with sports teams, coaches, and players within the Mid-Eastern Athletic Conference (MEAC). These activities provided him with temporary relief from the business school and helped sustain him during those very challenging early years.

With hiring issues to address and efforts to raise the department's standards, Dean Craig had his hands full with upgrading the accounting department at the same time he was upgrading all of the other departments within the business school. With so few African Americans holding PhDs in accounting, he faced significant challenges in hiring qualified faculty for the accounting program just like the other departments in the business school. Fortunately, the AACSB standards for accounting faculty considered MBAs and CPAs as academically qualified, since there was a shortage of PhDs in accounting prevalent throughout business school academia.

When he arrived in 1972, the accounting program aimed to teach students to apply their technical competence in accounting to solve business problems. This was achieved by providing a thorough understanding of accounting methodologies and theory, as well as the economic environment that accounting supports. Students were prepared for graduate study and accounting positions in both business and government, with a special focus on preparing for the CPA exam. The program was comprehensive, offering thirty hours of accounting credits within the curriculum.[4]

The accounting program was initially small. There were not many students pursuing accounting degrees at the business school. The class of 1967 had six accounting graduates, and the class of 1972 had twenty-nine graduates.[5] While the number of students significantly increased over this period, Dean Craig viewed the growth in enrollment and the number of graduates as an opportunity for the accounting department.

The accounting department had four faculty members, none of whom held PhDs or CPAs. One faculty member, Francis Covington, was an old colleague of Dean Craig's who held an MBA from the

University of Chicago.[6] He was married to Julia, a former student of Dean Craig's at South Carolina State College, who was also on the accounting faculty. She earned her MBA at Atlanta University. At the end of Dean Craig's first school year, they both left the faculty. Mr. Covington transitioned to the Dowdy administration, while Mrs. Covington joined Bennett College, an all-women's HBCU situated down the street from A&T.

After their departure, Mahesh Jain, Chandrakant G. Mehta, and Dean Craig taught accounting courses until the 1976–77 school year. Mehta earned his degree in business communications and an undergraduate law degree from Mumbai University, along with his MBA from Atlanta University. Jain, who had worked under Mahaffey and Watkins, had an MBA from Atlanta University and taught business courses. After Alexander's departure Jain added accounting courses to his teaching load and, along with Mehta, sustained the accounting department until Watkins was hired to lead it. Jain stayed with Dean Craig for a few years before leaving to pursue his PhD. Dean Craig noted that Jain had a genuine concern for his students, was an effective spokesperson for A&T, and was dearly missed by his students after his departure.

Since Dean Craig was the only one in the accounting department with deep knowledge in the field, most of the heavy lifting fell on his shoulders when it came to teaching the accounting courses. In his role as a professor, he was just as intentional as he was in his role as dean. He held students to high standards, and he encouraged them to pursue the highest credentials: MBA, CPA, or a PhD in accounting if they expressed an interest in academia.

Dr. Sharon Gary-Finney, the current chair of the Department of Accounting and Finance at the Earl G. Graves School of Business and Management at Morgan State University, was a senior when Dean Craig first arrived at A&T. She described him as the most professional and organized accounting instructor she had ever met. "He was structured in his presentation and kept his focus on the subject," she recalled. "Most accounting teachers at A&T during that time were not thoroughly educated in the subject matter and often strayed from it. Dean Craig did not, and I was truly impressed."

Gary-Finney grew up on a farm in North Carolina, and she described herself as "shy, sheltered, yet eager to learn." She noted that by observing Dean Craig, she decided that teaching at the collegiate level was a viable career option for her. "When I confided in him about my consideration of teaching as a career," she stated, "he urged me to pursue a PhD in accounting. I initially worked in public accounting, but eventually, I followed his advice."[7]

Among the students who took his accounting courses, Dean Craig had a relatively stable reputation. While Gary-Finney characterized him as encouraging, many students perceived him as tough. Mitch Martin, class of 1975, reflected on his experience in Dean Craig's classroom: "I had the pleasure—well, let's say, the experience—of studying tax accounting, cost accounting, and auditing under Dean Craig. He was one tough instructor. I appreciated his toughness more as I continued my studies and earned my MBA from the University of Wisconsin-Madison."[8] Dean Craig did not describe himself as tough, but rather, as "determined."

Although he had taken a position in leadership, once again Dean Craig was teaching several accounting courses. Like any professor, teaching required him to prepare for class, prepare tests, and grade papers. Of those tasks he found grading papers the most time-consuming, and he did not have graduate students, as he had observed at the University of Missouri, to assist him. He found a silver lining in grading papers, however. He used the opportunity to get to know his students and assess their academic standing. He wrote what he referred to as "love notes" on their assignments, addressing aspects like spelling, placement of dollar signs, and suggestions for improvement, a practice he carried over from his days at Lincoln University and FAMU.

While the accounting curriculum Dean Craig inherited was comprehensive, his challenge was finding academically qualified faculty to deliver it. Just as he did for the business administration program, Dean Craig navigated the faculty challenges using his strategy to identify potential faculty members and then persuade them to join A&T's business school. As with Gary-Finney, he also continued his practice of home-growing accounting PhDs.

After four years of working three full-time positions within the business school, Dean Craig finally had a breakthrough in hiring. In the 1976–77 school year, he made significant progress in hiring credentialed faculty for the accounting department. In the spring of 1975, he met Dr. Ladell Hyman at a professional conference at North Texas State University in Denton, Texas (now the University of North Texas). They were surprised to see each other, as chance encounters were often the only way to connect with African Americans holding these credentials during that time. Dean Craig successfully piqued Dr. Hyman's interest in joining A&T's accounting faculty and encouraged her to visit the program. She was impressed with what she learned and decided to join the business school. Both Jannette and Evelyn assisted with her recruitment by addressing various quality-of-life concerns, such as showing her around Greensboro, taking her shopping, and helping her feel comfortable with both the university and the city.

When Hyman joined the faculty at A&T, she brought the number of PhDs in the accounting department to two, including Dean Craig. They also both had MBAs and CPAs. She earned her undergraduate degree from the University of Arkansas, her MBA from Marquette University, her MAS from the University of Illinois, and her PhD in accounting from North Texas State University.[9] Hyman was appointed acting chair of the accounting department and taught Income Tax Accounting and Advanced Accounting, covering topics such as consolidations, business combinations, lease accounting, and governmental accounting. To fully grasp these subjects, a group of her students from the class of 1979, including me, supplemented her classroom instruction by spending many evenings in Merrick Hall working problems on the blackboard.

Other staff hired in that same year included Paul Thomas McGurr and William "Bill" Grubbs. McGurr held an undergraduate degree from John Carroll University, an MBA from the University of Denver, and he was also a CPA.[10] He was a professional in practice, on loan to the accounting department. Grubbs earned his undergraduate degree from East Carolina University and his MBA from UNC-Chapel Hill, and he was a CPA. His professional experience included three Big Eight accounting firms: Arthur Andersen, Price Waterhouse, and Touche Ross & Co. Although he did not hold a PhD, he added tremendous value and stability as a member of the accounting faculty.

In addition to being an accounting professor, Grubbs was also an educational entrepreneur in the field of accounting. He owned a Lambers franchise, covering the state of North Carolina, which offered a live course that prepared individuals to take the CPA exam. He served as the primary author of the Lambers textbook, and throughout his career, he produced multiple award winners for their performance on the CPA exam.[11] Grubbs was an excellent hire and a rarity as a professor at the business school for several reasons. He had unique teaching abilities that simplified accounting, making it easy to understand complex concepts. He was also one of only a few white professors at the business school at that time.

Grubbs taught Principles of Accounting I and II to sophomores. These courses provided foundational knowledge necessary to understand Intermediate Accounting I and II, which he taught in the junior year, as well as other accounting concepts taught by the other accounting professors. During the first week of the intermediate I accounting class in the junior year, Grubbs administered a comprehensive test covering all the concepts taught in Principles of Accounting I and II during the sophomore year. Students reacted to his comprehensive test in three ways: they changed their majors instead of taking it; they took it and changed their majors after they received their grade; or they took the test and continued on as accounting majors. With credentialed accounting professors so hard to find, Dean Craig found a gem in Grubbs to help raise the standard of the accounting program.

In reflection, Dan Moore, one of Grubbs's students, recalled, "He was tough and not shy about giving us five-hour exams. He designed them like a boot camp to prepare us to sit for the CPA exam."[12]

Dean Craig also leveraged Grubbs's talents to help educate his student population about the benefits of becoming a CPA. There was such a lack of CPAs in the African American community that young people were unaware of the profession. Dean Craig confided, "Initially, many students felt the CPA exam was not for us, so I had to encourage them to consider it. I urged them to prioritize it and shared with them its significance in my life, explaining that it was a testament to my professional development, it was a gratifying accomplishment, and a reward for the hard work in the classroom. It was something to be proud of, and it signified to the outside world patience, hard work, and that I had acquired a body of professional knowledge. I informed them that my CPA provided me with credibility as an accounting professor, something I believed was essential for encouraging and inspiring others. I have always believed that I should lead by example, as it is difficult to lead where you have not been."

Gary-Finney was the first among Dean Craig's students to pass the CPA exam. Upon hearing the news, he canceled all afternoon classes to convey to his students the significance of her achievement. While Finney was the first student of Dean Craig's era to pass the CPA exam, Broadus Sawyer became the first A&T graduate to achieve this milestone. In 1960, he was the sixtieth African American to obtain his CPA license and the fourth in the state of Maryland.[13] Holding an MBA from the Wharton School and a PhD in accounting from New York University, he was the seventh member of the pioneering MBA/CPA/PhD in accounting peer group alongside

Wilson, Mobley, Campfield, and others.[14] Early in his career, from the 1948–49 to the 1950–51 school year, Sawyer served on the faculty of A&T's business program[15] and later became dean of the business program at Morgan State University.

Dean Craig positively influenced Dr. HQ when she was a student to take the CPA exam. When she graduated in 1976, he encouraged her to take it, even funding two-thirds of the cost and allowing her to pay the rest to ensure she had some skin in the game. "At that time, I didn't think I could pass the CPA exam," Dr. HQ shared. "Dean Craig and Dr. Hyman were the only African American CPAs I knew. Although Dean Craig motivated me and my classmates by saying, 'You can pass the CPA exam and attend any graduate school you want,' I didn't believe him. I thought I would take the exam just for the experience, so I didn't bother studying for it."[16]

Although she did not pass any sections of the CPA exam on her first attempt, Dr. HQ scored in the sixties on all four parts. The passing grade was 75. Her scores reflected what Dean Craig meant. In her second attempt, she passed three parts, all except business law. She received her CPA license in 1978 while teaching at FAMU. Because of her success, Dean Craig rewarded her with an all-expenses-paid trip to A&T to speak with students about taking the CPA exam. She became a role model for others, even though she was initially apprehensive about tackling it.[17]

Dean Craig credits Grubbs with helping to demystify the CPA exam for A&T's students by "showing them that it did not bite; neither would it eat them up." Students at the business school needed convincing, since this was new to them, and they had few role models to emulate. Therefore, Dean Craig emphasized preparation and confidence in this area. He encouraged all of his students to believe in themselves and to prepare to justify their confidence, just as he had learned during his Morehouse days.

As the accounting program evolved, Grubbs also taught his Lambers CPA review course as a non-credit offering to prepare graduating seniors for the CPA exam. Students who took it had to fit it in their spare time. When I took that course during my senior year, I felt so guilty taking a break from studying that I carried my accounting books with me when I went to parties to soothe my guilty conscience about taking a study break. While seeking AACSB accreditation for the business administration program and developing the accounting department to meet the same standards, Dean Craig raised the bar for the quality of the accounting program, and students really had to dig deep to succeed.

With Hyman as acting chair of the accounting department and Grubbs, Hyman, and others effectively teaching, Dean Craig was able to relinquish his role of chair of the accounting department and most of the courses he taught. However, he continued to teach his favorite, Cost Accounting. He confided that there were "no volunteers to teach cost accounting." From his perspective, teaching cost accounting required a lot of concentration, and he taught it in a way that discouraged memorization, encouraging students to think critically. This approach, he believed, was essential, since accounting is a progressive field that is always evolving. As the business landscape changes, accounting must adapt as well. Therefore, he emphasized applying logic instead of rote memorization to help students grasp concepts.

For a time, accounting majors were required to take Dean Craig's cost accounting class to earn their degree, as there were no alternatives. For this he earned a reputation across the A&T campus not only for his efforts toward AACSB accreditation and how he inspired and motivated his students, but also for the rigor of the accounting program and his cost accounting course.

James Clausell, a member of the class of 1979, had a memorable learning experience with Dean Craig in his cost accounting class. He earned an A in the course, but Dean Craig deducted ten points from his final exam because he didn't include dollar signs next to the numbers in his calculated answers. As a result, he received a B in the course. He shared, "When I approached Dean Craig to negotiate, he explained that I might deserve the best in a job or a promotion, but personal preferences could influence the outcome. He further emphasized that the B would not hinder my progress. I always remembered that lesson: Be prepared to navigate disappointments and focus on the larger picture. Ultimately, I graduated Summa Cum Laude, joined the prestigious firm Coopers & Lybrand (now PricewaterhouseCoopers), became a CPA, and am now the managing partner of one of the most respected regional CPA firms on the East Coast, Clausell & Associates P.C."[18]

Dean Craig practiced equal opportunity for all students, as conveyed by Bonnie Rene Miley-Sims, class of 1979. She also earned an A in Cost Accounting up to her final exam in her senior year. "I received an F on my final cost accounting exam because I overslept and arrived late to class, so I only had half an hour to complete the final exam. Considering my relationship with Dean Craig, I thought he would show me grace and let me finish, but he didn't. My final grade in the class was a C. Disappointed, I met with him, prepared with a written script to guide our discussion about his decision and his refusal to give me more time to complete the final exam. I did not change his mind. When I stopped by his office to say goodbye after graduation, he reminded me of our exchange, emphasizing my courage in challenging his decision. He then offered words that helped me stay grounded throughout my career. He said, 'Remember to do that in the workplace. Stand up for yourself.'"[19]

Some students accused Dean Craig of favoring accounting students over those in other majors, but they were unaware of the challenges faced by Clausell, Miley-Sims, and so many others throughout the years. But once that narrative spread in the business school, people believed it. The real truth was Dean Craig worked diligently for all his students, regardless of their major. Francine Mitchell Verdine, class of 1983, ended her first semester at A&T with fifteen credit hours and a grade point average of 1.9. She visited Dean Craig in hopes of obtaining his signature to change her major from engineering to marketing. She explained, "Dean Craig asked me my grade point average, and I replied 1.9. He said, 'I can't do anything with that.' I had two sisters who excelled as accounting majors, and I tried to leverage that. I said, 'I'm Tanya Mitchell's sister.' Dean Craig responded, 'I can't do anything with that,' as he signed my transfer form. I then had the audacity to ask him for some money. He smiled and replied, 'I definitely can't give you any money.' Long story short, he facilitated my transfer and arranged for me to have work-study."[20]

"Sometimes kids showed up, and we did what we could for them," Dean Craig shared. "What the students didn't realize was that when the business administration program received accreditation in 1979, the accounting department had the lowest budget and relied heavily on external support. Following the decision to integrate the accounting profession, accounting firms, the AICPA, and other organizations provided generous financial support to help A&T and other HBCUs develop their accounting programs and offer scholarships to high potential accounting students. They were purposeful in their efforts, backing them up with funding." Because of external support, Dean Craig could secure scholarships for students willing to transition from other fields of study to accounting, and he did. Students stood to lose the scholarships if they switched back to a major other than accounting or failed to maintain their grades. "When we awarded scholarships, we required the students to strive for academic excellence in return," Dean Craig stated.

The first grant that Dean Craig personally received was from the Arthur Andersen Foundation, stemming from a relationship he developed with a partner, George "Bud" Beacham, while at FAMU. After he took the position at A&T, Beacham called to congratulate him on becoming a dean and to check in on how he was doing. Three weeks later, Dean Craig received a $3,000 check from the Arthur Andersen Foundation. "It was very kind of Bud to provide that grant. It was my first and it was euphoria when I awarded my first student scholarship of $150 from those funds," he recalled. "Arthur Andersen became a great friend of the business school."

Similar to his work with the business administration department, Dean Craig tackled the challenges he faced in developing the accounting program. Although he achieved improvements in both the program and faculty, he did not initially increase the number of graduates. In fact, the number of accounting graduates fell to twenty in 1979, down from twenty-nine graduates in the class of 1972,[21] the year Dean Craig joined the business school. The growth he desired for the accounting department did not materialize; however, the assumption is that it was due to the academic rigor he imposed on his students, the high expectations he set for them, and the reputation that had spread around campus about the accounting program and Dean Craig himself. It became common knowledge that if a student majored in accounting, Dean Craig would encourage them to pursue a CPA or a PhD in the field of accounting. Also, students had to take his cost accounting course and pass it to complete their degree.

Meanwhile, Dean Craig made another significant hire for the accounting department: Dr. Joseph "Joe" Boyd. He earned his undergraduate degree, Master of Accountancy, and PhD in accounting all from the University of South Carolina.[22] Boyd worked alongside Hyman for one year during the 1978–79 academic year. After her departure at the end of that year, he assumed the role of chair of the accounting department for the following three years.

In the classroom, Dean Craig continued his practice of imparting life lessons alongside the cost accounting material.

Terry Keith, from the class of 1977, remembered Dean Craig for the lessons he learned beyond accounting. He dedicated much class time to topics such as how to interview, how to dress, what to expect in the real world, and how to handle competition from other schools. "Dean Craig couldn't understand why I chose a job I had been working at for several years at Kroger, a grocery store in town, over an internship with the Big Eight. One evening, I looked up and saw him, saying, 'I came by to see why this job mattered more to you than an accounting internship with the Big Eight.' The next day, he gave a lecture on short-term gratitude versus long-term success. I knew it was aimed at me, just like the lecture he delivered when he came in early and spotted me parking my new car. In the end, it all worked out, and I am a proud and accomplished product of his teachings."[23] Keith continued his education and obtained an MBA from the University of Wisconsin-Madison.

Striving for the best and being your best at all times was what Dean Craig modeled, and he expected it from his administrative staff, faculty, and students alike. Everyone continued to contribute their personal best, making significant progress in upgrading the quality of all departments at the business school in hopes of attaining AACSB accreditation.

CHAPTER 15

We Made It

By the 1978–79 school year, enrollment at the business school was up to 1,088 students,[1] growing from a total enrollment of 645 students in 1966.[2] Of the 1,088, 576 (53 percent) were in the Department of Business Administration.[3] The areas of specialization in that department were Banking and Finance, Management, and Marketing,[4] taught by seventeen faculty members: ten with doctoral degrees, five who were in the process of completing doctoral dissertations, and two who were Juris Doctors.[5]

The business school was the fastest growing school on A&T's campus. Almost everyone—faculty, students, and administrative staff—was motivated and working hard, but no one was working harder than Dean Craig himself. His team was dependable, creative, and determined, and everyone persevered as they managed the growth at the business school while handling the rigorous changes necessary to meet the AACSB accreditation standards. The culture that Dean Craig aspired to build had taken root, inspiring everyone toward excellence.

Terry Williams learned firsthand at the graduation cookout for the class of 1979 that he had almost been kicked out of the accounting program during his sophomore year due to poor performance. It was Dean Craig who chose to give him a second chance. Fortunately, through his own initiative, Williams joined a study group with other accounting students to master core concepts, such as cost accounting and selected topics in accounting, especially in preparation for tests. "I was surprised to later hear that Dean Craig cited me as a role model for other students, saying, 'If Terry can do it, you can, too,'" Williams recalled.[6]

Pogue also felt the pressure to excel. In early spring 1978, he informed Dean Craig that, in his opinion, the Department of Business Administration was ready for accreditation. However, from Dean Craig's perspective, the standards were substantial and quite challenging, so he believed another year was necessary. Pogue proposed, and Dean Craig agreed, that he would write the introduction to the Self-Study Report that needed to be submitted to the AACSB to determine if the business program demonstrated enough potential to justify a site visit. Once he completed the introduction, Dean Craig took it home and reviewed it over the weekend. Impressed with what he read, they met on Monday and decided it was time to pursue accreditation. Dean Craig later told Jannette and Evelyn, "Ladies, we are moving full speed ahead. We are going for accreditation." He wasn't sure which of the ladies groaned, but all the focus at the business school turned to accreditation.

As a first step, Dean Craig appointed a committee tasked with completing the report, receiving assistance from faculty members across all business school departments. Dr. Willie Bailey, who chaired the Department of Business Administration, earned his undergraduate degree from Tougaloo College, a private HBCU in Tougaloo, Mississippi, and later completed both his MS and PhD at the University of Illinois at Urbana-Champaign.[7] The team spent months during the spring and fall semesters of 1978 preparing the Self-Study Report—gathering data, identifying gaps, and developing strategies and timelines to address them.

Dean Craig recalled, "The team I had in place mattered. Everyone contributed a little to the pot." Some faculty members wrote sections of the report, while others reviewed it; some gathered and analyzed data, and others researched questions. Jannette and Evelyn typed the report. It was a true team effort. In the winter of 1979, the day before the report was due, Jannette and Evelyn still had some typing left to finish. By 5:00 p.m., they were not yet done. The report was due to the AACSB headquarters in St. Louis, Missouri, the next day by 11:00 a.m. Disheartened by the amount of work remaining, Dean Craig called it quits and suggested the team submit it the following school year instead.

Pogue replied, "Do you hear those typewriters? As long as they're typing, I'm working."

At 7:00 p.m., Leon Warren, who led the placement office, stopped by with pizza. At 8:00 p.m., Brewer arrived and began proofreading. At 11:00 p.m., Brewer departed to go home. At midnight, Jannette said, "Good morning, Evelyn." Warren was asleep on the sofa. At 1:15 a.m., Evelyn took the report one floor up to Joyce Johnson so she could copy and bind eight copies. At 1:30 a.m., Jannette's husband called, prompting Warren to leave for home. When the eight copies were returned and reviewed, it was discovered that one section was missing. They addressed the issue, and by 3:45 a.m., the job was complete.

Dean Craig said, "Good night, Jannette. Good night, Evelyn. Thank you. Go home and don't come back until Tuesday."

Dean Craig and Pogue headed to the Pancake House to eat, unwind, and keep Pogue awake for his 7:00 a.m. flight to St. Louis to deliver the reports to the AACSB headquarters. When he left for the airport, Dean Craig went home, collapsed onto the sofa, and fell asleep. Before long, the doorbell rang. It was Pogue. Dean Craig panicked, fearing he had missed his flight to St. Louis. Pogue, being his resourceful self, explained that he had met an administrative assistant from the AACSB at the airport and loaded all eight copies of the report into the trunk of her car. He spent only forty-five minutes on the ground, got right back on the same plane that was returning to Greensboro, and traveled back in the same seat.

Unlike the 1969 Self-Study Report, which included recommendations necessary to meet the standards, this report addressed all aspects of how the Department of Business Administration fulfilled the AACSB accreditation standards. It covered the same areas: curriculum, faculty, research, business school operations, facilities, budget, library, and more. The team felt a deep sense of relief after completing and submitting the report for the AACSB evaluation. They were even more relieved when the evaluation indicated that they could proceed to the next step: a two-and-a-half-day site visit by an AACSB Peer Review Team.

The site visit occurred in the early months of 1979. The Peer Review Team consisted of deans from larger, more established AACSB-accredited business schools. Many of these deans had never visited A&T and were likely experiencing an HBCU campus for the first time. The objective of the site visit was to assess the quality of resources and the productivity of the business administration program, as detailed in the submitted report. The Peer Review Team met with Dean Craig, Pogue, and Bailey, along with select faculty and students, and the Vice Chancellor of Academic Affairs. They also toured the library, the placement center, and other key areas relevant to the business school's operations and productivity, ensuring alignment with the details outlined in the report. At the conclusion of the visit, the Peer Review Team held an exit interview with Dean Craig and Dowdy to share initial comments and observations. However, the team withheld its final decision on accreditation until the AACSB's annual meeting in the spring of 1979.

Everyone at the university—faculty, students, and leadership—plugged into the accreditation initiative felt both excited and anxious about the final decision. They recognized that achieving this goal would be a significant accomplishment for A&T. Most accredited business schools were major institutions of higher learning, including the elite universities. The deans of these schools established the AACSB and its standards, leading the organization since its inception. This was an opportunity for A&T, a small, public, historically black college in the South, to have its business program evaluated by the same educational standards as some of the nation's top business schools.

Both Dowdy and Dean Craig hoped that earning accreditation would significantly shift negative perceptions of A&T and HBCUs overall, positioning the business school and its students to compete on an equal footing with those from other AACSB-accredited business schools. Dean Craig also believed that this achievement would make hiring PhD faculty for the business school considerably easier. He had a lot of belief and a lot of faith, and he hoped for the best. "It was a challenging seven years to reach this point," he remarked, "but we understood that if we achieved AACSB accreditation, we might begin to receive more benefit of the doubt."

For those anxiously awaiting the results, it felt like spring would never arrive. When it finally came, the AACSB held its annual meeting at the Fairmont Hotel in New Orleans, Louisiana. Dean Craig and Pogue departed on Saturday for the four-day event. As they rode the hotel's elevator, Pogue nudged Dean Craig, gesturing for him to look at the woman riding up with them. It was none other than Ms. Lena Horne. They both maintained their composure, as if sharing an elevator with a celebrity was a routine occurrence for them. As the doors opened on other floors, people entering the elevator recognized Ms. Horne and some of them showed visible excitement. Ms. Horne turned to Pogue and said, "It's that way all the time, darling." Dean Craig remembered that Pogue simply smiled.

That Sunday, Dean Craig and Pogue held a forty-five-minute meeting with the AACSB Accreditation Board to address any remaining questions and concerns. When they reached the thirty-three-minute mark, the discussion ended. Thinking it wise to quit while they were ahead, Pogue said, "Thank you. It's been a pleasure." However, Dean Craig had other plans. He began discussing additional aspects of the business program to fill the remaining time.

"I figured they thought I was either very proud of our program or just crazy for continuing to talk during that extra time," Dean Craig shared. "Whatever the case, I filled the rest of that time explaining more details about our business program." As the meeting ended, there was no mention of whether the A&T's business program would be accredited.

The decision was to be announced on Tuesday at the Fairmount Hotel following the annual luncheon for all meeting attendees. Letters would be handed out in the hotel's main lobby after the luncheon, informing attendees which schools would or would not receive accreditation. On that day, lunch wrapped up around 2:00 p.m., after which Dean Craig experienced numbness in his right foot, prompting him to stay behind to stretch and regain feeling, delaying his arrival in the hotel's main lobby. Pogue had gone ahead. When Dean Craig arrived in the lobby, with excitement, Pogue exclaimed, "Where have you been? They're handing out the letters!" Since they only distributed letters to the deans, Pogue did not receive the letter.

When Dean Craig approached the table where the letters were being distributed, about twenty deans from the HBCU community gathered nearby. Deans from predominantly white schools within the UNC System also assembled off to the side. As he took the letter to open it, Dean Craig noticed his hands were shaking. He knew that if the business program didn't get accredited, they would have to wait another year before reapplying. Despite his trembling hands, he managed to open the letter and looked straight to the bottom, where he saw a message of congratulations. In his excitement, he dropped the letter, and it fell to the floor. Pogue picked it up and read it. With enthusiasm, he announced to the crowd, "We made it!" Sharing in the joy and pride of another HBCU achieving AACSB accreditation, the HBCU deans erupted into loud cheers that caught the attention of others in the lobby. They offered their congratulations and invited Dean Craig and Pogue to celebrate with them later that evening. They surprised the pair with tickets to see Ms. Lena Horne. Dean

Craig reminisced, "We had a table up front, close to the piano. When she sang 'Stormy Weather,' she came over to our table and stood next to Danny. We both smiled. She delivered a powerful and unforgettable performance that evening."

The following day, the AACSB hosted a ceremony at the Fairmount Hotel to honor the newly accredited business schools. The hotel featured elegant ballrooms adorned with chandeliers, vibrant carpets, and tall curtains. The room exuded luxury, and according to Dean Craig, it was "reminiscent of the red carpet events at the Academy Awards." Six universities received accreditation that year: North Carolina Agricultural and Technical State University, Boise State University, Duke University, Southern Methodist University, Vanderbilt University, and Winthrop University. The deans from the newly accredited schools stood behind a tall curtain while all other deans and representatives from business schools, both accredited and non-accredited, sat in the audience. When the president of the AACSB announced the newly accredited schools by stating each school's name, location, and its dean, the dean representing the school stepped out from behind the curtain.

When it was Dean Craig's turn, the president announced, "North Carolina Agricultural and Technical State University, Greensboro, North Carolina"—and, of course, his name: Dean "Kister" Craig. Escorted by Dr. James Bearden, Dean Craig stepped forward and walked up the aisle to find his seat. The first person he saw was Milton Wilson, who stood up and shook his hand. "Taking that walk was a very gratifying experience," Dean Craig recalled.

Dr. James Bearden served as dean of the business school at East Carolina University from 1968 to 1983, a traditionally white public institution of higher learning that was organized within the UNC System at the same time as A&T. He filled in as Dean Craig's escort for the chair of A&T's Peer Review Team, who could not attend the celebration. Bearden led the AACSB accreditation process for the MBA program at East Carolina University in 1976, while the undergraduate business program had already received accreditation in 1967. In 1976, the business program was the largest professional school on East Carolina University's campus, with fifty-five faculty members and 2,088 students.[8]

The celebration for the newly AACSB-accredited business schools continued later that evening with dinner sponsored by Dow Jones & Company at a soul food restaurant in the French Quarter. Dean Craig and Pogue felt right at home there. All the deans and representatives from the newly accredited schools were present, including Dr. Sam Richmond, dean of Vanderbilt University's MBA program, who sat at Dean Craig's table. He asked, "Kister, what is this North Carolina A&T?" Dean Craig responded playfully, "Sam, what's this Vanderbilt University?" Pogue kicked him under the table, acknowledging his mischief. Dean Craig's playful nature always worked to his advantage, and he recalled, "Sam and I shared a laugh, and that started a friendship that lasted for years."

Richmond served as the second dean of the MBA program at Vanderbilt's Owen School of Management. After joining in 1976, he identified sixteen strategic objectives to achieve, including enhancing the curriculum, increasing MBA enrollment, and raising students' GMAT scores, among others. In May 1979, marking the end of his third academic year and the start of the Owen School's second decade, he informed donors at a dinner that he had successfully completed twelve of his sixteen objectives.[9] Richmond also noted that perhaps the most significant achievement among his goals was that the Owen School received formal accreditation in 1979 from the AACSB, and out of 650 business schools in the United States, only seventeen were accredited at the master's level. Richmond acknowledged that Vanderbilt had joined the elite company of Harvard, Stanford, Chicago, Carnegie Mellon, Columbia, Cornell, and Northwestern.[10] With the accreditation of A&T, Dean Craig had earned the right to sit at the table with deans from these elite schools as well, along with his mentor Wilson.

When Dean Craig called Dowdy's office to share the good news, he was very excited and proud, congratulating Dean Craig and his team. The business program was the last of A&T's academic programs that qualified for national accreditation to obtain it. With the business program earning AACSB accreditation, Dowdy accomplished one of his most important strategic goals for the university. All the academic programs that qualified for national accreditation had achieved it.

A part of A&T folklore is how Dowdy delivered the good news to his boss, President William Friday, and his colleagues across the UNC System during the president's meeting later that week. Dowdy, who always wore suspenders, leaned back in his chair, tugged on his suspenders, and announced, "A&T's business administration program is now AACSB accredited." Several attendees applauded. President Friday asked, "Are you sure? I only have a couple of schools with that designation." His question made Dowdy uncertain.

Dowdy excused himself, left the room, and called Dean Craig, asking him to read the letter aloud, which he did. Feeling even more confident, when he returned to the room, he said, "President Friday, I repeat, the business administration program at A&T is now nationally accredited by the AACSB."

President Friday persisted with, "Are you sure?"

Dowdy leaned over and whispered to his colleague and friend Dr. Albert Whiting, the Chancellor of North Carolina Central University, "If Craig is wrong, he is a dead man!"

Weeks later, Dean Craig sent ten announcement cards detailing the achievement of AACSB accreditation for the business school to Dowdy. However, ten cards weren't enough for him. His assistant called and requested that he order one hundred additional announcement cards, prompting Dean Craig to place another order. Dowdy distributed announcement cards to every HBCU chancellor and many others within his extensive network.

Proud of the accomplishment, Dean Craig wanted the university and everyone—administration, faculty, and students—to benefit from all of the advantages of accreditation. One notable benefit was Beta Gamma Sigma, the honor society for AACSB-accredited business school students with high academic standing, which aims to encourage and recognize academic achievement in business studies. Following accreditation, Dean Craig and his team immediately began the process to establish a chapter to enhance the visibility of A&T and its business school and to provide student members with a recognized universal honor society for their resumes.

Beta Gamma Sigma has a rich history, arising from the merger of a commerce honor society with the same name founded at the University of Wisconsin in 1907 and two other similar societies: Delta Kappa Chi, established at the University of Illinois in 1910, and The Economics Club, founded at the University of California in 1906. Recognizing their common purposes, representatives from the three societies completed a merger that established Beta Gamma Sigma as the national honor society for collegiate schools of business in 1913. In 1919, the AACSB designated it as their scholastic honor society, limiting chapters to AACSB-accredited collegiate schools of business. Members of Beta Gamma Sigma often emerge as leaders across various sectors, including corporate, entrepreneurial, government, nonprofit, and academic fields. They include Nobel Prize winners, Olympians, inventors, CEOs of major global companies and nonprofit organizations, deans of top business schools, and others who contribute to society through social enterprise, service, and leadership.[11]

On April 16, 1980, A&T's business school held its first induction ceremony at the Hilton Inn, where thirty-six students and seven faculty members were initiated in the inaugural year. The faculty included Dr. Alice Kidder, Dr. Basil Coley, Dr. Michael Simmons, Dr. Meada Gibbs, Dr. Sylvia Bembry, Dr. Willie Bailey, and Dr. Quiester Craig. Dr. Robert "Bill" Howard was already a member of Beta Gamma Sigma.[12] The inaugural student members were Mary Beach, Alice Bellamy, Barbara Brasier, Katherine Burckley, Barbara

Campbell, Larry Carson, Clifton C. Craig, Emma Davis, Marc Edwards, Barbara Fulmore-Singleton, Ina Goocharan, Gwendolyn Green, Virginia Green, Edward Harding, Juanita Highsmith, Gloria Hughes, Hattie Issac, Maria Johnson, Johnny Lancaster, Deborah Long, Arden Kirk Lyles, Karen McLeod, Venay Mills, Brent Mondle, Debbie Neal, Allison Nordhoff, Constance Pinder, Shirley Pittman, Wildra Ray, Gwen Roach, Juliet Sampson, Patricia Scarboro, Vanetta Stringfield, Regina Tucker, Gerald Vaughan, and Joyce Willingham.[13]

Another notable feature was the Bronze Key Statue—a permanent structure weighing more than 100 pounds and standing over 52 inches tall. Beta Gamma Sigma encourages collegiate schools of business that establish chapters to install the Bronze Key Statue on their campuses, symbolizing a commitment to academic achievement and excellence. The Bronze Key Statue was positioned at the entrance to Merrick Hall.[14]

Another benefit was the opportunity to join Beta Alpha Psi, the honors organization for students, faculty, and professionals in accounting, finance, and financial information systems. Founded in 1919, it now has over 300 chapters on AACSB- or EQUIS-accredited college and university campuses, initiating over 300,000 members since its inception. EQUIS is another organization that accredits business schools abroad.[15] In 1983, the Zeta Sigma Chapter of Beta Alpha Psi was established. Dean Craig noted, "Our involvement in these organizations significantly changed the unfair negative perceptions of an HBCU, its business school, its students, its faculty, and its leadership."

Margaret Fiorentino, the executive director of Beta Alpha Psi during Dean Craig's tenure, expressed the organization's gratitude to Dean Craig and Dr. Mark Kiel, who chaired the accounting department for over 30 years, for their significant contributions to the Zeta Sigma Chapter at A&T. The chapter, she wrote, achieved superior status starting in 1985 and maintained it throughout Dean Craig's time. During that period, Fiorentino came to appreciate the spirit of

A&T, noting that the accomplishment of the Zeta Sigma Chapter "represented over thirty-one years of superior Aggie Pride!" During his tenure, Dean Craig ensured that his student members attended annual and regional meetings, as well as other Beta Alpha Psi activities and events.[16]

To further promote student development, Dean Craig and his faculty also encouraged student participation in various academic organizations, including the Business Administration Club, the Economics Club, the National Association of Black Accountants (NABA), and the ALOBEAEM Society, which were open to all students in their relevant majors. The acronym ALOBEAEM highlights the role of accountants in business with an ethical tone: Accounting is the Language of Business and the Ears and Eyes of Management. Dean Craig's predecessor, Dr. Herbert Watkins, organized the ALOBEAEM Society and established the first student chapter of the National Association of Black Accountants (NABA) on A&T's campus.[17]

NABA was established in 1970 as a national networking group for African Americans in the accounting profession after the CPA profession was integrated and the first hiring of African American CPAs and accountants in CPA firms and corporations. Cofounder CPA Frank Ross, one of nine founders of NABA and one of the first African Americans to become a partner in a Big Eight firm, wrote of NABA's creation: "The major accounting firms began hiring blacks, but did not help them assimilate into the workforce. They took the position that if they did anything special, they would be admitting that they were not hiring the right individuals. The few of us in the profession at that time said to ourselves that if the firms cannot do anything, then we need to step up and fill the void…"[18] In addition to providing a vehicle for networking, NABA has actively supported professional development of its membership, including students, by providing over $11 million in scholarship funding since its inception.[19]

At A&T's business school, NABA became a hub for professional development and a source of scholarships for accounting students. Students with a high grade point average were eligible for scholarships. For a period, A&T's accounting students received more NABA scholarships than those at any other school. "We encouraged our students to apply, assisting them in obtaining their transcripts, typing their applications, and having our faculty proofread their submissions," Dean Craig shared. "Students often procrastinated on deadlines, but we supported them to ensure they submitted their applications professionally and learned how to gain a competitive edge. The key lesson for the students was the importance of preparation."

Sarah Branch Cooper, an accounting major from the class of 2003, reflected on her activities during her time at the business school. "Once I entered the workforce, I truly appreciated all the training I received both inside and outside the classroom at A&T's School of Business & Economics. As a member of the ALOBEAEM Society, I developed soft skills, such as how to act professionally at a company happy hour when alcohol is flowing and when colleagues may get a little too relaxed. I also learned how to put together a resume and prepare for interviews. It seemed like every business class involved public speaking and team projects, both of which enhanced my leadership and interpersonal skills. Dean Craig helped me get involved in the University Honors Program, which provided me with opportunities to present at conferences and attend several trips with students from various disciplines at A&T. He truly embodied the NABA theme of that time, 'Lifting as We Climb.'"[20]

Dean Craig cultivated a culture at the business school where everyone strove for excellence. His standard of excellence became the norm, leading to significant improvements throughout the business school. He measured success by the accomplishments of his students.

Also, the external markers—AACSB accreditation, Beta Gamma Sigma, the Bronze Key Statue, and Beta Alpha Psi—denoted excellence and strengthened Dean Craig's claims of quality at the business school. Fundraising became significantly easier for him, and support for the business school increased. As graduates carried the spirit of excellence into the workplace, relationships with employers improved, facilitating student placement. When hiring PhDs, Dean Craig shifted the business school's perception from "worthy of consideration" to "we meet the standards like all other accredited institutions." However, he described the hiring process as "continuing to be a dog fight."

Even with external markers of validation, the negative perceptions of the business school and HBCUs did not dissolve in the minds of many PhD candidates and academic professionals. PhD candidates in business disciplines continued to be discouraged from joining the business school solely because it was located at an HBCU. Many deans and faculty at larger schools with significant endowments assumed HBCUs could not be peers in their eyes. However, after A&T's business program received accreditation, it had to uphold the same quality standards as larger institutions. This included research. It was an AACSB standard, a goal of the business school, and a requirement for faculty. "The assumption, once again, was that black colleges could not measure up," Dean Craig stated. "In hiring PhDs, the more established large institutions posed stiff competition for us smaller black schools in North Carolina."

Dean Craig recounted a memorable conversation he had with a PhD candidate after A&T's business school received AACSB accreditation. After explaining the mission and the business program, the candidate replied, "I respect what you're doing, but the salary difference compared to other schools I'm considering is too significant for me to overlook. You can't compete with what I'm being offered elsewhere."

He replied, "I didn't make you a salary offer. I'm just suggesting that you come visit our program."

"This person attended an HBCU for their undergraduate studies," Dean Craig recalled. "They visited and were amazed by our operations and curriculum. They did not believe we could match the salary offered by a predominantly white institution. They joined our faculty and became a fantastic recruiter for other faculty members with doctoral degrees in business. It was the external support we received that made this possible."

Dean Craig was relentless in pursuing everything he needed to succeed in his job. He kept a positive mindset and overcame the obstacles he confronted by moving forward, always with the end game in mind. By completing the AACSB accreditation of the Business Administration Department, Dowdy achieved his vision of obtaining national accreditations for all of A&T's academic programs that were eligible for such designations. Dean Craig thought it would take five years, but it took seven. Of what it meant to be a part of achieving Dowdy's vision, he would later say, "Those of us who grabbed ahold of Dowdy's coattails, we were just extremely proud to be a part of his administration."[21] With business and business education being dynamic, there was still more work to be done.

CHAPTER 16

Accreditation of the Accounting Program

Under Dean Craig, the accounting department consistently maintained strong leadership, with the next generation of African American faculty holding the MBA/CPA/PhD in accounting credentials. Dr. Ladell Hyman first exemplified this leadership, followed by Dr. Joseph Boyd, and then Dr. Mark Kiel, who each served as department chair. Boyd served under Hyman for one year and stepped into the role of department chair after her departure. He described the business school as "on the move" when he joined. The nearly completed accreditation process for the business administration program allowed him to gain valuable insights by observing the site visit and, as he stated, "the master himself, Dean Craig." He left at the end of the 1982–83 school year to assume the role of dean of the business program at traditionally black Norfolk State University in Norfolk, Virginia.[1]

Kiel, who joined A&T's business school in 1980 as a young assistant professor, worked under Boyd until his departure to Norfolk State and was later appointed chair of the accounting department. Kiel earned his undergraduate degree from Alabama State, his MBA from Atlanta University, and his PhD from the University of Georgia. While Kiel was at Atlanta University, Johnnie Clark, the first African

American woman to earn a PhD in accounting from the University of Georgia, inspired him to pursue his PhD in accounting.[2] With Kiel's generation, the number of African American PhDs in accounting increased, although still not significantly.

Dean Craig first became aware of Kiel while attending a conference sponsored by the AICPA Minority Initiative Committee, whose objective was to increase the representation of minorities in the CPA profession. To increase accounting faculty, the AICPA was assisting African Americans with pursuing their doctorates in accounting as a way to help HBCUs with the development of their accounting programs. About five or six doctoral candidates presented their dissertations at the conference. One was a student Dean Craig knew from FAMU, while another was Mark Kiel. Always being on the hunt for PhDs in the business disciplines, Dean Craig was observing the conference participants as a source for hiring. Initially, he was very interested in hiring a student who had impressed him with their presentation; that was, until Kiel took the stage.

He recalled, "Mark wore a powder blue suit, had one hand in his pocket, and all five-feet-four-inches of him exuded confidence and pride. I thought to myself, *Who is this quirky little guy?*"

As Kiel presented, Dean Craig was thoroughly impressed. "Mark was organized in his thoughts, delivered his material clearly, and infused humor in his presentation; his presentation had everything and more," Dean Craig recalled. "He captivated not only my attention but that of the entire audience."

Kiel was working at his alma mater, Alabama State University in Montgomery, as the chair of the accounting department at the time. Dean Craig began reaching out to encourage him to join the accounting department at A&T's business school. Kiel's response was indifferent. Because Dean Craig called him at home, he started to engage in conversations with Kiel's wife, Shirley. Through her, he piqued Kiel's interest in a faculty position at A&T. Dean Craig and Kiel conversed in November and December 1980, even though Dean

Craig did not have a position in his budget. He had grant funds, but he planned to reserve them for scholarships. He was interested in Kiel for the 1981–82 academic year, starting in August.

One day in December 1980, Dean Craig called Kiel to keep him interested in the position. To his surprise, Kiel asked, "When do you want me to start? What about next week?" Dean Craig explained his timing issue, and Kiel replied, "I can't wait for a position to open up." Through their conversations, Dean Craig had gotten to know Kiel and recognized many positives in hiring him. Aside from his excellent credentials and presentation abilities, he saw great potential for program development in Kiel. He also admired his light-hearted demeanor and outgoing personality. While he did not commit, he let Kiel know that he wanted him to join his team but would have to sort things out.

The following day, Dean Craig visited Vice Chancellor Rankin to request "borrowing" a position. This was a method the administration employed to create flexibility in hiring across the university. Deans could borrow faculty positions from future budget cycles, but they had to return them in the subsequent cycle. Focused, dedicated, and strategic in achieving his goals, Dowdy devised a plan where grants covered salaries for the first two to three years to onboard faculty. This approach had allowed Dean Craig to add faculty, though never to the extent he needed. Rankin informed Dean Craig that he had nothing available to lend. Dean Craig, however, was not discouraged.

Relying on his hope and faith, and with no funding for the position, Dean Craig invited Kiel to visit A&T and he accepted. During the trip, Kiel met Dowdy and Rankin and several faculty members within the accounting department. The meeting with Dowdy and Rankin was friendly, filled with laughter and warmth. Kiel's abilities were clearly demonstrated, and his personality shined. Overall, he made a very positive impression. When Dean Craig drove him to the airport for his return trip home, Kiel asked, "When are you going to make me an offer?" Knowing he had neither approval nor funds to support the position, Dean Craig took a chance and extended him an offer. Upon returning to his office, he called Rankin and asked, "Can I move forward?" Rankin replied, "Sorry, we have no available positions."

Dean Craig called Pogue, and they "got together to plot." He then returned to Rankin and said, "We need to act quickly. Mark is leaving Alabama State University, and he wants to join another HBCU. Other schools are eager to recruit him. These schools will offer incentives and do whatever it takes to bring him on board. As you know, most black colleges lack doctorates in accounting that also have a CPA license. If they hire Mark, it will give them a significant advantage in keeping up with the evolving needs of accounting programs. I suppose we will lose him, but thanks anyway for considering us." Of course, Dean Craig was unaware of the other schools Kiel was in talks with, but in his view, desperate situations called for desperate measures.

That evening, Dowdy called Dean Craig at home. He was in his competitive nature. He offered to lend Dean Craig a position for one semester, although he wanted it back in August and the salary was insufficient. Of course, Dean Craig accepted. After that exchange, the Dowdy administration always kept a position available for a part-time faculty member at the business school to support and accommodate Dean Craig's efforts.

Kiel started in December 1980. Upon joining the accounting department, he confided that he was "immediately impressed" by the number of talented young individuals Dean Craig had assembled as faculty members and his administrative and leadership teams. He quickly recognized Dean Craig's commitment to the growth and development of his faculty and felt confident that he had made a wise decision by joining the team. "I viewed the business school at A&T as an excellent place for me to pursue my passion for teaching and learning," Kiel recalled. "After a brief time working for Quiester,

I realized my passion for teaching could not be pursued in isolation. It had to be accompanied by other responsibilities to my students and my faculty colleagues. Quiester not only made me aware of these responsibilities but also showed confidence in me by appointing me as chair of the accounting department so that I could fulfill those responsibilities.[3]

"What I learned most from Quiester, through observation and his guidance, was that superior outcomes stem from capacity, high expectations, and a supportive culture. From my observations, he employed an effective and unique strategy for developing the intellectual capacity of faculty, students, and administrators throughout the organization. Being in such an environment early on, I recognized that organizations with high intellectual capacity can be challenging to manage. Talented individuals possess their own ideas and aspirations, creating a dynamic and often chaotic environment. Through Quiester's tutelage, I discovered that this dynamism and chaos are the lifeblood of an academic unit when a knowledgeable leader who is open to new ideas, listens intently, and genuinely cares."[4]

Kiel learned quickly, and upon becoming department chair, he immediately created some chaos of his own. As the new chair, one of his first actions was to retire Dean Craig from the classroom. Kiel viewed Dean Craig as the head of a growing business school and recognized that he was involved in many professional organizations. At that point, the business school was hiring and retaining academically qualified faculty while maintaining all of the AACSB standards. Because of this, he felt it was time for Dean Craig to stop teaching. Kiel acknowledged Dean Craig's strengths as a visionary and believed he could better use his time in that capacity. He negotiated with Dean Craig and convinced him to leave the classroom. Although it took time to implement, Dean Craig could no longer teach the Cost Accounting course.

As a new leader, Kiel dedicated himself to continually enhancing the accounting program to keep pace with changes occurring in accounting education nationwide. At that time, accounting educators were implementing several modifications aimed at advancing the accounting profession. Five-year accounting programs and independent schools of accounting were being established at business schools. To support this initiative, the AACSB set separate accreditation standards for accounting programs for the first time. Traditionally, accounting programs had been evaluated as an integral component of the business administration program.[5]

In early 1985, the accounting department at A&T's business school focused on reforming the accounting curriculum by integrating technology, strategizing to maintain the necessary financial and physical capacity for a high-quality accounting program, and recruiting talented students and faculty. Everyone worked hard, and the department made real progress, as measured by an established set of input and output metrics.[6]

By this time, Dean Craig and his team were beginning to prepare for the reaccreditation of the business administration program. They were all feeling optimistic about the state of the business school. Enrollment was increasing, and the success of the graduates was a testament to the quality of the business school's academic programs. Also, the business school had built a strong reputation for providing highly qualified students in the marketplace; it was graduating CPAs, and many students were pursuing advanced degrees, often at distinguished business programs. As they considered reaccrediting the business administration program, Kiel and Dean Craig also decided to pursue the next big goal: achieving AACSB accreditation for the accounting program as a standalone, just one year after the first accounting programs were accredited by the AACSB.

To advance this project, they first needed to win the chancellor's support. By that time, Dowdy's reign as chancellor of the university had ended. In *The A&T Register*, his students bid him farewell, saying, "Let us remember the meaning of a favorite word Dowdy used: tenacity. *Webster's* definition: the quality or state of being tenacious;

tending to hold fast; not easily pulled apart, cohesive and tough, persistent."[7] Tenacious he was in holding it together as the leader of the university during some of America's most tumultuous times, setting his most ambitious educational vision amid the turmoil of desegregating higher education in the South and leading his team to realize it while also inspiring his students.

Dr. Edward Fort was the new chancellor, having joined in the spring of 1981. He came to A&T after serving as chancellor of the University of Wisconsin colleges, a part of the University of Wisconsin System comprising fourteen two-year colleges. Chancellor Fort studied educational administration, earning a master's degree from Wayne State University and a doctorate from the University of California, Berkeley.[8] Shortly after establishing their goal to pursue accreditation of the accounting program, Dean Craig attended a meeting in downtown Greensboro with Chancellor Fort in attendance. As they engaged in conversation, he used the opportunity to introduce the idea and gain Fort's support, knowing it would accelerate their efforts. From years of working with Dowdy, Dean Craig understood that college presidents liked being leaders in academic accomplishments. When he approached Fort and introduced the idea of national accreditation for the accounting program, he emphasized that if A&T's accounting program achieved AACSB accreditation, it would be the first HBCU in the nation to have that designation.

Fort replied, "What did you say, Craig?" Dean Craig repeated that A&T would be the first. Fort replied, "Let's get it, Craig. And get a letter on my desk tomorrow morning detailing everything you need to make it happen." The following morning, Dean Craig and Kiel dictated the letter to Jannette and sent it over to Fort, as he had requested.

Accounting accreditation as a standalone program held higher standards than accounting programs as a part of the business administration accreditation, so several requirements were necessary. Within a short time, Dr. Nathan Simms, Vice Chancellor of Academic

Affairs and Dean Craig's new boss, had obtained everything on the list. This quick turnaround demonstrated the progress the university had made in its resources since the initial pursuit of accreditation for the business administration department in 1972, when Dean Craig started, and the initiative was unfunded.

In the following months, Dean Craig and Kiel dedicated their time to writing and reviewing the Accounting Department Self-Study Report for submission to the AACSB Accounting Accreditation Committee. They spent countless hours at the office and at Kiel's kitchen table, challenging each other on content, grammar, presentation, and virtually everything they could debate until they reached a consensus on how to showcase the various strengths of the accounting program. Thanks to the committed efforts of Kiel's staff assistant, Mary Hastye, the Accounting Department Self-Study Report was completed and submitted by the due date in the fall of 1985.

A few months later, when they received the initial assessment of the submitted report from the AACSB Accounting Accreditation Committee, Dean Craig and Kiel independently reviewed it. The committee's initial assessment was not positive; it indicated that A&T's accounting program was unlikely to receive accreditation. They recommended that the department not proceed to the next step, which involved a site visit by a Peer Review Team. Kiel was flabbergasted. He did not view their assessment as responsive to the submitted report. The weaknesses they identified were, in his view, strengths supported by success measures. When Kiel walked across the hall to Dean Craig's office, Dean Craig opened the conversation with, "Mark, they did not read our report!" Kiel responded with a series of expletives.

Since Dean Craig arrived at A&T in 1972, and by the time they submitted the Self-Study Report in 1985, the accounting department had greatly improved. The department was staffed with PhDs in accounting who were CPAs and MBAs, and they had been maintaining the status of academically qualified faculty consistent with the

AACSB standards since 1979, the year the business administration department received its first accreditation. Student outcomes were equally impressive. Graduates were being placed in top accounting firms and other upwardly mobile positions in private industry and government, as well as being accepted in top business schools and earning advanced degrees. There were plenty of examples of placement, promotions, and career success. Also, the number of students passing the CPA exam had steadily increased.

"We were small in size but strong in outcomes," Dean Craig shared. By then, Dean Craig had achieved his goal of increasing student enrollment in the accounting department; rising from twenty-nine in 1972 to 358 in 1985. "From our perspective," he stated, "the growth, productivity, and quality of the accounting program, along with the enhancement of its resources, were obvious."

After some discussion, Dean Craig and Kiel decided to exercise their right to request a visit from a Peer Review Team, a long-standing AACSB protocol in these situations. The meeting was granted, and they immediately began working on areas they knew required improvement. Meanwhile, they gathered the additional information requested by the AACSB Accounting Accreditation Committee and submitted it.

Aiming to impress, Fort paid for the Peer Review Team to stay at one of Greensboro's best hotels, the downtown Marriott. Three trips were made to pick up the committee members from the airport and transport them to the hotel. "The Peer Review Team was chaired by Dr. Milton Wilson, and other members included an accounting professor from a university in Ohio and an industry representative from the United States Government Accountability Office, and others," Kiel remembered.[9]

The visit began with a dinner at the Marriott Hotel. Present were the Peer Review Team, university administrators, community leaders, faculty, alumni, and others supporting the business school's efforts. Dean Craig, Kiel, and Dr. Georgia Bowser were also in attendance. Bowser, who chaired the business administration department, was responsible for its first reaccreditation. A graduate of North Carolina Central University, she earned her MS and PhD from the University of Wisconsin-Madison and was both a Fulbright Scholar and a Kellogg Fellow. Bowser had been part of the business administration department for eleven years, serving eight of those as chair.

The dinner meeting went well; however, there was a moment when a member of the Peer Review Team commented on the length of the dinner. Dean Craig felt somewhat unsettled by the comment, especially since he was already upset by the initial assessment of the accounting program. Nevertheless, he remained confident that the business administration program would be reaccredited because it had continued to advance since its initial accreditation. However, the initial assessment left him uncertain about the accounting program. Consequently, Dean Craig, Kiel, and Bowser adopted a team approach to both activities and relied on their faith in the hope of positive outcomes.

The Peer Review and business school teams gathered the next morning for breakfast. Several introductory discussions took place, and the Peer Review Team posed numerous questions to which the business school teams provided suitable and satisfactory answers. After breakfast, the Peer Review Team was escorted to their workspace in Merrick Hall. As Dean Craig and Kiel were returning to Kiel's office, Dean Craig remarked, "If they had read our report, they would know the answers to the questions they asked at breakfast." Kiel stayed silent, hoping that comment would not come up again, especially in the presence of the Peer Review Team. During the working portion of their visit, Kiel engaged with the team members on all issues related to the accounting program, while Bowser managed the business administration program. As always, Dean Craig shared his wisdom in both areas.

One area that came under scrutiny by the Peer Review Team was the integration and use of technology in the accounting program. They questioned whether the students were fully proficient in using computers, but their doubts quickly faded. During a student session in the computer lab, one member of the Peer Review Team asked a student several questions on that topic. The student not only answered the questions but also provided a full demonstration on how to perform the calculations using the computer. Satisfied with this result, someone on the Peer Review Team remarked, "Okay, next."

Overall, the working portion of the visit went well, as did the exit conferences. During the exit conference, Dean Craig, Bowser, and Kiel received a summary of the Peer Review Team's observations in their respective areas. There was no significant feedback that raised concerns. During the exit conference with Fort, he received an update on the Peer Review Team's two-day visit. Dean Craig made complementary closing comments and concluded with, "You did not read our report." Surprised that Dean Craig mentioned it again, Kiel quickly used his humor to change the subject, hoping for calm on that issue as a step toward ensuring a positive outcome for the accounting accreditation.

The next step for Dean Craig and his team was to defend their programs in a meeting with the Accreditation Committees of the AACSB. Dean Craig, Pogue, Bowser, and Kiel traveled to St. Louis, Missouri, for this meeting, which provided them with the opportunity to address any unresolved or questionable issues related to their pursuits. Overall, the meeting went well but there was no discussion on whether the two programs would be accredited.

The final decision regarding the initial accreditation of the accounting program and the reaccreditation of the business administration program was not revealed until the AACSB's annual meeting in April 1986. Dean Craig, Bowser, Pogue, Kiel and his wife, Shirley, all traveled to San Diego for the annual meeting, feeling confident that the business administration program would receive reaccreditation but feeling uncertain about the accounting program. Eagerly awaiting the results, they picked up their letters at the front desk upon arrival at the hotel. Just as Dean Craig had expected, the business administration program was reaccredited, and as they had all hoped, the accounting program was, too, making it one of sixty-one AACSB-accredited accounting programs nationwide, the only one local to the Greensboro area,[10] and the first for an HBCU.

At some point during their numerous working sessions, Kiel had asked Dean Craig if he could hold a party if the accounting program received accreditation. He requested the freedom to celebrate as he wished, and Dean Craig agreed. So, Kiel planned an extravaganza. He had a suite filled with food, drinks, and a crowd that included AACSB representatives, business school colleagues, HBCU deans, friends, and others. When Dean Craig arrived at the party about twenty minutes late, what he saw astonished him—Kiel stood in the middle of his bed, dressed in gym shorts with a sombrero on his head, smiling and jumping up and down in celebration. "That wasn't quite what I expected, but it all turned out okay," Dean Craig shared with a laugh.

In recognition of this achievement, the *Journal of Accountancy*, the trade magazine for the accounting profession, published an article titled "Accreditation: A First for a Black School—A&T's Accounting Program Recognized by the AACSB." A&T became the first HBCU ever featured in this publication in the eighty-one years since its inception.

"I was proud of our accomplishment in earning AACSB accreditation for the accounting program at A&T's School of Business and Economics," Dean Craig stated. "We had come a long way from a history of no CPAs or PhDs in accounting on the faculty to now having a nationally recognized accounting program. This was groundbreaking for us and HBCUs, and Mark's leadership in this area was phenomenal."

Dean Craig described Kiel as a fantastic leader for the business school's accounting department, indicating that he made a remarkable impact by enhancing resource productivity and developing the accounting program. He was an excellent instructor and leader, offered a fresh voice, possessed academic qualifications, and was an avid golfer. "Mark accepted all golfing invitations on behalf of the business school, not me," Dean Craig shared. "Our work was a team effort. Mark and I were great colleagues, and best of all, we became great friends. His wife, Shirley, remarked that I always showed up at their house when she was cooking."

By the late 1990s, enrollment at the business school had increased, perceptions of competitiveness were high, and undergraduate degrees were offered in Accounting, Finance, Management, Management Information Systems, Marketing, Transportation, Economics, Administrative Services, and Data Processing. At that time, Dean Craig was able to hire an even larger percentage of faculty with terminal degrees. Almost 90 percent of the faculty held PhDs; however, most positions still were not competitively funded in the state budget and therefore required external support. In hiring PhD candidates, he still had to address negative perceptions.

A typical response from some PhD candidates at that time was, "Before you waste your time, here are the offers I have."

Dean Craig would respond, "I was prepared to offer you $5,000 to $10,000 more than that." Still, the perceptions remained that an HBCU couldn't compete. "People questioned how we managed to make it work. We were financially struggling, but we had to do what was necessary to stay competitive," Dean Craig explained. "Our goal was to ensure everyone was competitively compensated within our state budget, but that issue was still being addressed when I retired."

Ultimately, Dean Craig built a faculty known for its rigor and high standards—dedicated individuals deeply committed to driving meaningful change. Each person exhibited unique strengths and valuable contributions, standing out in both the classroom and in their research. They genuinely cared for their students, helping them reach their full potential. Despite their success, some faculty members expressed concerns, primarily because they believed that Dean Craig's expectations were too high. For instance, he required all faculty to hold office hours and to be available to assist students, as he made himself accessible and felt they should do the same.

"Dean Craig was there to make a difference," Dr. Michael Simmons recalled. "He was concerned about the student's welfare, education, performance, and their futures, and he expressed his commitment to these issues in every faculty meeting. Research became imperative for faculty, and as things changed, such as technology, he required us to evolve with the times. He emphasized that we were there for the students, and he wanted us to help them secure internships, full-time employment, and acceptance at prestigious institutions for professional degrees. His care for students was contagious, and nothing validates that more than the actions of a couple of my students years after they left A&T."[11]

Simmons shared that later in his career he received a phone call from two former students, Emel Jenkins and Joseph Lopez. Both were working for the U.S. Department of Labor and met for the first time at a conference in South Africa. During their discussions, they discovered common threads in their majors, A&T, and him. "They called me to express their appreciation for the support they received while at A&T, which brought tears to my eyes," Simmons stated. "Dean Craig always knew what he wanted. He made it clear in our faculty meetings and held those who didn't meet the commitment accountable."

One example of holding faculty accountable was demonstrated in an account that was included in an article in the *Greensboro Daily News* (now *Greensboro News and Record*) around the early 1980s. It was reported that Dean Craig shared that he was happy that he recruited a PhD from a major university until the faculty complained about the "kind of pressure Craig was applying," saying he "might as well go back to his more prestigious former employer." In recalling the incident, it was reported that Dean Craig said, "I had a student assist him in packing. He had come [to A&T] to retire. But we're not running a rest home."[12] He shared his philosophy with his faculty: "Unless our students can be competitive in the marketplace, we can't justify our existence as a school."[13]

Dean Craig and his team's efforts benefited countless students. Many have found success across various sectors, including business, education, government, entrepreneurship, and nonprofit. Some advanced to the C-Suite of major corporations, while others enjoyed prosperous careers in middle management. Some even launched CPA firms, and many pursued academic careers, becoming administrators, professors, and business school deans.

In terms of accounting, A&T emerged as a leading institution in the nation for graduating African American accountants and CPAs. By 1998, over 300 CPAs had graduated from A&T, comprising more than 5 percent of all African American CPAs in the country.[14] Several became the first African American seniors and managers in their respective offices at major CPA firms, and some are now partners in Big Four and large regional firms.

Kiel shared proudly, "The first A&T student to become a partner was Reginald Enoch at Deloitte." Additionally, Dr. HQ remembered the names of several students who made partner at major firms: Princess Palmer at KPMG, Antoinette Lockett and Doyt Jones at PricewaterhouseCoopers, and Jamelia Livingston at Ernst & Young. Others who made partner in major firms included Priscilla Bullock, Brian Moore, Melanie Glover, and Christina Griffin Howard.

Christina, a double major in accounting and Spanish from the class of 2000, is currently a partner at FORVIS, one of the top ten audit and consulting firms worldwide. Her initial thought was to spend two to three years in public accounting, based on her early experiences in the field. She explained. "When I first interviewed for an intern position, I noticed that the firms would send African American staff and first-year managers to A&T for recruitment, but never any black partners. That observation carried over during my internship at Ernst & Young; partners were generally white men. When I brought this up in a discussion with Dean Craig, he challenged us to 'change the narrative.' In terms of becoming partners in public accounting, he introduced the 'why not you' concept to us students, effectively planting the seed for me and many others."[15]

Becoming a partner at a CPA firm is no small feat. Viewing no challenge as too great for his students, Dean Craig inspired and empowered them to create change and make a difference, just as he learned at Lab High and Morehouse College. Not only did he inspire them, but he also provided valuable advice to help them succeed. "He made it clear that you can't do things alone," Christina recalled, "because support and assistance can push you even further. I took that to my job in public accounting, along with the understanding that I had to be my own advocate. I also needed to recognize opportunities and take advantage of them to become a partner."[16]

In his role as dean, the essence of what Dean Craig loved about teaching materialized—his deep commitment to the professional success of his students. Seeing them accomplish big goals confirmed what he always believed. "I always knew if we got our toe in the door we could get through," he shared. Little did he know just how his commitment would play out in impacting the American business school ecosystem at large.

CHAPTER 17

Impacting the Business School Ecosystem

Influencing change in the American business school ecosystem was another significant aspect of Dean Craig's life's work. As a professor at land-grant institutions South Carolina State College, Lincoln University, and Florida A&M University, and dean at A&T, he had firsthand knowledge of the major challenges faced by public black colleges in establishing AACSB-accredited business programs. He described the situation saying, "Resources were suspect at best." This meant inadequate funding hampered an institution's ability to develop and maintain quality business programs. The long-term impact of segregated education and the lack of access to corporate careers also contributed to the underdevelopment of business schools at HBCUs and the shortage of African American business school faculty. Dean Craig strongly believed that the few accredited business schools at HBCUs and those aspiring to be accredited would struggle to achieve long-term sustainability if the pool of African American PhDs in business disciplines did not increase.

Dean Craig influenced this area by sitting at multiple tables, remaining committed to his beliefs, and advocating for essential changes. He engaged with professional organizations, starting at Lincoln University of Missouri and continuing for several years after his retirement in 2013. He supported the professional organizations he joined and worked to promote their missions while also championing change, to enable HBCUs to develop high-quality, AACSB-accredited business programs and provide their students with opportunities to pursue professional careers in corporate environments.

The first professional organization Dean Craig joined was the American Accounting Association (AAA) while he was at Lincoln University. The AAA is the largest community of accountants in academia, dedicated to shaping the future of the accounting discipline through teaching, cutting-edge research, and publications. Its history dates back to 1916, when the organization was founded to unite thought leaders for research in the accounting field.[1] The AAA celebrates those who make significant contributions to research through their induction into the Accounting Hall of Fame.[2] In 2024, there were 120 members of this elite club, including three African Americans: Dean Craig's hero, Dr. William Campfield, who was inducted in 2019 as the 98th member; Dean Craig's former boss, Dr. Sybil Mobley, who became the 109th member when inducted in 2021;[3] and Frank Ross, NABA cofounder and one of the early African American partners in a Big Eight firm, who was the 119th member inducted in 2024.[4]

Members of the AAA volunteer their time and are assigned to various committees. Dean Craig viewed committee work in professional organizations as an excellent networking opportunity and a valuable learning experience. As he engaged in committee work, he built relationships with colleagues, learned how to design programs, and had opportunities to influence activities that addressed the challenges faced by the profession and HBCUs in strengthening their accounting programs. His committee work at the AAA focused on accounting education and initiatives to fulfill the organization's mission. He completed a two-year term as a member-at-large on the AAA Council and served on both the Committee on Accounting

Education and the Committee for the Future Professorial Supply.[5] Dean Craig's approach to participating in professional organizations served him well. He became well-known amongst his peers, as Dr. HQ confirmed: "When I started attending the AAA meetings, people would look at my name tag and see A&T. The first questions asked were, how is Quiester, and how is Mark Kiel?"

While at FAMU, Dean Craig became more familiar with the AICPA, as his boss, Mobley, was active in the organization. He joined the AICPA, and by attending conferences and other professional events while learning more about the AICPA's programs that encouraged, supported, and provided opportunities for African Americans and other minority students to pursue accounting as a career, he developed an interest in the organization. When he joined A&T as dean, he continued his membership and became more engaged as a leader and dean.

As a dean, he met Sharon Donahue, the Director of the Committee on Recruitment from Minority Groups. As director, she worked to increase minority participation in the accounting profession, a goal established by the AICPA when it integrated the profession in the late 1960s. Similar to the AAA, members volunteered their time and were assigned to various committees, enabling Dean Craig to support the AICPA's core mission while also influencing its programs to increase minority participation in the accounting profession. The AICPA committees he participated on included the Professional Practices Committee, the Scholarship Committee, various faculty development committees, and the Committee on Recruitment from Minority Groups, which he chaired for a term.

One approach the AICPA took to help diversify the profession was to assist HBCUs in developing their accounting programs. Scholarships were funded for students, and various initiatives were implemented to enhance accounting faculty. Financial support was provided for faculty travel to professional development activities, including events sponsored by the AICPA's Faculty Development

Committee. During Memorial Day weekend, the AICPA held three-day workshops in New York City. Summer institutes were also organized to keep faculty updated on the latest technical developments in the profession and to highlight further career opportunities available in the accounting field. The Faculty Development Committee also, for a time, worked to increase the number of African American PhDs in accounting. That is how Dean Craig met Mark Kiel.

Dean Craig was thankful for the external funding and programs provided by the AICPA because they significantly benefited the accounting programs at HBCUs. He remembered that the support went a long way, because the accounting programs at black colleges were initially small. He shared, "The accounting scholarship funds we received from the AICPA, accounting firms, and others helped educate many of our students, and the faculty development programs they provided were essential in enhancing the competency of our faculty in the early stages of our development."

By participating in those workshops and serving on committees, Dean Craig formed lasting friendships with Donahue and other representatives from the AICPA. Through these experiences, he also connected with practitioners in the accounting field, corporate executives, business school deans, and faculty from both HBCUs and larger, more established business schools, along with others committed to supporting the AICPA initiatives to diversify the accounting profession and corporate America. During a meeting of the AICPA Committee on Recruitment from Minority Groups in the late 1970s or early 1980s he met Bernard "Bernie" Milano, a long-time KPMG employee who started as an auditor in their Philadelphia office and rose to the executive level, leading the company's recruitment initiatives and the KPMG Foundation. In addition to the AICPA, Milano also participated in professional meetings of the AAA, the AACSB, and other professional organizations, and he attended meetings with business school academics. As their paths continued to cross, Dean Craig and Milano formed a relationship that lasted over forty years.[6]

Milano recalled, "Quiester was great at asking questions. There was that call: 'Bernie, I am forming an advisory council for A&T's School of Business and Economics. Will you serve on it?' No one says no to Craig, so I accepted the opportunity, not realizing my phone would ring a little later with the next Craig question. 'Now that you are on my advisory board, will you serve as chair?' Then, many years later, it was my turn. With outstanding alumni serving on the advisory board, shouldn't you appoint my replacement? His response was priceless: 'Yes, just as soon as I retire.'"[7]

"Bernie was a tremendous asset as chair of our business school advisory board," Dean Craig recalled. "He also recruited accounting students from A&T for KPMG. We accomplished a lot together throughout our careers."

After the business administration program gained accreditation in 1979, A&T became a full member of the AACSB. As part of an organization of business school deans, Dean Craig became actively involved and was appointed to several committees, including budget, standards, and more. He also participated in various Peer Review Teams and, over the years, conducted peer reviews at larger, established schools and HBCUs, including Morgan State University, South Carolina State University, and Norfolk State University.

Dean Craig especially valued his time on the Standards Committee because it allowed him to deepen his understanding of the AACSB standards and how they were developed. As a newcomer to accreditation, he exchanged notes with fellow deans, gained new insights, and discovered innovative methods that others employed to maintain the AACSB accreditation standards and integrate continuous improvement into their business programs. As his relationships developed with other deans in the AACSB, he prioritized engaging in discussions with them to gain their perspectives on various issues.

One issue of particular importance to him was the shortage of African American PhDs in business disciplines, which he faced while gaining accreditation of A&T's business school. In addition to financial resources, hiring academically qualified faculty was the most challenging standard he encountered in building an accredited business program. Once this issue was raised, he was determined to advocate among his fellow deans at traditionally white institutions for producing more minority PhDs in the various business fields. As his AACSB dean peer group did not experience any negative impact because of this issue, their perspective differed. Therefore, they consistently responded that they could not find minority students interested in pursuing PhDs in the business disciplines or that none applied to their programs.

Dean Craig's perspective was unique as he was the tenth African American to earn a PhD in accounting, achieving this milestone in 1972. He viewed these issues through the lens of an African American working at an HBCU. With firsthand experience of the challenges in hiring PhDs in business disciplines, he understood their origins and persistence if left unaddressed. Furthermore, he recognized that as HBCUs were just beginning to develop their undergraduate business programs, they could not yet produce African Americans with doctorate degrees in these fields. He believed that, for black colleges to effectively enhance the quality of their business programs, it was essential to increase the number of African American doctoral faculty. The difficulties he faced in hiring PhDs emphasized this issue, and he knew the talent pool needed to grow to give black colleges "a fighting chance" at establishing AACSB-accredited business programs. His conviction stemmed from his own experiences, and he consistently advocated for his beliefs. On this matter, Dean Craig was called into the Morehouse tradition and persistently kept the dialogue alive among his AACSB business school dean peers from traditionally white institutions.

Dean Craig's persistent advocacy resonated with some of his colleagues. Dr. Jerry Trapnell explained, "When I became dean of the business school at Clemson University, I became more involved with the AACSB. Quiester and I collaborated closely and became better acquainted. We served on Peer Review teams and participated in committee work together. In 2004, I became the Chief Accreditation Officer at the AACSB, and our paths continued to intersect. We often saw each other. He was well-known and highly respected.

"I particularly remember one meeting that Quiester led at the AACSB. It was a gathering of a small group of deans and AACSB department heads with varying personal experiences and backgrounds. He addressed the need for diversity, equity, and inclusion long before this topic gained traction in corporate circles. As he spoke, I reflected on my upbringing. I grew up in a small, segregated town in Georgia in the early 1950s. Neither of my parents attended college, but for my brother and me, going to college was nonnegotiable. My father owned a business and employed African Americans, though he did not always reflect kindly on them. Quiester's talk was a catharsis for me. It was an eye-opener in dealing with societal issues and helped me understand how to address injustices. He helped me understand how to be a better person, and for that, I have immense respect for him. I learned a lot from Quiester. He is a wonderful person who helped people, including me, see and do the right thing."[8]

In the early 1990s, there were fewer than 300 minority (African Americans, Hispanic Americans, and Native Americans) PhD professors in accounting, finance, information systems, management, and marketing combined in the entire United States.[9] This low number reflected the lingering effects of segregation, which hindered the development of higher education across all fields at HBCUs, particularly in business, as African Americans were excluded from professional careers in corporate America. Due to these low numbers and his personal experience in hiring business school faculty, Dean Craig continued to engage in spirited discussions and advocate with his fellow AACSB deans for the necessity of producing more African American business school PhDs at predominantly white institutions. As he persisted on this issue, the second attempt to address the problem occurred in 1989, after the AICPA's initiative to assist accountants in obtaining their PhDs was terminated.

To Dean Craig's delight, a group of academics and supportive organizations launched a program called the Minority Summer Institute (MSI) to address the issue. During the summer, a cohort of "high potential" minority undergraduate juniors and seniors was invited to the University of Michigan, where they were introduced to careers in academia across all five business disciplines to encourage them to pursue this career path.[10] The AACSB and GMAC, the organization that administers the GMAT test for business school admission, sponsored the program.[11] Although the MSI program was well-intentioned, well-attended, and well-executed, it was unsuccessful. After four cycles and 131 graduates, the efforts to create a pipeline of minority students pursuing doctoral degrees in business disciplines failed. Only one student pursued a doctoral degree, leading to the program's closure.[12]

"I applauded the effort," Dean Craig shared, "and naturally, I was disappointed that the program was unsuccessful. I was actively involved and traveled to Dearborn each summer to support it as a leader, advocate, and role model. Several students from A&T's business school were participants. Although the program ended, there was still a need to grow the pool of African American PhD business school faculty. It was a problem that was not going to resolve itself."

Meanwhile, the early 1990s marked one of the longest periods of economic growth in U.S. history, largely fueled by the personal computer and the emergence of the Internet, which ignited the technology boom.[13] During this same period, unemployment fell from 7.4 percent in 1993 to 5.4 percent in 1996, reaching a low of 3.9 percent in 2000.[14] In many areas, the issue was less about the unemployed and more about locating employable workers. Another changing factor in the United States was demographic trends. The population was becoming "bigger, older, and more diverse."[15] Given these factors, skilled workers from diverse backgrounds were in demand, leading to intense competition among companies for hiring and retaining talent. However, the pool of diverse candidates remained limited. Consequently, business schools faced pressure from business leaders to produce more graduates, including those from diverse backgrounds.[16]

The convergence of these factors became evident to Milano, the KPMG partner who led university recruitment and eventually rose to lead all human resource functions. He learned of an incident at KPMG that nearly cost the firm a client due to a lack of diversity. In a debriefing with the audit team, the CEO of a prominent public retail company with a largely female customer base challenged the all-male KPMG audit team, stating, "To understand our business, you need to understand our customer base." In response, a top female audit leader was quickly assigned to the team, which pleased the CEO.[17]

As a result of this incident, Milano became increasingly urgent in his efforts to hire a more diverse workforce. He had been exploring ways to recruit more women and minorities while also pondering why more African Americans, Hispanic Americans, and Native Americans were not entering the accounting profession.[18] By this time, the attacks on affirmative action during President Ronald Reagan's administration had taken root, and the efforts from the late 1960s to diversify the accounting profession had curtailed. Understanding the "social and business trends influencing corporate human resources," Milano recognized the strong business case for hiring a diverse workforce. This issue was often discussed in the committee and board meetings he attended with his corporate human resource counterparts and peers in the accounting and business education sectors.[19]

As these issues were explored, the "dismally low rates of minority enrollment in business education" became a focal point for this group, often discussed during breaks, in side conversations, and occasionally on formal meeting agendas. Differing perspectives on the issue emerged. Generally, one group of problem solvers felt frustrated that all options for change had been exhausted. In contrast, the other group remained optimistic and energized about finding new solutions. Among the optimistic problem solvers were Milano, Hammond, Dr. Melvin Stith, and Peter Thorp, Milano's counterpart at Citibank, who was facing the same challenges.[20]

As discussions continued within this group, they became aware of research highlighting various reasons for the low number of minorities completing higher education. Scholars such as Dr. James E. Blackwell and Dr. Claude M. Steele, who explored this topic, concluded that "minority students were disadvantaged by stereotyping and the lack of role models and mentors who resembled them," especially in business, due to the scarcity of minority professors in business disciplines across American business schools.[21] Another paper written by a white scholar named Dr. John Elliott, who led the Cornell University doctoral program, emerged suggesting a need for greater inclusion.[22]

These theories were validated by Hammond, who had written her dissertation on minority representation in the accounting profession. As a white student with three degrees, she recalled encountering very few minorities among her professors. As a researcher, she confirmed her experience by surveying one hundred doctoral-granting universities, asking three questions about African Americans: How many are on your faculty? How many are doctoral students? And how many PhDs have you produced? Her mailbox was flooded with responses, overwhelmingly indicating zeros. Another research project led by Hammond found that the college majors chosen by students of color were often influenced by knowing a person of color in that field who served as a role model and mentor.[23]

After reviewing all of this information, a shift in perspective emerged among the optimistic problem solvers. Their new viewpoint acknowledged that attracting more minorities to become business school faculty at traditionally white institutions could increase the number of minorities pursuing business degrees as undergraduates,[24] thus increasing the labor pool. Another facet of this new perspective was exemplified by business school dean Dr. Melvin Stith. Stith began his tenure in 1991 as dean of the business school at Florida State University and was one of the few African American deans leading a prominent, traditionally white business school.[25] He earned his undergraduate degree from Norfolk State University, an HBCU, and his MBA and PhD in marketing from Syracuse University.[26]

As the new dean at Florida State University, Stith infused the business school with fresh energy and ideas, promptly setting an ambitious and focused agenda to "position the forty-year-old undergraduate program among the nation's best and largest, build new facilities, and multiply the endowment severalfold." He successfully accomplished these goals, and the university's leadership was pleased with his accomplishments. He also set a goal to increase the representation of minorities in the business doctoral program; however, that goal faced resistance when faculty members accused him of lowering academic standards by admitting so many minority students. Committed to his objective and confident in his approach, Stith addressed the issue by presenting statistics that demonstrated that the overall performance on the admissions exam of his minority doctoral students was higher than that of their nonminority peers. He responded to queries raised by the university provost, stating, "If the football coach can recruit nationally, so can I." Under Stith's leadership, the Florida State University College of Business gradually became a national leader in producing African American doctoral PhDs in business disciplines.[27]

As good friends, Dean Craig appreciated Stith's leadership in this area. Stith demonstrated that traditionally white business schools could produce more minority PhDs in business disciplines, the very issue Dean Craig had consistently championed among his fellow AACSB deans. Milano and Thorp were equally impressed by Stith's success in producing minority PhDs at Florida State University. With renewed optimism, Milano reached out to Dean Craig to share the business community's interest in exploring changes in business education as a way to create a more diverse employee population. As a persistent advocate for this issue, Dean Craig was more than thrilled.[28] He stated, "I knew that if the business community were involved, people would have to listen because large companies are the customers of business schools."

Sharing common interests, the four—Craig, Stith, Milano, and Thorp—formed a formidable team and joined forces to explore changes in this area. Dean Craig lived the issue and understood its long-term implications. Stith demonstrated that a major university could produce more minority PhDs in business fields. And, conscious of the predicted population trends and shifts impacting employment, Milano and Thorp were dedicated to finding solutions to create a more diverse workforce for their companies. They also had the support of corporate giants.

Their first collective effort to explore the new strategy—to increase the number of minority PhDs in business disciplines in the classroom as a means to increase the number of minority students studying business—was to analyze the MSI model that had failed to establish a pipeline for minority business school PhDs in the early 1990s. They discovered that the lack of successful outcomes stemmed from targeting the wrong audience. Traditional beliefs suggested that most individuals in their late-20s and beyond were unlikely to make a career change to become a professor; however, they learned that this theory did not hold true for the minority population.

Minority students, many of whom were the first in their families to secure a corporate job with a middle-class income and who faced student loans, could not afford to dedicate an additional four to seven years of unpaid time pursuing a PhD, immediatley after obtaining their undergraduate degree. They were however, most susceptible to abandon their aspirations of climbing the corporate ladder mid-career. Milano and Thorp had observed these trends in their companies for years. With this refined perspective, the four realized that these individuals might represent a more suitable audience to target for a career transition to business school academia. Their next challenge was how to find them.[29]

Given the history of African Americans in the accounting profession, the underrepresentation of minorities was particularly notable in the area for which Milano recruited. Research by Hammond at that time indicated that while African Americans comprised 12 percent of the U.S. population, only 1 percent were CPAs.[30] By the early 1990s, KPMG executive Robert Elliott's professional achievements had secured him the position of assistant to the chairman at KPMG and a role on the firm's strategic planning committee. Like Milano, Elliott was familiar with employment trends in the accounting sector, including the need for a more diverse workforce. As he gained national recognition, he was also elected chairman of the AICPA for a term. Milano and Elliott had maintained a close relationship since working together at KPMG's Philadelphia office early in their careers, and Milano occasionally sought Elliott's insight on important matters, as he had a reputation as a "visionary, a source of intellect with an uncanny ability to see, interpret, and act on the big picture."[31]

In August 1992, the AAA honored Elliott with its annual Wildman Medal Award for his professional achievements in advancing theory and practice in the accounting profession. This honor included a cash award of $2,500, which was traditionally donated back to the AAA. However, considering the interconnected issues of global competitiveness, diversity in business, and the necessity of access to education and educators as role models for minorities, Elliott decided to break with tradition. When he accepted the award, he announced that he would donate the funds to establish a program to "financially support African American doctoral students in accounting programs who would one day become professors."[32] Recognizing that the amount was too small for its intended purpose, Elliot triple-matched it on the spot, bringing the total to $10,000. He also revealed that Milano and the leaders of the KPMG Foundation would match that amount, raising the total to $20,000. He then told a stunned crowd, "I'm very pleased that the AICPA would match that, bringing the total to $40,000."[33]

Dean Craig recalled Elliot's announcement that evening. "I was at Bob's table. He did a wonderful thing by donating those funds. He sparked a fire in a very important area. He was always an outstanding professional and a personable, caring person."

The $40,000 seed funding was sufficient to support two of the several applicants competing for the accounting doctoral student fellowships. More importantly, it drew public attention to the issue that Dean Craig had been advocating for, which Stith demonstrated as feasible and which Milano, Thorp, and Elliot regarded as crucial to their future business needs. Elliot's surprise announcement began a "new era in pursuing greater diversity in business education."[34] It led to the founding of The PhD Project.

The PhD Project, established in 1993, initially aimed to increase the population of African American doctoral students in accounting, aligning with KPMG's business objectives. As the concept of The PhD Project evolved, it expanded to include all underserved minority groups—African American, Hispanic, and Native American—as well as all five business school disciplines: management, marketing, finance, information systems, and accounting. As of its thirty-second year, The PhD Project had raised the number of minority PhDs in these five business disciplines from 294 in 1994 to over 1,500.[35] Dr. Scott Cowen, President Emeritus of Tulane University and a former AACSB President later wrote of the initiative, "The PhD Project proved that a diverse faculty attracts a diverse student body, which ultimately leads to increased diversity and inclusiveness in the workplace and boardroom."[36]

The PhD Project achieved such success in increasing the number of minority PhDs in the business disciplines because of Eliott's next move, which was even more significant. After launching the initiative with the $40,000 seed funding, he later said to Milano,

"It's time to declare victory and close it down," referring to KPMG Foundation's twenty-year investment of millions of dollars in advancing academic accounting research. "If we can do for diversity what we've done for research in auditing and tax, we will have made a lasting difference."[37] Shortly thereafter, in the fall of 1993, the KPMG Foundation trustees authorized Milano to discontinue the research program and reallocate the funds toward establishing more diverse business school faculties. They also announced the establishment of the KPMG African American Accounting Doctoral Students program to support some of the other applicants who applied for fellowships. Lastly, they entrusted Milano to make it all happen.[38]

The PhD Project was established in less than a year, from the formulation of the core idea to its first conference. There were many contributors, including business school deans, heads of doctoral programs, African American business school professors, the former director of the MSI program, representatives from GMAC, the AACSB, and others interested in this issue.[39] Key to shaping the initiative was understanding the issues faced by minority doctoral students at traditionally white business schools. In a series of meetings, thoughts and feelings were shared by Michael Clement, an African American accounting doctoral student studying at Stanford who had worked with Thorp at Citibank;[40] Dr. Carolyn Callahan; and Sandra Shelton, a doctoral student from the University of Wisconsin-Madison, and others.

Clement, Callahan, Shelton, and many others discovered common threads in the isolation and alienation they experienced as doctoral students in a predominantly white environment. Often, being the sole African American pursuing such a degree at their respective universities, they thought they were the only ones in the United States pursuing such a degree. Also, the isolation they felt was so severe that they highlighted the mental toughness and resiliency needed to succeed in completing their PhD program in those environments.[41] To address the isolation issues, Doctoral Student Associations for each business discipline were established as a foundational element of The PhD Project to connect students for support, networking, and mentorship. Dean Craig became a charter member of the Accounting Doctoral Student Association and never missed a summer conference.

Getting at the heart of the new perspective that drove the creation of The PhD project, an aha moment occurred during a planning meeting when a white academic asked Shelton why she thought the number of African Americans at the front of the classroom would encourage more minority students to pursue business degrees. Shelton's logical, practical, but unexpected response was: "Having an African American professor benefits all students. All students have to realize that they can learn from someone who is of a different background. If students want to succeed in business, they must respect the opinions of others who are different from them," causing the meeting participants to realize that The PhD Project would not only benefit minority students but all students.[42]

In the end, less than a year after the initiative was conceived, in December 1994, the first conference of The PhD Project took place at the Hyatt O'Hare Hotel in Chicago. Representatives from the four founding sponsors—KPMG, Citibank, the AACSB, and GMAC—attended, along with representatives from Chrysler and Texaco, the corporate sponsors. The marketing program generated 570 applications from interested parties. Of these, 285 applicants met the screening criteria for being doctoral-program-ready and were invited to the conference, with all expenses paid. Only nineteen of the 285 did not attend.[43] Dozens of minority business school faculty and current doctoral students from across the country attended to provide insights on the journey, career, and rewards of becoming a PhD in one of the five business disciplines to the prospective doctoral students.[44]

Everyone contributed to keeping the spirit of The PhD Project alive. Dean Craig highlighted the issue and persistently advocated for change among his AACSB business school dean peers. Milano noted, "Craig took a stand on diversity and got the AACSB on board with The PhD Project." Stith showed that change was possible at a majority institution, Elliott sparked the initiative, and Milano was the driving force and guidance the project needed to become a reality.[45] In 2011, a Hall of Fame was created for The PhD Project, and Dean Craig, Milano, and Stith, along with Dr. Andy Policano and Dr. John Elliott, were the inaugural members.[46]

"The PhD Project became a significant resource for identifying minority faculty," Dean Craig stated. "I utilized it as a resource and hired more than fifteen professors who participated in the program. I encouraged my students interested in academia to apply to The PhD Project, and at one point, A&T had the highest number of students going through the program. The PhD Project achieved remarkable success in increasing the number of minority faculty in business disciplines. However, despite the larger pool of minority PhDs, HBCU business schools still had to persevere and persist. The competition for hiring business school faculty remained very competitive for black colleges."

It was written that from the very beginning, Dean Craig was "one of the strongest, most reliable sources of encouragement and information for not only the people who created The PhD Project but all of its doctoral students and professors."[47] He joined The PhD Project's Academic Advisory Council and Project AHEAD, a planning group aimed at increasing diversity in administrative roles at the department chair and dean levels, especially at HBCUs, and attended every annual conference of The PhD Project, even in the early years following his retirement. He mentored applicants, doctoral students, and faculty, and the individuals he connected with greatly appreciated his advice, support, and mentorship.

Callahan, who has experienced a distinguished career as a full professor and administrative leader, remarked: "Dean Craig touched many lives, both directly and indirectly. While he can take the most pride in those who attended A&T, he encouraged and supported many others. In fact, many of us owe our academic accomplishments at traditionally white institutions, in no small part, to him. His can-do, must-do attitude inspired me. I view all my successes since our first meeting in 1994 as small miracles, grounded in his kindness, generosity, and capacity to recognize God's gifts in so many others."[48]

While mentoring doctoral students in The PhD Project, to convey his point, Dean Craig drew inspiration from Dr. Benjamin Mays, who served as the president of Morehouse College during his time there. Dr. Mays used memorable sayings and quotations, employing metaphors that resonated with his students, helping them retain the core message he wanted to impart. The students Dean Craig interacted with while participating in The PhD Project compiled the following list of his sayings, which they referred to as "QUIESTERISMS."

- Stand up to be seen; speak up to be heard; shut up to be appreciated.
- You can't teach what you don't know.
- Don't wait for the hammer to fall.
- He had an unlimited budget and spent it all in the first week.
- [Colleague]: Whenever that word comes, you're going to get it.
- If you come with nothing to the dance, you won't dance.
- As long as we keep on keeping on, we can make it.
- I've said all I'm going to say; you have every right to disagree. When you're done disagreeing, I am going to say it again.
- That goose ain't worth its dinner.
- We need to stop preaching sometimes and start to listen to our own sermons.
- Aim high, it's no more difficult to shoot the feathers off an eagle than it is to shoot the fur off of a skunk.

As a Morehouse Man trained in social consciousness and driving change, Dean Craig played a pivotal role in creating opportunities for success in business schools for African Americans and other underrepresented groups, both at HBCUs and traditionally white institutions. In reflection, he stated, "What my experiences confirmed is that having a seat at the table is crucial for making change. You must have a seat at the table if you want your interests to be represented. And when it feels challenging to stand up and speak out, that's when it's needed most. Silence on important issues doesn't foster an opportunity for change. A risk is always involved in speaking up, but you must consider whether the rewards outweigh the risks. The reward far outweighed the risk in terms of increasing the number of African American business school faculty. From my point of view, this was something that needed to be done, and I was pleased to be a part of it."

In other areas, Dean Craig advocated for and influenced change in ways he believed would benefit underrepresented groups, always considering his student population. One such initiative was his interest in the North Carolina Association of CPAs' proposal to increase the required hours of coursework to sit for the CPA exam. He believed this proposal would disadvantage his student population, as it would raise the credit hours of course work from 120 to 150, requiring 30 additional hours of coursework after completing an undergraduate degree. In his view, additional hurdles in obtaining the CPA license would likely deter his student population from pursuing it. Recognizing the potential impact of this change on his student population, he successfully secured Dr. HQ as a representative on the committee to present an alternative perspective, and together, they successfully persuaded the association to consider their viewpoint as the rules were revised.

Clearly, Dean Craig's contributions through his leadership and committee work at leading professional organizations such as the North Carolina Association of CPAs, the AICPA, the AAA, the

AACSB, and others positioned him to build relationships and earn respect among his peers. His persistent advocacy for change was combined with diplomacy, enabling him to gain support for the changes he believed were necessary for the profession, especially since African Americans and other underrepresented groups had so much "catching up" to do. As evidence that his colleagues perceived his advocacy positively, he received a call that shocked him in the fall of 1992.

CHAPTER 18

A Season of Recognition

Dean Craig's accomplishments at A&T's business school and within America's business school ecosystem ushered him into a season of recognition and awards starting in 1985. He received many accolades and secured his place in history as the first African American and the first HBCU representative to achieve several honors. He also gained recognition beyond the professional organizations to which he belonged, receiving awards and acknowledgment from nearly every area of his life's journey.

The National Association of Black Accountants (NABA) was the first professional organization to recognize him. In 1985, he received the Distinguished Service Award from NABA, recognizing his dedication to advancing the organization's mission. Later, when his former student Dan Moore served as the national president of NABA, Dean Craig received the President's Award, and he also earned the NABA Accounting Legend Award.

After building a high-quality AACSB-accredited business school with student success as one of its primary measures, A&T honored him with the Administrator of the Year Award at the May 1986 Commencement Ceremony. The University of Missouri-Columbia, where he became the first African American to earn a PhD in accounting, recognized him with a Business and Public Citation Merit Award in 1987—an award given annually to alumni for their career accomplishments; involvement with the college through board activities, recruitment, or other collaborative programs; and financial support of the college. Recipients are chosen by a vote from the entire faculty.

Next came recognition made possible by an old friend. In 1988, Obrie Smith, an older student whom Dean Craig befriended while teaching at Lincoln University, honored him as an educator by including him in a collection of original oil paintings entitled "Gallery of Greats: Black Educators…Building the Foundation." As Smith rose through the ranks to become Director of Corporate Communications at the Miller Brewing Company, he managed the "Gallery of Greats" project as part of the 1988 Black History Month celebration. Dean Craig, along with six other black educators, appeared in this exhibit alongside notable African Americans: John Hope Franklin, Carter G. Woodson, W.E.B. Du Bois, Alain LeRoy Locke, and Mary Frances Berry. The unveiling took place at the U.S. Department of Education and toured various cities across the United States for two years.

One of the tour stops was A&T, where the portraits of Dean Craig and John Hope Franklin, one of America's most accomplished historians and educators, were unveiled. Chancellor Fort spoke at the event, and Jannette, Evelyn, Pogue, Kiel, and Warren were among the many attendees. Dean Craig's sister, Doll, was present for the occasion and he recalled how she telephoned everyone in the family to let them know about the exhibit featuring Baby Bro. She also sent them a picture of his portrait, which was later hung in his living room.

Dean Craig was among impressive company with all the featured educators, including Franklin, who garnered many distinctions and awards. He was particularly known for his scholarly reappraisal of the American Civil War era and the importance of the black struggle in shaping modern American identity. Franklin also contributed to the legal brief that led to the historic Supreme Court decision, *Brown v. Board of Education of Topeka*, and developed African American studies programs at colleges and universities. Franklin drove over to A&T from Duke University, where he taught, for the unveiling.

"Being part of that collection was a profoundly humbling experience," Dean Craig recalled. "I was thankful for Obrie's friendship, our professional relationship, and I was especially moved by the honor he bestowed upon me. It was incredibly gratifying. As I met the others featured in the exhibit and learned about their accomplishments, it became even more gratifying."

In 1991, Dean Craig received two awards: the North Carolina Association of CPAs honored him with the Outstanding Educator Award in recognition of his significant contributions through teaching and active involvement in the accounting profession, and Clark Atlanta University, where he earned his MBA, awarded him Outstanding Alumnus of the Year.

Then came the phone call in 1992. Dean Craig was at home the day he received it. The caller asked if a group of members could submit his name to the nominating committee to serve as president of the AACSB International for the upcoming year. The membership elects the president, who serves a one-year term leading the organization, by majority vote. Shocked, Dean Craig responded, "You guys are full of it. I'm not sure I want to play that game."

The response was, "Quiester, I think you are scared."

Dean Craig replied, "No, but there is no way they will elect me."

While speaking, Dean Craig reflected on his upbringing at home where he learned faith, and his training at Lab High and at Morehouse, where he was challenged to go out and make a difference in the world and achieve meaningful accomplishments. At the same time, he felt anxious about his chances of being elected as the first African American and the first dean from an HBCU to lead this prestigious organization of business school deans with such a long-standing history.

He continued, "There's no such thing as anyone from North Carolina A&T serving as president of the AACSB. But if you want to give it a shot, go ahead."

With Dean Craig's consent, the group submitted an application that included a headshot and his curriculum vitae which also outlined his involvement with the AACSB. It was a member's committee work that earned them this honor.

"I thought the headshot would definitely kill my chances," Dean Craig shared jokingly. "The application was submitted to the nominating committee, and I was too shocked to question it."

One month later, Dean Craig received another call. He thought it would be a rejection, but instead, he learned he was one of three candidates. Soon after, he received another call from the nominating committee informing him of his official appointment as president, making him both the first African American and the first HBCU representative to serve as president of the AACSB in the organization's seventy-seven-year history.

After processing his mixed emotions of feeling both honored and shocked at the same time, Dean Craig realized he was facing a significant responsibility. He immediately turned his attention to preparing for the challenge ahead. He understood some of the inner workings of the organization from his committee work, and for what he didn't know, he had the support of the AACSB board members and staff, both of whom provided him with tremendous assistance during his tenure.

In his role as president, he addressed the concerns of members and standards for accreditation, and ensured program quality and productivity to make business schools the best they could be in terms of brand, quality, students, and faculty. He presided over meetings—some regional, some national, and some international—and attended others as a guest to fulfill his responsibilities. A highlight for him was leading the annual meeting, which drew a large crowd since most members attended and business schools seeking accreditation were informed of their success.

Dr. Anthony "Tony" Nelson, a management major from A&T's business school who graduated in the class of 1980, attended an

AACSB meeting when Dean Craig was president. Nelson did not have a personal relationship with Dean Craig during his time at the business school, only having glimpsed him briefly over the years, including the moment Dean Craig handed him his diploma. It was Pogue who facilitated their connection, and Nelson got to know Dean Craig better after earning his MBA and PhD in management information systems from the University of Pittsburgh and accepting a position as an assistant professor at the University of Missouri-St. Louis. Although Nelson knew Dean Craig was heavily involved with the AACSB, he was uncertain about the extent of that involvement. When Dean Craig visited St. Louis for a meeting, he invited Nelson to lunch at the event site.

Nelson described their encounter. "I met Dean Craig in the hotel lobby, where he told me about the great things happening at A&T. Afterward, we walked into a large banquet hall filled with a sea of white people. As we passed the tables, Dean Craig spoke to many individuals, and it was clear that they all knew him. I felt extremely proud to be his guest and to see that my former dean was so popular.

"I felt anxious when he walked to the head platform for the dignitaries and VIPs. Honestly, I was worried I would be embarrassed in front of thousands and have to return to a seat elsewhere in the banquet hall. But instead, Dean Craig pointed to one of the seats at the head table and said, 'You can sit here.' I thought he had either lost his mind or was the boldest black man alive," Nelson said, laughing. "Fortunately, neither was true. During the luncheon program, he was introduced as the president of the AACSB, which surprised me. I was overwhelmed with pride for my alma mater that day."

During his time as president, Dean Craig represented the AACSB and member schools at the Global Management Development Forum in Barcelona, Spain. At the lunch meeting, he had to toast a very important visitor who was Spanish. Fortunately, those in attendance were fluent in both English and Spanish, because his Spanish was quite shaky; he knew only enough to say yes or no. That experience led him to suggest to his students that they study a foreign language as an elective. He observed the business world becoming more global and knew this would provide students with the opportunity to study abroad.

The AACSB's annual meeting, which Dean Craig presided over, brought his career experiences full circle. The meeting took place in Seattle, Washington. For that trip, he insisted that Jannette and Evelyn join him and Pogue. After years of hard work and personal sacrifice, he wanted to share this experience with his core team, the JED Principle, which he had relied on for so much over the years and to whom he attributed much of his success. They flew on a 747 jet from Greensboro, stopping in Atlanta, Georgia, before reaching their final destination. Dressed in jeans, sneakers, and A&T shirts and caps, they all represented the university well. As usual, Pogue was the first to spot the chauffeur standing in the airport, holding a sign that read: "Quiester Craig." They approached the chauffeur and he led them to a long white stretch limousine for their ride to the hotel.

Over 1,000 business school deans and representatives from around the world attended the annual meeting. For the keynote speaker at the annual luncheon, Dean Craig selected A&T alumnus Reverend Jesse Jackson, Sr. On the day of his speech, he arrived at the hotel and entered the event through the kitchen, stopping to shake hands with the kitchen staff.

When Dean Craig stood up to introduce Reverend Jackson, Jannette later remarked that he did something he often did when telling a joke. Dean Craig remembered the moment. "I reached up, adjusted the knot of my necktie, and pushed it up, but I didn't tell a joke that time. At that moment, I muttered under my breath, 'Mama, look at your baby son now.'"

That was a significant moment for Dean Craig. He had been nurtured both at home and in school to succeed, but he could have never imagined while growing up as "Baby Bro" in Montgomery, Alabama, amidst extreme segregation that he would earn such an opportunity. He stood there as the president of an international organization of business school deans from across the globe, the first African American and the first HBCU representative. Dean Craig had undeniably reached the mountaintop, and with Mr. and Mrs. Craig looking down on him, he was immensely proud that their baby boy was making history by diversifying the landscape of America's business school education in a number of ways.

Reverend Jackson's keynote speech was titled "Yale or Jail." He urged the audience of business school deans to diversify their student enrollment, noting that it costs more to place young men in jail than to support their education at Yale. He also emphasized the power of education in transforming individual life trajectories and, given the history of education for African Americans in this nation, he noted that there was still work to be done. After the luncheon concluded, Reverend Jackson stayed to take photos with interested audience members and Dean Craig introduced him to key individuals, including Milton Wilson, the pioneer of AACSB accreditation at HBCUs.

From Dean Craig's perspective, serving as president of the AACSB was a great honor for him, his team, his students, and A&T, bringing pride to the business school alumni. The university gained significant recognition because its business and accounting programs earned national accreditation, along with his leadership during that term as AACSB president and his role in the annual meeting. These achievements helped boost the school's reputation in the global business school community. "Quiester not only served but also advanced the AACSB, helping it to embrace a wider range of schools," Trapnell recalled. "He ensured there was greater representation from HBCUs and smaller traditionally white institutions."

During his year as president, Dean Craig received a budget to visit ten to twelve small schools, including several HBCUs, where he received a warm welcome on every campus. He built connections with business school deans and university presidents, encouraging them to pursue AACSB accreditation, which he believed was crucial for enhancing the value of their business schools and, importantly, for their students. At HBCUs during that time, program improvement was not yet a guaranteed outcome, as choices were still being made because of limited resources.

In 1994, Beta Alpha Psi, the national accounting honor society, recognized Dean Craig as the Beta Alpha Psi Accountant of the Year in Education.

The University of Missouri acknowledged his many achievements in 1998 with their Distinguished Alumni Award. He is featured on the website of the University of Missouri's Trulaske College of Business as the first African American to earn a PhD in accounting.

Another recognition occurred in 2000 when Dean Craig was elected to serve a two-year term as president of Beta Gamma Sigma, the national honor society for business schools worldwide. In this role, he became the first African American and the first representative from an HBCU to hold this position. While serving as president of Beta Gamma Sigma, he was interviewed for an article published in the organization's trade magazine.

When asked about the significance of his selection, its implications for Beta Gamma Sigma as a whole, and whether he offered a different perspective than previous presidents, he shared: "First of all, I was flattered. It never occurred to me that I would be asked to serve as president. But when I was, I didn't hesitate. I think the whole idea stemmed from an assessment that I truly believed in what the organization was doing and, therefore, I could move around the country, representing it, making speeches, and attending induction ceremonies. I think this was an explosion in terms of the idea that we were fully diversifying management education. I think it also conveyed that quality comes in various shapes and sizes. A lot of times, people attribute quality only to the schools they know about. But I think when I became president of Beta Gamma Sigma, the general consensus was that there must be some quality in schools like North Carolina A&T. Otherwise, the membership would not have even considered me. I was very grateful for the opportunity. I interacted with schools—large, small, research ones, you name it.[1]

"As to having a different perspective than previous presidents, the one thing that I may have leaned on a little harder was to make certain that smaller traditionally white schools and predominantly minority schools got involved and took advantage of their eligibility to Beta Gamma Sigma. That wasn't so much from a Beta Gamma Sigma standpoint, but from the standpoint of these schools. So, you can call that a perspective, but I think it was a personal mandate. But as far as leadership, I was part of a team that included the administrators and staff of Beta Gamma Sigma, and we were in a continuing flow to advance the mission and virtues of Beta Gamma Sigma, and from that perspective, I just happened to be from an HBCU."[2]

While serving as president of Beta Gamma Sigma, Dean Craig faced the difficult task of sending a message to the global membership to acknowledge the tragic events of September 11, 2001, recognizing the impact on Beta Gamma Sigma members, and offering thoughts and prayers to the worldwide community. "That was a very somber time," he noted. Earlier that same year, he presided over the Student Leadership Forum. During his tenure as president, the organization had more than 335 chapters and 440,000 members.

In 2001, he was selected to serve on the Strategic Development Board at the University of Missouri-Columbia Trulaske College of Business. The Board's mission is to advance the college's strategic initiatives.

Dean Craig appeared on "The Greensboro 100 List of Movers, Shakers, and Makers," published by *The Carolina Peacemaker* in 2002. When he interviewed for the dean's position at A&T in 1972, the individuals he met who were on that list impressed him, and because of his focus and diligence, he earned his rightful place on it, too.

Just one year later, in June 2003, the business school received an unexpected gift of $200,000 from Wachovia Bank to establish the Quiester Craig Endowed Scholarship Fund. This endowment in his name recognized all he had contributed to A&T's business school and his demonstration of leadership in supporting the growth and development of other HBCU business schools. Wachovia also donated $50,000 to commission a sculpture, named Progress, that stands on the grounds of the business school.[3]

An even bigger recognition came to Dean Craig the following year. On April 14, 2004, the university dedicated a state-of-the-art building, constructed as an annex to Merrick Hall to expand the business school. During the ceremony, the building's name was unveiled: Quiester Craig Hall—both honoring him and surprising him. He immediately recognized the value of the modern facility, knowing it would help strengthen efforts to recruit top students and academically qualified faculty while advancing the business school's operations into the twenty-first century.

The new building provided a spacious suite on the fourth floor for Dean Craig and his administrative team. He had a large office with a stunning view of Aggie Stadium. Even though he enjoyed his lovely new office with brand-new furniture, he kept his old, large, patched-up brown leather desk chair that had been gifted to him years earlier by a group of his students. Additionally, the Bronze Key Statue that accompanied the Beta Gamma Sigma Chapter was moved to the new front entrance of the business school.

The expansion of the business school was long overdue. Space in Merrick Hall had been tight since the beginning of Dean Craig's tenure, and he had worked around these constraints for many years. In fact, the 1969 Self-Study Report stated that the nearly new (at the time) Merrick Hall, which housed the business school, lacked a functional design for training business and industry professionals. Because the math department was also located in the building, the business school had access to only seventeen classrooms, and offices were shared by two faculty members. There were four laboratories—one each for accounting, statistics, business machines/typing, and shorthand—that accommodated only twenty to thirty students.[4] Steps were taken to improve conditions for the business school for AACSB accreditation, including relocating the math department to Crosby Hall; however, the space remained cramped as enrollment in the business school increased. Professors often brought in extra chairs to accommodate students, and, unsurprisingly, the overcrowding led to student complaints.

Faye Mitchell Moore, a 1972 graduate who took several of Dean Craig's accounting classes, vividly remembered the ordeal: "One day, at the beginning of the semester, Dean Craig said in class, 'Don't worry about the overcrowding in this area. There will be a pop quiz every day, and each quiz will count toward your final grade.' He then dismissed the class. After a few days, there was more space in the classroom, and fewer extra seats were brought in, a trend that continued every time the class met. On the last day to drop or add courses, Dean Craig announced that he was available to sign off on any request to drop the course. At the next class meeting, the classroom looked more like hen's teeth—few and far apart."[5]

"That was not an intentional strategy for space management," Dean Craig shared, chuckling. "The teaching method of daily pop quizzes was to encourage studying and active participation in the learning process. Our goal was to provide excellence in business and accounting education to prepare students to be competitive in the marketplace. So, I taught in a way to make sure my students knew the material since accounting knowledge is a building block. That teaching method encouraged our students to be diligent in their studies."

In 2005, Dean Craig received the Milton Wilson Award from the National HBCU Business School Deans Roundtable (the HBCU Deans Roundtable). This award recognizes Wilson's pioneering leadership in establishing the first AACSB-accredited business school at Texas Southern University and repeating it at Howard University. Founded in 1999, the HBCU Deans Roundtable emerged from informal gatherings of deans from the HBCU community. It was started with twenty-two founding schools, including Alabama A&M University, Chicago State University, Howard University, Morehouse College, North Carolina Agricultural and Technical State University, and Tuskegee University, among others.

The organization evolved as more deans from HBCU business schools began exploring AACSB accreditation. To avoid reinventing the wheel, a group of HBCU deans held meetings informally to share knowledge and build on the successes of those who had already achieved accreditation. As momentum grew for this group, their meetings were scheduled in conjunction with the AACSB meetings, which played a crucial role in increasing the membership of HBCU business school deans within that organization. One advantage of the meetings was that the deans became acquainted with available business school faculty, whom they were eager to learn about. Since the meetings proved effective, they formalized this group into the Roundtable and sometimes invited guests to learn about the triumphs and challenges of HBCU business schools. Dean Craig's colleague Jerry Trapnell was a frequent visitor. "I attended several meetings of the HBCU Deans Roundtable with Quiester. Within that peer group, he was known as the Dean of Deans."[6] Upon invitation, AACSB-accredited HBCU deans also supported other HBCUs with program development by sharing insights gained from their experiences.

Dean Craig's unwavering commitment to maintaining the highest standards of excellence in business school education made his work a frequent topic in local news. Many published articles in the *Greensboro News and Record,* covered by Jack Scism in his early years and later John Newsome, *The Carolina Peacemaker, The Triad Weekly*, and *The Carolina Times* documented his accomplishments. On a national level, several A&T students graced the cover of *Business Week Magazine* and were pictured inside with Dean Craig in June 2001 when an article entitled "Big Strides at Black B-Schools" was published, highlighting the successes achieved and challenges faced by business schools at HBCUs. By that time, there were eighty business programs at black colleges enrolling 250,000 students.[7] Within academia, *The Chronicle of Higher Education* featured Dean Craig in an article in July 2007 entitled "At North Carolina A&T, He Means Business."

Dean Craig also contributed to the community by serving on several boards of organizations dedicated to improving the quality of life for their constituents. These organizations included the Salvation Army, the Greensboro Workforce Development Commission, the United Way, and a Washington, DC-based nonprofit, The Institute of American Business, which aimed to encourage the development of funding for minority businesses. He was also on the board of directors of Greensboro-based financial institutions, such as Mutual Savings & Loan of Greensboro and First Peoples Savings and Loan. He remained devoted to his religious faith as a member of Providence Baptist Church, where he served for years as its Chief Financial Officer.

Dean Craig earned high regard in every arena he entered, recognized for his contributions and role in facilitating organizational change. While he transformed organizations, he also changed people. His influence on people was most evident in the impact he had on his A&T students, who appreciated, cherished, and revered him for the mentoring, support, advice, and nurturing he provided during his forty-one years as dean.

CHAPTER 19

Student Impact: In Their Own Words

From the moment he arrived at A&T's business school in 1972 until his retirement in 2013, the culture that Dean Craig established endured, was consistently applied, and transformed the lives of thousands of students. Within this culture, students received a high-quality business education and, most importantly, were supported in ways that enabled many to succeed in their careers and in life beyond their expectations. Dean Craig left a lasting impact on his students, which is best understood through the stories they share of their experiences at A&T's business school and beyond.

Because of the tight budget in the business school's early days, Dean Craig lacked funds to travel to recruit students or to develop a recruitment strategy. He welcomed the students that showed up to major in business, and he often recruited at the school's fall registration or while walking around campus. Terry Worrell Glover, a second-generation Aggie and marketing major from the class of 1979, was one such student whom Dean Craig recruited at the fall registration. She recalled, "At the start of my freshman year, when I entered the gym to register for classes, I was uncertain about my major. As fate would have it, I walked right into Dean Craig. He smiled, engaged me in conversation, and before I knew it, I was at the business school table reviewing the curriculum for an accounting major. I began with accounting, but after returning from my summer internship with General Motors, I decided to switch my major to marketing. I was so afraid that he would be disappointed, but instead, he was both supportive and encouraging."[1]

Just as Dean Craig found students, they often found him, as shared by Job McCoy, a business management major in the class of 1983.

Job's parents were typical textile workers in South Carolina, earning meager incomes. His mother recognized the value of education, which led her to work and save to fund college educations for four of her nine children. She sent Job to A&T in the fall of 1979 with just over $900, but that amount did not cover his tuition and fees. Since he could not meet his financial obligation, a woman in the bursar's office asked him about his major. When he said business, she sent him over to the business school to speak with Dean Craig.[2]

"When I sat down with him in his office, I explained my financial dilemma and shared my academic and athletic abilities," Job remembered. "I will never forget what Dean Craig said to me next. He said, 'Young man, if you have the courage and motivation to come to my office expressing a desire to attend A&T and major in business administration, let me take a look at your high school transcript. If your grades are as good as you've indicated, I will provide you with an academic scholarship for the amount necessary to attend school.' He also mentioned, 'I know Coach Don Corbett. If you're interested in trying out for the basketball team, I'll send you over to meet with him as well.'" Job received a partial academic scholarship to close his financial gap with a commitment for it to last as long as he met Dean Craig's academic standards.[3]

"Sometimes kids showed up, and we did what we could for them," Dean Craig recounted. "The fundraising that was done at the business school to secure external support made an education possible for many of our kids."

Dean Craig's recruitment methods, combined with students choosing business as their majors and the unfair conditions that blacks faced in segregated America, contributed to the varied profile of the early students at the business school. The 1969 Self-Study Report identified student quality as needing improvement, noting that "some students" graduated with honors. Out of the 76 graduates in 1968, 5 percent graduated with honors.[4]

As Dean Craig worked to enhance the quality of programs and faculty at the business school to prepare for accreditation, he also focused on improving student quality to meet the standards. The AACSB used SAT admission scores as a primary indicator of student quality, alongside other criteria such as participation in enrichment activities, job placement rates, the number of students pursuing advanced degrees, and community service involvement. Although SAT scores varied widely among the student population at the business school, Dean Craig believed that student quality was present. "It was determined by what we were asking our students to do," he shared, "and it shifted as we encouraged them to achieve more. It required some support to get students on track, but as they began to understand the advantages of their business education, their personal drive to excel became the norm." His belief in his students and his approach to motivating them proved effective. In 1979, the year the business program received AACSB accreditation, 35 out of 124 graduates, or 28 percent, were honor students, an increase of 23 percent since 1968.[5]

As the business school budget increased, the AACSB standards for student quality quickly became a priority, leading to the implementation of more recruitment strategies. The goal was to identify students with a record of exceptional academic performance and demonstrated achievements to increase the number of incoming freshmen within the competitive range. Dean Craig's strategy was to populate the business school with students who graduated at the top of their high school class.

To achieve this goal, he made recruitment a collaborative effort, involving administrative staff, department chairs, faculty, and alumni. Alumni played an essential role by identifying high schools in their respective cities from which students were recruited. Occasionally, alumni hosted recruitment events, such as the dinner organized by Mitch Martin, George Hand, and James Clausell on the top floor of the Westin Peachtree Plaza, which overlooks Atlanta. Several students were recruited at that event. Dean Craig and his team traveled to high schools in several states, including North Carolina, South Carolina, Virginia, Georgia, and Alabama.

One visit was to a gifted and talented school in Virginia. Dean Craig and Kiel recruited the school's first, second, and fourth-ranked African American students. One student they recruited was Dawn Harris. She graduated from the Transportation and Logistics Institute, becoming the first business school student to achieve a 4.0 grade point average and earning the title of valedictorian of the university. Over time, several of Dean Craig's students earned that title upon graduation.

During the same trip to Virginia, Kiel recruited Lynn Poindexter for the accounting program. She became the first African American student to receive a financial award from the AAA, achieving this for two consecutive years. Her accomplishment brought recognition to A&T, the business school, and the accounting program. Dean Craig and Kiel also visited Montgomery, Alabama, the dean's hometown, where they successfully recruited two top African American students from Sidney Lanier High School, which had been a state-of-the-art high school exclusively for white students when he was a young boy. Although he had walked past that school hundreds of times, this recruitment trip was the first time he entered it.

Recruitment efforts attracted more top students to the business school, creating another challenge for Dean Craig. He needed to provide students with compelling reasons to choose A&T's business school. This required additional funding for scholarships, as the business school was now competing with more established institutions for top graduating high school seniors. Similar to hiring academically qualified faculty, this remains a competitive area for HBCUs, since better-established schools have larger endowments. To accomplish this goal, Dean Craig worked diligently on proposals to different companies and foundations to increase the amount of scholarship funding at the business school.

Even while attracting top academic students, there was still a need for support, coaching, and mentoring. Throughout Dean Craig's tenure, he encouraged the faculty to be patient with students. His philosophy was that each student required something different, and he urged his faculty to follow his example and meet students where they were. As part of the business school culture, he developed a "medicine bag" full of tools to motivate students, build their confidence, and prepare them for the workplace. He set high expectations and rewarded those who met them with scholarships and internships. As explained by Tamara Harrison Long and John Alexander, caring was woven into the business school's daily activities. Ongoing support and mentoring were provided, and students were also exposed to positive role models.

Tamara, an accounting major from the class of 1986, started her journey at UNC-Chapel Hill, and her first accounting course was not going well. She was in a class of 350 students, her professor did not know her, and her advisor suggested she change her major. After a few days of reflection, she changed universities and enrolled at NC A&T State University, the school her high school teacher had recommended she attend from the start.[6]

"When I became an Aggie in the fall of 1982, it didn't take me long to realize that I wasn't just a student," Tamara recalled. "I had been adopted into a family and culture of professors and administrators who maintained unwavering standards of excellence yet nurtured me with a love that reminded me that even my best efforts always had room for improvement. Dean Craig, whom I affectionately call big ole Papa Bear, set the bar for everyone in the business school. And when I or any of my classmates fell below that standard, we could count on a first-class trip straight to his office."[7]

John, a business administration major from the class of 1991, shared a similar view: "There is no place where I could have benefited more. Dean Craig attracted and recruited the best professors, who demanded excellence from their students. The environment he created was unique in that it was both very professional and very demanding, while also giving us students a sense that we were valued and that our well-being was genuinely cared for."

Exposure to role models was a key strategy that Dean Craig employed to motivate his students and help them understand how a business school education could shape their lives. The business school alumni played a vital role in this effort. After graduating and entering the business world, many returned to campus to share their positions, experiences, and success at their various companies. Their message often emphasized the importance of working hard, taking studies seriously, and keeping priorities in check. They encouraged students to believe in themselves, their faculty, and A&T, assuring them that graduating from the business school would make them competitive in the marketplace. Many students who previously lacked exposure to corporate America took their advice to heart and became role models for future students as they entered and succeeded in the workplace.

Alumni spoke with students in classrooms, and the student newspaper occasionally featured them. One example occurred in 1982 when *The A&T Register* highlighted three accounting alumni—Dan Moore, Faye Mitchell Moore, and Mitch Martin—in an above-the-fold, front-page article after they visited the business school during homecoming weekend. Accompanied by a striking photo of Faye Mitchell Moore seated in a large, high-backed chair while the other two perched on its arms, the article showcased their career achievements. Dan became the first African American manager in his office at Arthur Andersen. His wife, Faye, was the first African American woman to achieve the same title at her office at Peat Marwick Mitchell. Mitch ascended to vice president and chief financial officer at Cable Atlanta after completing a tenure with Arthur Andersen. All three were CPAs.[8]

Dean Craig sought to prepare his students academically, believing that such preparation would instill confidence, which is essential for successfully competing in corporate America or pursuing higher education. Joe Wilson, who described himself as "a very raw product from a small town in North Carolina," felt fortunate to receive both nurturing and tough love from Dean Craig during his time at A&T's business school. He did not want to find himself back home on the family's farm.[9]

"I was flattered that my early academic success caught Dean Craig's attention," Joe recalled. "Initially, I tried to minimize my interactions with him because I saw little benefit in him witnessing how much development I would need to become a business professional. As time passed and my confidence grew, I started to genuinely appreciate how fortunate I was to have access to him. I viewed Dean Craig as an incredible role model. I will never forget the anxiety my classmates and I felt about taking his cost accounting class. Ultimately, that experience was transformative. He demonstrated how much success I could achieve if I remained focused and worked hard."[10]

Joe quickly abandoned his career in auditing at what was Coopers & Lybrand after joining in 1982 to use his accounting training in the broader financial world. "At that time, investment banking was hot. I didn't really know what it was, but it sure sounded exciting. Lacking any real appreciation for how challenging that transition would be, I applied to several business schools and set out to pursue a career in investment banking. One of my greatest regrets is that I didn't seek Dean Craig's advice during this time. I still don't understand why I didn't. Perhaps I was embarrassed because I felt

I would never become the kind of accounting professional he had trained me to be.[11]

"I was shocked to receive a full tuition scholarship to the Johnson School at Cornell. I had concerns about my ability to compete in a rigorous, case-based curriculum. However, I discovered once again that my house had been built on solid ground. At A&T's business school, I had been taught how to think, survive, and win. I was pleased when I received words of congratulations from Dean Craig after Citigroup promoted me to managing director. It was ironic that my A&T classmate, Pat Miller Zollar, received her promotion from Lehman around the same time. As I reflect on my experiences, I can't help but believe that I am one of Dean Craig's greatest success stories. How else would he describe his role in transforming a small-town farm boy into a financial executive that lasted on Wall Street for over forty years? It's a testament to the remarkable program he developed at A&T's business school to prepare students to be highly competitive in the particular area."[12]

Scholarships and internships served as Dean Craig's secret motivators for his students. Students who received scholarships valued them and worked hard to achieve the excellence Dean Craig expected, particularly if they wished to retain their scholarships. One such student was Angela Cain, a marketing major from the class of 2006. When she arrived as a freshman, she was uncertain about how she would afford her dream of attending college at A&T.

"So, during the first week of school, I marched into Dean Craig's office to introduce myself and make my case," Angela recalled. "We exchanged pleasantries and then got down to business. He presented me with my first challenge, asking, 'Why should I help you?' I responded, 'Because I am a hard worker, a focused student, and I live by the motto: To whom much is given, much is required. I promise to pay it forward in some way.' He smiled in that sly, quirky way of his and told me that if I could prove I was worth it, he would support me. He asked me to come back with my first quarter grades, and I did.[13]

"As soon as I walked into his office, I was prepared to proudly share my four A's and one B. I barely had time to say, 'Hey, Dean,' before he responded, 'Don't hey me with that one B!' I was shocked. How did he know I had one B? He had hundreds of students; how in the world did he know my grades? He did this throughout my academic career. Every time I visited Dean Craig; he was aware of my grades and how I was performing in each class. There were a few instances when I was slightly afraid to see him because I knew what he would say. But we kept our promises to each other." Angela later obtained her MBA from the Kellogg School of Management at Northwestern University.[14]

According to Dawn Stroud, an accounting major from the class of 1996, scholarships sometimes came with additional commitments. "I had to join Toastmasters as a condition for keeping my scholarship. I wasn't fond of public speaking, so I wasn't excited about making this commitment. However, that experience taught me one of the many life lessons I learned at the business school. Sometimes, you have to engage in activities you might not enjoy to improve yourself. Other valuable lessons, directly imparted by Dean Craig and the faculty, included how to properly shake hands, which side of your shirt to place your name tag, what to order during business meals, how to dress for success, and much more. I have since passed these life lessons on to my own sons."[15]

Regarding internships and full-time employment as another motivator, Dean Craig strongly emphasized that students should interview for as many opportunities as possible. From the very beginning, the Career Center was part of the team, supporting all recruitment efforts for the business school. They ran advertisements and articles in *The A&T Register*, highlighting when recruiters would be on campus and the positions they sought to fill. These opportunities included institutions of higher education that offered students the chance to pursue advanced degrees. To ensure students were prepared for interviews, Dean Craig discussed appropriate business attire, oftentimes referring some individuals to his tailor for alterations—at his expense.

No one was better than Dean Craig in helping students secure internships, as Sylvia Andrews, class of 1978, recounted. "A few days before the semester ended in my junior year, Dean Craig stopped me in the hallway and invited me to his office. Feeling surprised and somewhat in awe, I thought I was going to be reprimanded for something I had done wrong. It was quite the opposite. He was looking for a student to apply for an internship at Procter & Gamble's National Headquarters in Cincinnati, Ohio. He asked me to write a letter explaining why I believed I should be considered for the internship and to return it to him within a few days. He assured me he would handle the rest. Within weeks of giving him my essay, I received an internship offer, took my very first plane ride, and lived in Cincinnati with three other interns near the P&G campus. This was my first exposure to a Fortune 500 company and working in corporate America. That experience was a game changer for me, as I got to see marketing and advertising in full swing."[16]

Sometimes, Dean Craig had to work a bit harder to secure internships for students, as they avoided responding to invitations to his office for their own reasons. In retrospect, Teresa Davis Lassiter, an accounting major from the class of 1989, described her reasons as inexcusable. "I kept receiving messages from Ms. McKeathen and Mrs. Suggs, inviting me to meet with Dean Craig. I kept ignoring those messages. Finally, one day, as I entered Merrick Hall from the Crosby Hall side, I saw him standing in the middle of the hallway near his office. In my infinite wisdom, I decided to take the stairs to the second floor and walk across the building to reach the other end of the first floor, hoping to avoid him. However, being the perceptive person that he is, he intercepted me as I made my way down the stairwell and escorted me to his office. He wanted to let me know that he had arranged a summer internship for me with The Equitable in New York City. Needless to say, that internship was one of the best experiences I've ever had."[17]

Internships were not limited to the corporate environment. Dean Craig placed his students in various sectors. Melba Pridgeon Batey, a marketing major from the class of 1979, interned in the office of Governor James "Jim" Hunt in Raleigh, North Carolina, the state's capital. She had a remarkable work experience, and Governor Hunt's kind gesture has remained with her to this day. After her internship concluded, Governor Hunt invited Melba and her mother to the Governor's reelection inaugural ball. He provided round-trip car service for them, and at the ball, he spoke about the work Melba completed during her internship.

On his mission to enhance student quality at the business school in the early years, Dean Craig did not always support a work-play balance for his students in Merrick Hall. India Atkins Jackson began her journey as an accounting major in 1975, and after a few meetings with Dean Craig, he advised her it would be best not to join A&T's Blue & Gold Marching Machine as an extracurricular activity. India had been very active in her high school band as a cheerleader and in other activities, and she still graduated with honors. "I wanted to continue my extracurricular activities at A&T, so I went ahead with my plan and became a majorette in the band. My reasoning was that this was a better choice than being a cheerleader, because being a majorette was limited to the football season, allowing me ample time for studying.[18]

"After many mornings and evenings of practice, game day finally arrived. As we prepared to take the field at halftime, excitement filled the air. We marched onto the field and performed for the visiting team's side. Then, we turned to face the cheers of hundreds of Aggies and showcased our skills for the home team's side. My excitement and smile quickly transformed into sheer shock when I spotted Dean Craig standing on the sideline, larger than life, staring me down. I wanted to melt into the playing field. The rest of the weekend was a complete blur, knowing I had to face him on Monday morning. We talked, he advised, and I changed my major to marketing. Still,

I spent many hours under his mentorship. I always knew where to find sound advice, even though I didn't always follow it. Throughout it all, I understood he wanted what was best for me."[19]

Pledging a sorority or fraternity was another distraction, according to Dean Craig. Diane Frost Hill, class of 1977, was called to Dean Craig's office, deferring her dream of joining Delta Sigma Theta. "At the time, I was a second-semester senior, and Dean Craig discussed the importance of maintaining my grade point average during the critical period when he was preparing for accreditation. He suggested that I could pledge in the graduate chapter if I truly wanted to engage in community service, which was my reason for wanting to join a sorority. I took his advice to heart and followed it. To this day, I have no idea how he knew I had even attended a rush meeting," Diane concluded with a hint of amazement.[20]

Although Dean Craig discouraged students, many still managed to pursue their desired extracurricular activities without his knowledge. One such student was Pamela McCorkle Buncum, class of 1981. "After I was elected president of the Student Government Association, Dean Craig called me into his office to express his concerns about how this new role might affect my plans to graduate. Surprisingly, I had managed to fly under the radar until then. When I arrived, we engaged in small talk, and he congratulated me on my election. Then, he hit me with the big question. He asked sternly, 'Pam, tell me, do you plan to major in SGA or accounting?' Before I could respond, he patiently outlined my academic standing and what it would take to meet his expectations, emphasizing the importance of finishing strong. I listened intently, my pride bruised, but I left determined not to disappoint either him or myself.[21]

"In the end, he helped me stay focused on my schoolwork and was always there to applaud my efforts as SGA President. I remember that the fall semester of 1980 was a bit tumultuous because Chancellor Dowdy announced his retirement from the university, which, in fulfilling my presidential duties, took even more time away from my studies. I spoke on behalf of the student body at his campus retirement ceremony, and afterward, Dean Craig found me in the crowd. He placed his hands on my shoulders, looked me square in the eyes, and told me that if I could stand there in front of all those people with that kind of self-confidence and knock the ball out of the park like I just did, then I was capable of accomplishing anything I set my mind to," Pamela shared.[22] While Dean Craig continued to challenge his students regarding their grades, over time, he relaxed a bit, showing appreciation for the value of a multidimensional college experience.

Challenging students to meet his high expectations was at the top of Dean Craig's list for motivating and empowering them. He had a "shoot for the stars, you might hit the moon" approach to setting expectations. Or, as he put it, "Aim high; it's no more difficult to shoot the feathers off an eagle than it is to shoot the fur off of a skunk."

By the time Willie A. Deese, who was part of the Merrick Hall Auditorium Insurrection, arrived at A&T, he was already accustomed to high expectations like those Dean Craig implemented at the business school. Willie said, "When I met Dean Craig, I realized he was a strict disciplinarian, no-nonsense, work-around-the-clock kind of guy whose meter was always set on excellence, which I had left at home. My father, Fred Deese, was a janitor at Davidson College during the day, a landscaper after work and on weekends, and a farmer in his spare time. His mantra was, 'Do your work good, and when you do, there will always be demand for what you do.' He worked all the time, so he believed all of his kids should do the same. I went to college to escape his authority, and who did I meet? My father with a PhD, Dean Craig.[23]

"In my initial encounters with Dean Craig, I found him intimidating, intolerant, overbearing, and unnecessarily demanding. Those were some of my nicer thoughts. By the time I turned twenty-one, I began to understand why he was so demanding, similar to my father.

They both prepared me for the challenges I would face in life. So, when I got knocked down, as I did on several occasions throughout my career, I was able to get up and continue striving for the excellence they both demonstrated and demanded. In my adulthood, they have been my heroes, my advisors, my confidants, my counselors, and most importantly, my friends."[24]

Willie enjoyed a forty-year career, rising to the C-suite and ultimately retiring as Executive Vice President of Merck & Co. and President of the Merck Manufacturing Division, an American multinational pharmaceutical company. He serves on various corporate boards, and President Joe Biden appointed him to the President's Board of Advisors on Historically Black Colleges and Universities. As the largest alumni financial contributor to A&T, the School of Business and Economics was renamed the Willie A. Deese College of Business and Economics in 2020, while the Merrick Hall Auditorium, where the insurrection occurred, is now named the Fred and Janie Deese Auditorium in honor of his parents. Thanks to Willie's philanthropy, the Deese Clock Tower beautifies A&T's campus, and the Deese Ballroom in the student center provides a lovely gathering space for the A&T community.

Students at the business school considered themselves fortunate to receive Dean Craig's support, guidance, and mentorship. This role was one that people either loved or loathed. Regarding mentoring, Mitch Martin, a member of the class of 1975, may have gotten the best of it from Dean Craig. "I first met Dean Craig when I was summoned to his office during my freshman year in the first semester. The moment I saw him, my first thought was, what a giant of a man. Little did I know how true that was. He spoke to me about needing good students to help build the business school. At the time, this meant little to me because I was considering transferring to High Point College on a basketball scholarship. I ultimately stayed at A&T, since he offered to cover my tuition as long as I maintained a good grade point average. While attending the business school, his watchful eye kept me on track. He encouraged me to pursue internships, which were an integral and invaluable part of my college experience. He helped me decide to defer work and get my MBA. When I began my career in public accounting, he guided me through the political landscape. He was the first person I called when I received a major job offer, and he advised me on my most critical career decisions, including starting a CPA firm and later diversifying my business interests to become one of the largest minority-owned airport concessions in the country, with over 500 employees.[25]

"When my CPA firm celebrated its tenth anniversary, I felt incredibly proud to have Dean Craig there. On the worst day of my life, my father's funeral, my sadness and emptiness were lifted when I unexpectedly saw [Dean Craig] sitting in the church pew. He always made time to listen and encourage me, and he has been a dear friend, confidant, and mentor throughout my entire time knowing him."[26]

Dean Craig got to know his students well. While he supported them, he also challenged them to be the best they could be. According to Cheryl Duncan-Gill, a class of 1979 accounting major, Dean Craig had a special gift: "his uncanny ability to see things in a person that they may not see in themselves."[27] Shandi Barksdale Starks, an accounting major from the class of 1993, confirmed Cheryl's observation. "My first year in Merrick Hall, I began to notice this very tall man that so many people had warned me about. I did a great job of avoiding him until one day he tapped me on my shoulder and asked, 'When are you planning to come introduce yourself to me?' I inquired how he knew my name, and he replied, 'I know everyone who is in my pocketbook.'"[28] Being in Dean Craig's pocketbook meant being on scholarship.

"Another time, he saw me in the hall and advised me to stop wearing flats, invest in a good pair of heels, and learn how to walk in them. Self-conscious about my height, I avoided wearing heels until he told me to use my height to my advantage and stand out even more among my peers. I followed Dean Craig's advice, bought those heels, learned how to walk in them, and they worked well with my corporate dress; but more importantly, they helped build my confidence," Shandi concluded.[29]

Dmitri Stockton, an accounting major from the class of 1986, echoed Cheryl's observation and Shandi's experience. "Words cannot truly express the impact that Dean Craig had on all of us who were fortunate enough to be influenced by him. Whether it was his many words of wisdom, or his relentless advocacy for each student who lived by the 'Craig Playbook,' just as he prescribed it, [he] produced student outcomes that were unmatched among many of his peers. I believe it amazed all of us how well he understood exactly what each of us needed and when we needed it. It was almost as if he possessed a certain predictive ability that was never wrong, and he delivered his assessments with a level of directness and clarity that was incredibly helpful to his students."[30]

Dmitri leveraged his first job at Arthur Andersen into a position in GE's financial management program. After joining the corporate audit staff, he received ongoing promotions that ultimately led him to the C-suite. He worked across various GE divisions, holding titles such as managing director, chief risk officer, chief marketing officer, and chief executive officer of GE Capital Bank in Switzerland. As President and CEO, he also led GE's consumer finance expansion in banking throughout Eastern Europe, restructured GE Capital Global Banking during the financial crisis, and was later appointed a senior vice president and recognized as one of the top forty leaders globally of the GE Company by its board of directors.[31]

After a decade abroad, Dmitri returned to the United States to lead the restructuring and sale of GE's $120 billion asset management business as chairman, president, and CEO. Following the sale, he remained at GE as a special advisor to the chairman of the company until his retirement in 2017. Since retiring, he has served on various corporate boards, including Deere & Company and Target Corporation, and he began a private equity career as an advisor and investor.[32]

"Reflecting on my background, I did not have the typical upbringing of a corporate senior executive," Dmitri said. "It was much different from the assumptions people made when they thought I held a Harvard, Wharton, or Stanford MBA and possibly had a head start in life. I was raised on a farm in a small town called Stoneville, North Carolina, and also in Martinsville, Virginia, in a single-parent household. We were not wealthy. I graduated from an HBCU, and entering college, I wasn't the obvious candidate for academic success. To my mother's credit, she was persistent in guiding me to engage with life and connecting me with the right academic opportunities. After our visit to A&T's business school, she felt confident I would be well cared for after meeting Dean Craig and Dr. Kiel.[33]

"My career success is directly correlated to the support and guidance I received at A&T," Stockton continued. "Thanks to Dean Craig's leadership, the business school was a special place and life-changing in many respects. He fostered a culture where there was a group of people who invested in me: Dr. Georgia Bowser, Dr. Kiel, Mrs. Suggs, Ms. McKeathen, Mrs. Shirley Kiel, Ms. Mary Hayste, and Dr. Pogue, to name a few. I remember the countless times I was in Dr. Pogue's office, not only learning course material but also discovering how to make the right choices in life. This support has been a lifelong journey, as these individuals have followed my progress as a corporate leader, a husband, and a father."[34]

Jannette maintained a list to track graduates in leadership and other management positions in business, the nonprofit sector, government, education, and as entrepreneurs. "It grew to be a very impressive list over the years," Dean Craig shared proudly.

Before the rise of social media, Jannette's list was often challenging to keep current as people changed jobs, leading Dean Craig to sometimes discover the successes of his students by chance. One day, while browsing through a magazine, he stumbled upon an article titled "Top Paid Women in Corporate America" and recognized a name and face that looked familiar. He inquired with Jannette about her identity, and she confirmed it was Donna Scott, an accounting graduate from the class of 1979. "I quickly tracked Donna down," Dean Craig recalled. "We had a phone conversation, and she updated me on her career, and we both shared a moment of pride. I felt like a proud papa. There are many stories like this with numerous students advancing in their careers and representing A&T exceptionally well."

Donna Scott James had an illustrious career that landed her in the C-Suite at Nationwide Insurance. With her bachelor's degree in accounting and her CPA license, she began her career at Coopers & Lybrand, now PricewaterhouseCoopers, before transitioning to Nationwide Insurance. Over ten years, she quickly ascended the corporate ladder, holding positions such as Director of Tax-Sheltered Products, Corporate Vice President of Human Resources, Executive Vice President, and Chief Administrative Officer and President of Nationwide Strategic Investments. In these roles, Donna became the first African American to serve on Nationwide's executive committee and the first to lead one of its operating divisions.[35]

Looking back, Donna said, "I considered studying engineering, but thanks to Dean Craig, I received more scholarship money to study accounting. Without that scholarship, I wouldn't have been able to attend college. The foundation for my success, both professionally and personally, was established with the support and guidance I received from him. When I failed, he held me accountable and provided a path to recover and learn from my setbacks. When I succeeded, he made sure I understood my obligation and the privilege of giving back and paying it forward.[36]

"I'll never forget how he took a group of us to dinner before graduation. It was my first time at a table with more napkins, knives, and forks than I ever thought I'd need. That moment prepared me for a lifetime of learning how to be confident and competent, regardless of the task or how unfamiliar the circumstances might be. My opportunities in life have been endless in spectrum and abundant in quality because of my beginnings and learnings at A&T's business school."[37]

After Nationwide, Donna's opportunities continued to expand. She operates her own business advisory services practice, serves on several corporate boards, and currently chairs the board at Victoria's Secret & Co. She cofounded a nonprofit, The Center for Healthy Families; acts as co-executive director of the African American Leadership Academy; and chaired the National Women's Business Council by presidential appointment under President Barack Obama.[38]

Another one of Dean Craig's students, who, like Donna, earned a few firsts of her own as an African American, is Dr. Cynthia Williams Turner, class of 1990. She joined the audit staff at Ernst & Young before obtaining her MA and PhD in accounting from Ohio State's Fisher College of Business. She was the first African American woman to earn a PhD in accounting at the Fisher College of Business and the first African American to serve on their business school's leadership team, where she currently works. Turner is a highly sought-after facilitator and guest speaker on the topics of diversity, equity, and inclusion (DEI), whose contributions brought her nationwide recognition.

"I am who I am today as an educator, scholar, and leader because of the extraordinary impact Dean Craig had on me as a student at A&T," Cynthia shared. "I am forever indebted to him, and I promised him when he retired that every day I would work earnestly to pay it forward."[39] In her current leadership role at the Fisher College of Business, Cynthia advocated for Donna to receive an honorary doctorate from Ohio State University.

Dean Craig's students have entered various career sectors. Lynn Perry Wooten, class of 1988, chose education as her career path and is now a university president. "In the words of Marian Wright Edelman, Dean Craig has been a lantern on my path, guiding me through my educational journey. It all began when I was in high school. I received a letter from A&T about the accounting program. Little did I know how that letter would change my life until I met the person behind it. I enrolled at A&T in the accounting program, where I learned to achieve academic excellence under the guidance and mentorship of Dean Craig. He always expected the best from his students and invested in us so we could realize our full potential. He became my mentor, champion, and sponsor, and from him, I learned what it means to put students first. The mentoring I received from him empowered me to honor my heritage, focus on the present, and trailblaze toward the future. Because of this, each day I give my best efforts toward mentoring others."[40]

Lynn truly embraced Dean Craig's expectations. Not only did she excel academically, but she graduated as the valedictorian of her class. She is now a CPA with an MBA from Duke University's Fuqua School of Business, a PhD in business administration from the University of Michigan Ross School of Business, and a Certificate in Advanced Educational Leadership from Harvard University's Graduate School of Education. Lynn made history as the first African American appointed as the ninth president of Simmons University.[41]

Drawing on the concepts taught by Dean Craig, Hilda Pinnix-Ragland, an accounting major from the class of 1977, achieved remarkable success as she advanced her education and career. She earned her MBA from the Duke University Fuqua School of Business, completed graduate studies in taxation at St. John's University, and finished the Executive Program at Harvard University's Kennedy School of Government. Hilda began her career as an accountant at Colgate-Palmolive Company; however, she left to join Arthur Andersen at the encouragement of the audit team, where she became one of the first African American seniors in the New York Office.[42]

Later, Hilda became a financial analyst at Progress Energy, which merged with Duke Energy. She leveraged her financial background to rise to a C-suite position at Duke Energy, where she became the first African American officer—a role she held until her retirement. Within the energy sector, she chose "a road less traveled," where few women—and even fewer African American women—ventured to lead the operations of Duke Energy, delivering energy to a customer base of 600,000. "I often thought about Dean Craig and his teachings throughout my career, especially as I traveled around the world speaking as an energy expert at conferences. The excellence that he expected of me provided a strong foundation guiding my achievements."[43]

While Dean Craig nurtured his business school students and those he met through The PhD Project, he also extended his generosity to students he encountered in other ways. One of them was Melissa M. Oliver, a music major in the College of Arts and Sciences and a member of the class of 2001. With no money and far from home, she applied for work-study, hoping to ease the financial strain. "I spoke to the assistant in the financial aid office and told her I was a hard worker and could do or try anything. She looked at me and said, 'Now, honey, I only have one place on campus that needs a student worker, but all the other students begged me not to assign them to this department.' I slightly frowned and asked which department needed help. She responded, 'It's the dean's office in the School of Business and Economics with Dr. Quiester Craig. Some students say he is an enormous grizzly bear that will growl at you for the slightest things, but really, he's just a big generous teddy bear who holds students accountable for their actions. If you just do your job, you will be fine.' She ended our conversation with, 'Young lady, I think you can handle it. Just do your job.'[44]

"I took my paperwork to Dean Craig's office and met two of the nicest women in the world, Ms. Evelyn and Mrs. Jannette. They both immediately said the same thing: 'Just do your job, and you'll be fine.' Mrs. Jannette picked up the phone, called Dean Craig, and asked if I could come in to meet him. I heard a loud voice coming through both the wall and the phone, saying, 'Yeah, yeah, send her in.' My heart started racing as she opened the door. I saw him sitting in that humongous brown leather chair. He stood up to greet me with a handshake, and from that moment on, he was always inviting, encouraging, and simply amazing to watch. He became a father figure to me and someone with exemplary character to follow.[45]

"Many students were terrified of Dean Craig, but I am incredibly grateful that I took everyone's advice and just did my job, as it gave me the opportunity to meet such an extraordinary man and get to know the big, generous teddy bear that he is. He always encouraged me academically to never give up, no matter what I faced. He also supported my boyfriend, who might have withdrawn from college if not for his words of wisdom. His leadership helped so many, and I truly appreciate all he did to assist me throughout my collegiate journey. Seeing him at my wedding was the icing on the cake."[46]

Dean Craig never forgot the commitment he made to himself that cold, rainy night in Augusta, Georgia, when he found himself stranded and a kind farmer gave him a ride to the bus depot. From then on, he made it his mission to help his students and anyone else who needed support. After that experience, he adopted "If I Can Help Somebody" by Mahalia Jackson as his favorite song. He helped everyone he could, provided they showed a willingness to help themselves.

Leroy Thornton Edwards, Jr., a student who graduated from A&T's business school, returned for a visit early in Dean Craig's tenure. He expressed his desire to pursue an MBA. Since A&T did not offer an MBA program, Dean Craig took him across town to the business school at the University of North Carolina at Greensboro to meet Dean David Shelton. Their meeting resulted in a full scholarship that allowed Leroy to pursue his MBA. After earning his degree, he built a career in brand management with several major corporations, then used that experience to start The Edwards Companies, a distribution business for snack foods, petroleum, and beer and wine beverages. He wrote about his connection, saying: "I have an unbreakable bond with Dean Craig for the support he gave me."[47]

As an outsider looking in, Trapnell summed it up based on his observations during numerous visits to A&T's business school. "With Quiester, it all boiled down to the student. He treated them with kindness and care, offering them great encouragement. He wanted them to expect challenges, work hard, and earn their success. There was no compromise on expectations; he elevated their performance. He expected them to reach their potential and made them understand that if they worked hard and applied themselves, they would succeed.[48]

"I was amazed by his memory and his ability to know his students so well. That is a talent I struggled with throughout my career. I can see him in the hallway. He knew when to push or nudge a student or when to give them a kick in the pants. He understood what button to press to motivate them. He would place a hand on a shoulder or give a fatherly talk. He recognized when it was time to do it, and he knew how to do it. It was stunning to watch. I have never met another dean who could replicate the rapport that Quiester had with his students. I could see that his students revered him. The students he touched think the world of him.[49]

"Quiester was a giant of a man physically, personality-wise, and otherwise. He wielded power at A&T and was a force to be reckoned with. He did the right things for people. He had a humbleness about him, and he always thought of others and found a way to help them succeed,"[50] Trapnell concluded.

Dean Quiester Craig was a trailblazing academic with an extraordinary record of service in academia. He helped to diversify business school education, the accounting profession, and corporate America while inspiring his students. Although his days of teaching and influencing are over, his legacy lives on through the countless individuals and organizations he touched. His impact is a testament to the power of faith, belief, hard work, caring, and compassion—attributes he learned in his early life at home and at school. Dean Craig's story remains a guiding light for those striving to make a difference, reminding them that a single individual can leave an indelible mark on the world and the people they touch, echoing his legacy throughout time and for generations to come.

EPILOGUE

After Dean Craig's retirement in 2013, he was succeeded by Dr. Beryl McEwen. She earned her master's and doctorate degrees from Southern Illinois University at Carbondale and her bachelor's degree from the University of Technology, Jamaica. She has demonstrated leadership in business education, strategic planning, academic accreditation, and classroom teaching, as evidenced by a long and growing list of awards from professional organizations, including the National Business Education Association and the North Carolina Department of Public Instruction Business Education Hall of Fame.[1]

Beryl expressed her admiration for Dean Craig, highlighting his diverse skill set, dedication, strong work ethic, and the invaluable gifts he offered to his students and so many others. She recalled Dean Craig's story about why he served for forty-one years, holding the door open for his students—just as the older black men in Montgomery, Alabama, did for him and his classmates during their youth—allowing them to place their coins in the farebox and take their time to walk to the back of the bus, so the driver would not pull off.[2]

The Willie A. Deese College of Business and Economics (Deese College) is currently led by former student, Dr. Kecia Williams, PhD, CPA, who was inspired by Dean Craig. She continues to uphold the student-centered values developed during his leadership. In Fall 2025, enrollment at the Deese College totaled 2,071—almost three times the 726 enrolled in 1968, when the university completed the 1969 Self-Study Report. The class of 2024 graduated 286 students, a 921 percent increase from the twenty-eight graduates in 1968.[3] Through its undergraduate and graduate programs, the Deese College continues to have a significant impact on its student population.

The Deese College houses five departments with undergraduate programs in **Accounting and Finance,** offering degrees in accounting and finance; **Business Information Systems and Analytics**, offering degrees in business information technology and business analytics; **Economics**, offering degrees in economics with concentrations in business and law; **Management**, offering degrees in management with concentrations in business administration, entrepreneurship, international management, and management information systems; **Marketing and Supply Chain Management**, offering degrees in marketing, marketing with a sales concentration, and supply chain management.

The graduate programs include a Master of Accountancy and a Master of Business Administration, with concentrations in accounting, general business, and human resource management.

All programs at Deese College remain accredited by the AACSB, and the college's vision is to be a national leader in global business education that transforms students' lives. The business school is ranked No. 77 (tie) out of 133 by U.S. News Best Business Schools.[4]

In August 2024, the American Accounting Association awarded Dean Emeritus Quiester Craig, MBA, CPA, PhD their Lifetime Achievement Award for his trailblazing work and extraordinary service to the accounting profession. Later that year, he passed away on December 12, 2024 at the age of 88. His family laid him to rest on December 20th at Providence Baptist Church in Greensboro, surrounded by love, prayer, song, and shared memories. On February 6, 2025, his former student and the son of Reverend Jesse Jackson,

Sr., the Honorable Jonathan L. Jackson of Illinois in the U.S. House of Representatives, honored his life and legacy during the Extension of Remarks section of Congress, writing him into the Congressional Record.

AFTERWORD

There has always been intellectual capacity in the African American community, going all the way back to George Washington Carver and before. He had brains, skills, and power but no opportunity to develop his numerous inventions into commercially viable businesses. Until the Civil Rights Act of 1964, there were limited opportunities for people of color in the corporate arena. The scope was restricted as to what people of color were permitted to do; we were pushed to the clerical. My devotion to HBCU business school education was to provide an opportunity for kids who might not have gotten their chance. *Dean Quiester Craig, February 2024*

Dr. George Washington Carver's favorite poem, "Equipment," embodies the spirit in which Dean Craig built the culture at A&T's business school that inspired his students.

"Equipment"
By Edgar A. Guest

Figure it out for yourself, my lad,
You've all that the greatest of men have had,
Two arms, two hands, two legs, two eyes,
And a brain to use if you would be wise.
With this equipment they all began,
So start for the top and say: "I can."

Look them over, the wise and great
They take their food from a common plate,
And similar knives and forks they use,

And similar laces they tie their shoes.
The world considers them brave and smart,
But you've all they had when they made their start.

You can triumph and come to skill,
You can be great if you only will.
You're well equipped for what fight you choose,
You have legs and arms and a brain to use,
And the man who has risen great deeds to do
Began his life with no more than you.

You are the handicap you must face,
You are the one who must choose your place,
You must say where you want to go,
How much you will study the truth to know.
God has equipped you for life, but He
Lets you decide what you want to be.

Courage must come from the soul within,
The man must furnish the will to win.
So figure it out for yourself, my lad.
You were born with all that the great have had,
With your equipment they all began,
Get hold of yourself and say: "I can."

ACKNOWLEDGMENTS

I want to express my heartfelt gratitude to everyone who contributed to completing this book. First and foremost, I am incredibly thankful to my family (especially my grandsons, Omar Jr. and Nygee) and friends for their unwavering support and encouragement throughout this journey. Their belief in my vision and their prayers have been a constant source of motivation. Thank you for understanding my absences due to my commitment to this project, which culminated into seven years of research and writing aimed at "filling in the sketch" of Dean Craig's journey, which he generously shared to make this book possible.

I would also like to thank the alumni, faculty, and administrators at North Carolina Agricultural and Technical State University, as well as Dean Craig's colleagues and special friends who contributed to *The Letters of Gratitude to Dr. Q* project, providing a solid foundation for telling this story. Each contributor, listed on page 328 and 329, offered invaluable insights into their experiences with Dean Craig. While only a selection of the letters was used in this story, they all greatly helped inspire and shape this work. A special thanks to Willie A. Deese, for whom the Deese College is now named, for not only sharing his stories for *The Letters of Gratitude to Dr. Q* project but also for his support and assistance in helping me execute it.

I also want to express my sincere gratitude to Dean Craig's colleagues and friends: Mr. Bernie Milano for providing me a book at our first meeting that detailed the evolution of The PhD Project; Milano's wife, Dr. Sharon Gay Pierson, whose pointed me to her published work that addressed Dean Craig's early education, shining light, for the first time, on laboratory schools on HBCU campuses during the Jim Crow Era; and Dr. Theresa Hammond for her book documenting the history of the pioneering African American Certified Public Accountants, which prominently featured Dean Craig. The historical context provided by each source greatly enriched my understanding of Dean Craig's legacy.

Special thanks to Dr. Anthony "Tony" Nelson, an alumnus of the Willie A. Deese College of Business and Economics and the current dean of the business school at North Carolina Central University, for introducing me to Bernie Milano, and for providing valuable perspectives on academic topics in his role as dean. Thanks to my Delta Sigma Theta Sorors and friends Francine Wright, Dianne F. Young, Bonnie Newman Davis, and Phyllis Bivins-Hudson for your referrals that provided resources that helped advance this project. I also thank my Soror, accounting classmate, and friend Cheryl Duncan-Gill for being my local connection to Dean Craig, and offering valuable insights, comments, and encouragement throughout this process.

I sincerely acknowledge the institutions and individuals who graciously provided access to their archives and collections, often assisting with my research. Special thanks to James Stewart, Harvey Long, Edward Love, and Ms. Gloria Pitts at the F.D. Bluford Library at North Carolina Agricultural and Technical State University; Mark Schleer at the Inman E. Page Library at Lincoln University; Avery L. Daniels at the Miller F. Whittaker Library at South Carolina State University; Kris Ford at the Archives at The Atlanta University Center, Robert W. Woodruff Library; and Dr. Joseph Hushcroft, Jr., the former Interim Dean and Dr. Lisa Owens-Jackson, Chairperson of the Department of Accounting and Finance at the Willie A. Deese College of Business and Economics at North Carolina Agricultural and Technical State University. Your support significantly enriched my research.

Sincere thanks to Barry Cohen at AdLab Media Communications, and my editors, Lyric Dodson of Editing by Lyric, Sabrina Butler at Unpolished Words, and my designer, Monique Mensah at Make Your Mark Publishing Solutions. Your support and guidance in helping me bring this book to print are greatly appreciated. I could not have gotten it done without you.

I also want to thank my dear friend and the former chair of A&T's accounting department, Dr. Mark Kiel, whom I met through my sister, his student Cassandra "Zoe" Mitchell, over forty years ago while he was completing a faculty internship at a Big Eight firm in New York City. We became and have remained friends, which, in retrospect, seems destined for this project. Mark, I appreciate your advice, support, encouragement, honesty, feedback, and the time you devoted, as you consistently supported me throughout this journey. Thank you so much for being part of this experience.

Finally, I thank Dean Craig for the kindness he showed me as a business school student, which changed the trajectory of my life. His actions planted a seed of gratitude in my heart that endured for over forty-five years, inspiring me to undertake this project. When I approached him about writing his biography, he admitted that he had not considered documenting his life's work but was proud of his achievements. He then said, "I will provide you with the sketch, and you can fill in the blanks." For seven years, we did just that, and I am forever grateful that he entrusted me with sharing his inspirational story. My only regret is that he did not live to see the finished product. However, I hope his insights within these pages resonate with and inspire all who read them.

Thank you to everyone listed below for your contributions to the *Letters of Gratitude to Dr. Q* project in 2016. Your letters were compiled and presented to Dean Craig under the title *Letters of Gratitude to Dr. Q: An Anthology from the Heart*. Each of your expressions of gratitude truly moved him. A copy of the compilation of letters is archived at the F.D. Bluford Library, North Carolina Agricultural and Technical State University.

Akins Jackson, India
Alexander, John
Andrews, Sylvia L.
Barksdale Starks, Shandi
Black Cohen, Donna
Branch Cooper, Sarah
Burch, Charles "Chuck"
Burton, Kenneth Bowman
Butler Buckner, Kia
Butler, James F.
Byrd, David H.
Byrd, Donald R.
Cain, Angela
Callahan, Dr. Carolyn
Carlton Thompson, Cynthia
Carosella, Christina
Carter, Mike
Chiles-Neal, Dr. Ethel
Clausell, James A.
Clayton, Clarence
Coley, Dr. Basil
Conrad II, Charles J.
Cornelius, Dr. Cathy
Cozart, Ulysses J.
Crawford Edwards, Chiquita
Curtis, Garland
Davis Lassiter, Teresa
Davis Thornton, Jini
Deese, Willie A.
Duncan-Gill, Cheryl
Eccles Register, Beverly
Ellis, Barbara J.
Florentino, Margaret
Franklin, Jacqueline
Frost Hill, Diane
Gaines, Robert G.
Gary-Finney, Dr. Sharon
Gay Pierson, Dr. Sharon
Gillard, Monate Denise
Glover, Dr. Hubert D.
Gray Steed, Cheryl
Gray, Quintin
Green, Virginia L.
Griffin Howard, Christina
Hammond, Dr. Theresa
Harrison Long, Tamara
Henderson, Dr. Ronda B.
Howze, Jr., Robert L.
Hunt, Keith
Jones Collins, Karen
Jones Higgs, Valencia
Jones Johnson, Cathy

Jordan, Yolanda
Keith, Curtis
Keith, Melvin
Keith, Terry
Kiel, Dr. Mark
King, Timothy
Kirkland, Jonathan Crawford
Martin Sr., Chancellor Emeritus Harold
Martin, Mitch
Martin, Vaughn M.
McCants Williams, Ericka
McCorkle Buncum, Pamela
McCoy, Job
McEwen, Dr. Beryl
McKeathen, Evelyn
McMurray Washington, Cynthia
Meeks-Blount, Denise
Milano, Bernard J.
Miles, Dr. Angela K.
Miley Sims, Rene "Bonnie"
Miller Zoller, Patricia
Mitchell, Cassandra Zoe
Mitchell, Tanya Y.
Mitchell Verdine, Francine
Moore, Daniel H.
Moore, Faye M.
Nelson, Dr. Anthony "Tony"
ogilvie, Dr. dt
Oliver, Melissa M.
Owens-Jackson, Dr. Lisa
Pace Kirk, Angie
Perino, Tara
Perry Wooten, Dr. Lynn
Pinnix-Ragland, Hilda
Ponder II, Randall D.
Prather-Kinsey, Jenice
Pridgeon Batey, Melba
Rainey, Antionette
Ray, Devon
Raynor-Jones, Kim
Raynor, Yvonne
Redden, Barbara
Robertson, Carl
Sanders-Harrod, LaDeirdre
Scott James, Donna
Scott Reid, Bonnie
Scott Sea, Denecia
Shelton, Dr. Sandra W.
Smith, Jasper
Spells, Michael
Stockton, Dmitri
Stringfellow, Jacqueline D.
Stroud Cole, Dawn
Suggs, Jannette M.
Thompson Bernard, Akilah C.
Tidwell, Ponce DeLeon
Walker Bingham, Verdina
Walker-Samon, Tamika
Welch, Cecily VM
West, Jimmie
White, Wendi
Williams Smith, Dr. Kecia
Williams, Percy "Pete"
Williams, Terry
Willams Turner, Dr. Cynthia
Williamson, Joel
Wilson, Joseph
Worrell Glover, Terry

PERMISSIONS ACKNOWLEDGMENTS

Dean Quiester Craig Collection, Folder 1, University Archives and Special Collections, F.D. Bluford Library, North Carolina Agricultural and Technical State University, Greensboro, North Carolina.

Office of the Chancellor, Lewis Carnegie Dowdy Collection, University Archives and Special Collections, F.D. Bluford Library, North Carolina Agricultural and Technical State University, Greensboro, North Carolina.

The University Archives at the Inman E. Page Library, Lincoln University, Jefferson City, Missouri.

SC State Historical Collection & Archives, Miller F. Whittaker Library, South Carolina State University, Orangeburg, South Carolina.

Morehouse College Torch, 1957, Morehouse College Printed and Published, Atlanta University Center Robert W. Woodruff Library.

The Archives at the Willie A. Deese College of Business and Economics, North Carolina Agricultural and Technical State University, Greensboro, North Carolina.

A White-Collar Profession: African American Certified Public Accountants Since 1921 by Theresa A. Hammond. Copyright © 2002 by the University of North Carolina Press.

END NOTES

Chapter 1

1 North Carolina A&T State University, "The House That Dean Craig Built," *The Alumni Times*, April 2023, https://relations.ncat.edu/pubs/alumnitimes/2013/mar14/dean-craig.html.

2 Dr. Harold Martin, *Personal letter of gratitude to Dr. Q*, October 2016.

3 Martin, *Personal letter*.

4 Kimberly Fields, "Aggies Celebrate Dean Craig's Legacy," *The A&T Register*, April 24, 2013, https://ncatregister.com/3213/uncategorized/aggies-celebrate-dean-craigs-legacy/.

5 Fields, "Aggies Celebrate Dean Craig's Legacy."

6 Fields, "Aggies Celebrate Dean Craig's Legacy."

7 Fields, "Aggies Celebrate Dean Craig's Legacy."

8 Fields, "Aggies Celebrate Dean Craig's Legacy."

9 Fields, "Aggies Celebrate Dean Craig's Legacy."

Chapter 2

1 Sharon Gay Pierson, *Laboratory of Learning: HBCU Laboratory Schools and Alabama State College Lab High in the Era of Jim Crow* (Peter Lang Publishing, Inc., 2014), 208.

2 John Newsome, "The Business School Is Dean Craig," *Greensboro News & Record*, June 23, 2013, https://greensboro.com/news/local/the-business-school-is-dean-craig/article_8dbbd0de-dacf-11e2-9136-0019bb30f31a.html.

3 Jack Scism, "Priorities: Quiester Craig Has Kept His In Order," *Greensboro News & Record*, May 19, 1986

4 Newsome, "The Business School Is Dean Craig."

5 Maia Cucchiara, "New Goals, Familiar Challenges?: A Brief History of University-Run Schools," *Perspectives on Urban Education* 7, no. 1 (Summer 2010): 96, https://eric.ed.gov/?id=EJ894472.

6 Paul Erickson, Neal Gray, Bill Wesley, Elizabeth Dunagan, "Why Parents Choose Laboratory Schools for Their Children," *NALS Journal* 2, no. 2 (2012): 1–8.

7 Erickson et al. "Why Parents Choose Laboratory Schools for Their Children."

8 Cucchiara, "New Goals, Familiar Challenges?" 96.

9 Pierson, *Laboratory of Learning*, 184–185.

10 Pierson, *Laboratory of Learning*, 185.

11 Cucchiara, "New Goals, Familiar Challenges," 96–99.

12 "University Archives," University of Missouri, December 2014, https://muarchives.missouri.edu/c-rg8-s8.html.

13 Pierson, *Laboratory of Learning*, 39–40, 75, 223.

14 Pierson, *Laboratory of Learning*, 100–102, 106, 110.

15 Pierson, *Laboratory of Learning*, 111–14, 126, 128.

16 Pierson, *Laboratory of Learning*, 9, 134, 140–41.

17 Pierson, *Laboratory of Learning*, 95.

18 Pierson, *Laboratory of Learning*, 209.

19 Pierson, *Laboratory of Learning*, 194–95.

20 Pierson, *Laboratory of Learning*, 195–96.

21 Pierson, *Laboratory of Learning*, 196.

22 Pierson, *Laboratory of Learning*, 196.

23 Pierson, *Laboratory of Learning*, 199.

24 Pierson, *Laboratory of Learning*, 201.

25 Pierson, *Laboratory of Learning*, 196, 201–203, 215.

26 Pierson, *Laboratory of Learning*, 189–90.

27 Pierson, *Laboratory of Learning*, 180.

28 Pierson, *Laboratory of Learning*, 183.

29 Pierson, *Laboratory of Learning*, 183.

30 Jessica Pettus Rankin, "School to End Session Friday," personal scrapbook newspaper clipping, June 1948.

31 Pierson, *Laboratory of Learning*, 200.

32 Pierson, *Laboratory of Learning*, 200.

33 "The 1920s Education: Topics In The News," Progress Through Curriculum Changes, https://www.encyclopedia.com/social-sciences/culture-magazines/1920s-education-topics-news.

34 Pierson, *Laboratory of Learning*, 49–51.

35 Pierson, *Laboratory of Learning*, 180.

36 Pierson, *Laboratory of Learning*, 177–78.

37 Dr. Harold Martin, *Personal letter of gratitude to Dr. Q*, October 2016.

38 Pierson, *Laboratory of Learning*, 213.

39 Pierson, *Laboratory of Learning*, 203.

40 The Fund for Advancement of Education, *They Went to College Early* (April 1957).

41 Pierson, *Laboratory of Learning*, 96.
42 Pierson, *Laboratory of Learning*, 151.
43 Pierson, *Laboratory of Learning*, 153.
44 Pierson, *Laboratory of Learning*, 158.
45 Pierson, *Laboratory of Learning*, 157–58.
46 Pierson, *Laboratory of Learning*, 160.
47 Newsome, "The Business School Is Dean Craig."

Chapter 3

1 "Graves Hall," City of Atlanta, GA, accessed June 26, 2025, https://www.atlantaga.gov/government/departments/city-planning/historic-preservation/property-district-information/graves-hall.
2 W.E.B. Du Bois, "The Cultural Missions of Atlanta University," *Phylon (1940-1956)* 3, No. 2 (2nd Qtr., 1942): 106.
3 "Our Stories: Sophia B. Packard and Harriet E. Giles, Founders," Spelman College, accessed April 2020, https://www.spelman.edu/about-us/news-and-events/our-stories/stories/2020/04/11/sophia-packard-and-harriet-giles.
4 "Morehouse 5 to Play S.C. State," *Alabama Tribune*, December 9, 1955, 7.
5 "Morehouse, Fisk Tangle Tonight," *The Atlanta Journal*, January 4, 1957, 15.
6 "Davis v. Prince Edward County," BvB, accessed April 2025, https://brown65.the74million.org/davisvprince.
7 "Biography: Barbara Rose Johns Powell, 1935–1991," Robert Russa Moton Museum, accessed April, 2025, https://motonmuseum.org/learn/biography-barbara-rose-johns-powell/.
8 Freddie C. Colston, *Dr. Benjamin E. Mays Speaks: Representative Speeches of a Great American Orator* (University Press of America, Inc., 2002), 16.
9 Clayborne Carson, "Martin Luther King Jr.: The Morehouse Years," *The Journal of Blacks in Higher Education*, no. 15 (1977): 121.
10 Leonard Ray Teel, "Benjamin Mays: Teaching by Example, Leading through Will," *Change* 14, no. 7 (1982): 15.
11 Teel, "Benjamin Mays," 15–16.
12 Colston, *Dr. Benjamin E. Mays Speaks*, 12–13.
13 "A History of Morehouse School of Religion," Morehouse School of Religion, accessed June 26, 2025, https://www.themorehouseschoolofreligion.org/history/.
14 Carson, "Martin Luther King Jr.," 121.
15 Colston, *Dr. Benjamin E. Mays Speaks*, 16.
16 Teel, "Benjamin Mays," 15–16.
17 Colston, *Dr. Benjamin E. Mays Speaks*, 14.
18 Colston, *Dr. Benjamin E. Mays Speaks*, 15.

[19] Teel, "Benjamin Mays," 15.
[20] Teel, "Benjamin Mays," 22.
[21] Teel, "Benjamin Mays," 22.
[22] Teel, "Benjamin Mays," 19.
[23] Theresa A. Hammond, *A White-Collar Profession: African American Certified Public Accountants Since 1921* (The University of North Carolina Press, 2022), 24.
[24] Hammond, *A White-Collar Profession*, 24.
[25] Edward Jones, "Morehouse College in Business Ninety Years—Building Men," *Phylon Quarterly* 18, no. 3 (3rd Qtr., 1957): 237–38.
[26] Stephanie Capparell, "How Pepsi Opened Door to Diversity," *The Wall Street Journal*, January 9, 2007, https://www.wsj.com/articles/SB116831396726171042.
[27] "Harlem's Ron Brown and Sylvia Fitt The New Pepsi Cola 1950," *Harlem World*, May 3, 2015.
[28] Capparell, "How Pepsi Opened Door to Diversity."
[29] Capparell, "How Pepsi Opened Door to Diversity."
[30] Capparell, "How Pepsi Opened Door to Diversity."
[31] Knowledge at Wharton Staff, "How Corporate America Came to Recognize Diversity, One Pepsi at a Time," Knowledge at Wharton, February 28, 2007, https://knowledge.wharton.upenn.edu/article/how-corporate-america-came-to-recognize-diversity-one-pepsi-at-a-time/.

Chapter 4

[1] Theresa A. Hammond, *A White-Collar Profession: African American Certified Public Accountants Since 1921* (The University of North Carolina Press, 2022), 111.
[2] United States Commission on Civil Rights, "Equal Protection of the Laws in Public Higher Education," 1960.
[3] Dawn Byron Hutchins, "Laboring in the Shade," *Connecticut Explored*, February 9, 2021, https://connecticuthistory.org/laboring-in-the-shade/.
[4] Leroy Davis, "John Hope at Brown University: The Black Man Who Refused to Pass for White," *The Journal of Blacks in Higher Education,* (1998–1999): 122.
[5] Hutchins, "Laboring in the Shade."
[6] Clayborne Carson, "Martin Luther King Jr.: The Morehouse Years," *The Journal of Blacks in Higher Education*, no. 15 (1977): 125.
[7] Joseph A. Pierce, *Negro Business and Business Education: Their Present and Prospective Development* (HarperCollins Publishers, 1947), 275.
[8] Pierce, *Negro Business and Business Education*, 277.
[9] Clark Atlanta University, "The First Phylon Institute and Twenty-Fifth Atlanta University Conference," *Phylon* 2, no. 3 (3rd Qtr., 1941): 275–88.

[10] Lauren A. Wendling, "Higher Education as a Means of Communal Uplift: The Educational Philosophy of W.E.B. Du Bois," *The Journal of Negro Education* 87, no. 3 (2018): 285, 292.

[11] Alex Benson Henderson, "Heman E. Perry and Black Enterprise in Atlanta, 1908–1925," *The President and Fellows of Harvard College* 61, no. 2 (summer, 1987): 217.

[12] Henderson, "Heman E. Perry and Black Enterprise in Atlanta, 1908–1925," 219.

[13] Henderson, "Heman E. Perry and Black Enterprise in Atlanta, 1908–1925," 225.

[14] Henderson, "Heman E. Perry and Black Enterprise in Atlanta, 1908–1925," 217.

[15] Henderson, "Heman E. Perry and Black Enterprise in Atlanta, 1908–1925," 224.

[16] Henderson, "Heman E. Perry and Black Enterprise in Atlanta, 1908–1925," 229.

[17] Henderson, "Heman E. Perry and Black Enterprise in Atlanta, 1908–1925," 229–30.

[18] Henderson, "Heman E. Perry and Black Enterprise in Atlanta, 1908–1925," 231–2.

[19] Henderson, "Heman E. Perry and Black Enterprise in Atlanta, 1908–1925," 237.

[20] Henderson, "Heman E. Perry and Black Enterprise in Atlanta, 1908–1925," 237.

[21] Henderson, "Heman E. Perry and Black Enterprise in Atlanta, 1908–1925," 237.

[22] Henderson, "Heman E. Perry and Black Enterprise in Atlanta, 1908–1925," 237.

[23] Henderson, "Heman E. Perry and Black Enterprise in Atlanta, 1908–1925," 233.

[24] Robert J. Alexander, "Negro Business in Atlanta," *Southern Economic Journal* 17, no. 4 (1951): 456–57.

[25] Alexander, "Negro Business in Atlanta," 457–58.

[26] Alexander, "Negro Business in Atlanta," 462.

[27] Hammond, *A White-Collar Profession*, 26.

[28] Atlanta University, *The Atlanta University Bulletin* (The Catalogue) 3, no. 102 (1957–1958): 221–22.

[29] Atlanta University, *The Atlanta University Bulletin* (The Catalogue) 3, no. 102 (1957–1958): 223–25.

[30] Association for the Study of African American Life and History, "Editor's: Former Students," *Negro History Bulletin* 26, no. 7 (1963): 207.

[31] Atlanta University, *The Atlanta University Bulletin* (The Catalogue) 3, no. 102 (1957–1958): 145.

[32] Atlanta University, *The Atlanta University Bulletin* (The Catalogue) 3, no. 102 (1957–1958): 52–54.

[33] Atlanta University, *The Atlanta University Bulletin* (The Catalogue) 3, no. 102 (1957–1958): 146.

[34] Atlanta University, *The Atlanta University Bulletin* (The Catalogue) 3, no. 102 (1957–1958): 149.

Chapter 5

1 State University System of Florida, "Statistics of land-grant colleges and universities 1958/1959," HathiTrust, accessed August 2024, https://babel.hathitrust.org/cgi/pt?id=ufl.31262088525224&seq=57&q1=%22South+Carolina+State+College%22.

2 William C. Hine, "South Carolina State College: A Legacy of Education and Public Service," *The 1890 Land-Grant Colleges: A Centennial View* 65, no. 2 (Spring 1991): 196.

3 Hine, "South Carolina State College," 224.

4 Hine, "South Carolina State College," 197.

5 Hine, "South Carolina State College," 221.

6 "Acts against the education of slaves South Carolina, 1740 and Virginia, 1819," Thirteen PBS, accessed May 2024, https://www.thirteen.org/wnet/slavery/experience/education/docs1.html.

7 Hine, "South Carolina State College," 224.

8 Hine, "South Carolina State College," 217.

9 Hine, "South Carolina State College," 212–14.

10 Hine, "South Carolina State College," 213.

11 Hine, "South Carolina State College," Preface XV.

12 Hine, "South Carolina State College," Preface XV.

13 "David (Deacon) Jones," Pro Football Hall of Fame, accessed July 2023, https://www.profootballhof.com/players/david-deacon-jones/.

Chapter 6

1 Susan T. Hill, "The Traditionally Black Institutions of Higher Education 1860 to 1982," National Center for Education Statistics, 1982, 113.

2 Hill, "The Traditionally Black Institutions of Higher Education 1860 to 1982," 113.

3 Albert P. Marshall, *Soldiers' dream a centennial history of Lincoln University of Missouri* (Lincoln University, 1966), 1–3, https://bluetigercommons.lincolnu.edu/lu_history_book/2/.

4 "Five Communities Change a Nation," Separate Is Not Equal: Brown v. Board of Education, Smithsonian Museum of American History Behring Center, accessed January 2024, https://americanhistory.si.edu/brown/history/4-five/five-communities.html.

5 Carole A. Williams, *The Black/White Colleges: Dismantling the Dual System of Higher Education* (U.S. Commission On Civil Rights, 1988), 13.

6 "Missouri State Archives: Timeline of Missouri's African American History," Missouri Digital Heritage, accessed January 2024, https://www.sos.mo.gov/mdh/curriculum/africanamerican/timeline/timeline6#:~:text=MISSOURI%20

STATE%20ARCHIVES,of%20Missouri%27s%20African%20American%20History&text=Judge%20Sam%20Blair%20of%20the,students%20on%20June%2027%2C%201950.

7 Marshall, *Soldiers' dream a centennial history of Lincoln University of Missouri*, 29.

8 Cynthia J. Chapel, "Shifting history, shifting mission, shifting identity: The search for survival at Lincoln University (Jefferson City, Missouri) 1866-1997" (diss., Oklahoma State University, 1997), 360.

9 Arlene Levinson, "Historically Black, Now Mostly White At Lincoln University, Social Life Is Segregated Even If Classes Are Not," *Associated Press*, December 16, 1999, https://www.washingtonpost.com/wp-srv/WPcap/1999-12/16/002r-121699-idx.html.

10 Levinson, "Historically Black, Now Mostly White."

11 Levinson, "Historically Black, Now Mostly White."

12 Chapel, "Shifting history, shifting mission, shifting identity," 353.

13 Chapel, "Shifting history, shifting mission, shifting identity," 359–60.

14 Levinson, "Historically Black, Now Mostly White."

15 Marshall, *Soldiers' dream a centennial history of Lincoln University of Missouri*, 30.

16 Chapel, "Shifting history, shifting mission, shifting identity," 353.

17 Marshall, *Soldiers' dream a centennial history of Lincoln University of Missouri*, 30.

18 Sara Weissman, "An HBCU in Predominantly White Surroundings," *Muddy River News*, June 17, 2022, https://muddyrivernews.com/politics/an-hbcu-in-predominantly-white-surroundings/20220617091838/.

19 Marshall, *Soldiers' dream a centennial history of Lincoln University of Missouri*, 30.

20 Harry Kendall Dowdy, Jr., *Crimson Waterfall* (Dog Ear Publishing, 2016), 86.

21 "Economic Department Offers Corporation Course," *The Lincoln Clarion*, January 8, 1965, 1.

22 "Economic Department Offers Corporation Course," *The Lincoln Clarion*, January 8, 1965, 1.

23 "Business Depart. Offers New Majors," *The Lincoln Clarion*, January 16, 1960.

24 "Business Depart. Offers New Majors," *The Lincoln Clarion*, January 16, 1960.

25 "New Accounting Course," *The Lincoln Clarion*, January 11, 1963.

26 Lincoln University, "Department of Economics and Business," *Lincoln University Bulletin 1967–1968*, Fall 1967.

27 Chapel, "Shifting history, shifting mission, shifting identity," 353.

28 Chapel, "Shifting history, shifting mission, shifting identity," 360.

29 Chapel, "Shifting history, shifting mission, shifting identity," 354.

30 Chapel, "Shifting history, shifting mission, shifting identity," 354–55.

31 Chapel, "Shifting history, shifting mission, shifting identity," 354.

32 "Recruiter Schedule," *The Lincoln Clarion*, November 10, 1967.

[33] "Business Students Dominate Campus," *Jefferson City Post Tribune*, November 25, 1970.
[34] "Business Administration Largest Dept. At Lincoln U.," *Jet Magazine*, December 24, 1970, 19.
[35] "Business Administration Largest Dept. At Lincoln U.," 19.
[36] "Business Students Dominate Campus," *Jefferson City Post Tribune*, November 25, 1970.
[37] James D. Edwards, "Public Accounting in the United States, 1928–1951," *The Accounting Review*, 1956: 444–471.

Chapter 7

[1] Haskins & Sells, "Haskins & Sells, certified public accountants, A History of the origin and growth of the firm, 1895-1935," *Haskins and Sells Publications Deloitte Collection*, January 1, 1935, 3–4.
[2] James D. Edwards, "Public Accounting in the United States, 1896–1913," *The Accounting Review*, April 1955, 241–42.
[3] Haskins & Sells, "Haskins & Sells, certified public accountants," 3–4.
[4] Edwards, "Public Accounting in the United States, 1896–1913," 241–42.
[5] Theresa A. Hammond, *A White-Collar Profession: African American Certified Public Accountants Since 1921* (The University of North Carolina Press, 2022), 3.
[6] Stephen A. Zeff, "How the U.S. Accounting Profession Got Where It Is Today: Part I," *Accounting Horizons* 17, no. 3 (2003): 190.
[7] Charles W. Wootton and Carel M. Wolk, "Development of the big eight accounting firms in the United States, 1900-1990," *The Accounting Historians Journal* 19, no. 1 (1992): 1–2, https://egrove.olemiss.edu/aah_journal/vol19/iss1/1.
[8] Wootton and Wolk, "Development of the big eight accounting firms," 4.
[9] Wootton and Wolk, "Development of the big eight accounting firms," 6.
[10] Wootton and Wolk, "Development of the big eight accounting firms," 10.
[11] Wootton and Wolk, "Development of the big eight accounting firms," 10.
[12] Wootton and Wolk, "Development of the big eight accounting firms," 10.
[13] Hammond, *A White-Collar Profession*, 2.
[14] Hammond, *A White-Collar Profession*, 47–49.
[15] Hammond, *A White-Collar Profession*, 17–18, 21, 23, 30.
[16] Hammond, *A White-Collar Profession*, 8, 23.
[17] Hammond, *A White-Collar Profession*,147–49.
[18] Hammond, *A White-Collar Profession*, 5.
[19] Hammond, *A White-Collar Profession*, 31.
[20] Hammond, *A White-Collar Profession*, 147–49.

[21] Charlene Rhinehart, "Meet 'General Lucas': The First Black Person to Become a Certified Public Accountant in New York," *Black Enterprise*, February 21, 2021, https://www.blackenterprise.com/meet-general-lucas-the-first-black-person-to-become-a-certified-public-accountant-in-new-york/.

[22] Hammond, *A White-Collar Profession*, 103.

[23] Hammond, *A White-Collar Profession*, 5.

[24] Edwards, "Public Accounting in the United States, 1928–1951," 460.

[25] Hammond, *A White-Collar Profession*, 31.

[26] Hammond, *A White-Collar Profession*, 24.

[27] Hammond, *A White-Collar Profession*, 2.

[28] Hammond, *A White-Collar Profession*, 6.

[29] Hammond, *A White-Collar Profession*, 67–68.

[30] Hammond, *A White-Collar Profession*, 67–68.

[31] "The Civil Rights Act of 1964: A Long Struggle for Freedom," The Library of Congress, accessed September 2020, https://www.loc.gov/exhibits/civil-rights-act/civil-rights-act-of-1964.html.

[32] Hammond, *A White-Collar Profession*, 76.

[33] Hammond, *A White-Collar Profession*, 76–77.

[34] Hammond, *A White-Collar Profession*, 77–78.

[35] Hammond, *A White-Collar Profession*, 78.

[36] Hammond, *A White-Collar Profession*, 78.

[37] Hammond, *A White-Collar Profession*, 82–83.

[38] Hammond, *A White-Collar Profession*, 79–81.

[39] Hammond, *A White-Collar Profession*, 105.

[40] Hammond, *A White-Collar Profession*, 7.

[41] Hammond, *A White-Collar Profession*, 104.

[42] Hammond, *A White-Collar Profession*, 15.

[43] Hammond, *A White-Collar Profession*, 113.

[44] Hammond, *A White-Collar Profession*, 5–7.

Chapter 8

[1] Rachel Wimpee, "The Birth of the Modern MBA," *Rockefeller Archive Center*, November 1, 2019, https://resource.rockarch.org/story/the-birth-of-the-modern-mba/.

[2] Dereck Barr-Pulliam, "An Assessment of Dr. William L. Campfield's Contributions to Diversifying Accounting Education and Practice," (February 24, 2012): 10, https://papers.ssrn.com/sol3/papers.cfm?abstract_id=1908752.

[3] Dereck Barr-Pulliam, "An Assessment of Dr. William L. Campfield's Contributions," 6–7.

[4] Dale L. Flesher, Helen G. Gabre, "NABA: Forty Years of Growth," *Journal of Accountancy*, December 1, 2009, https://www.journalofaccountancy.com/issues/2009/dec/20092033.html.

[5] "William Louis Campfield," American Accounting Association, accessed June 2014, https://aaahq.org/Accounting-Hall-of-Fame/Members/2019/William-Louis-Campfield.

Chapter 9

[1] Annette Singleton Jackson and Leedell W. Neyland, *The Florida A&M University School of Business and Industry, SBI: The Sybil Collins Mobley Years, A Historical Perspective* (The Florida A&M University Foundation, 2013), 7–8.

[2] Jackson and Neyland, *The Florida A&M University School of Business and Industry*, 7–8.

[3] Jackson and Neyland, *The Florida A&M University School of Business and Industry*, 8.

[4] Jackson and Neyland, *The Florida A&M University School of Business and Industry*, 9.

[5] Jackson and Neyland, *The Florida A&M University School of Business and Industry*, 10–11.

[6] Jackson and Neyland, *The Florida A&M University School of Business and Industry*, 9–10.

[7] Jackson and Neyland, *The Florida A&M University School of Business and Industry*, 9.

[8] Jackson and Neyland, *The Florida A&M University School of Business and Industry*, 12–15.

[9] Jackson and Neyland, *The Florida A&M University School of Business and Industry*, 14.

[10] Jackson and Neyland, *The Florida A&M University School of Business and Industry*, 13–14.

[11] Jackson and Neyland, *The Florida A&M University School of Business and Industry*, 26–27.

[12] Jackson and Neyland, *The Florida A&M University School of Business and Industry*, 26.

[13] Jackson and Neyland, *The Florida A&M University School of Business and Industry*, 27.

[14] Jackson and Neyland, *The Florida A&M University School of Business and Industry*, 14.

[15] "Kenneth Wilbur Perry Obituary," *The Anderson News*, September 12, 2012, https://www.news-gazette.com/obituaries/kenneth-perry/article_88c9680a-3a58-54b9-b452-fbe82bf009d0.html.

[16] "Kenneth Wilbur Perry Obituary," *The Anderson News*.

[17] Robert F. Smith, "Celebrating the 100th Anniversary of the First African American CPA: John W. Cromwell Jr.," Personal Blog, January 20, 2021, accessed March 2021, https://robertsmith.com/blog/celebrating-the-100th-anniversary-of-the-first-african-american-cpa-john-w-cromwell-jr/.
[18] Jackson and Neyland, *The Florida A&M University School of Business and Industry*, 11–12.
[19] Jackson and Neyland, *The Florida A&M University School of Business and Industry*, 15–16.
[20] Jackson and Neyland, *The Florida A&M University School of Business and Industry*, 16.
[21] Jackson and Neyland, *The Florida A&M University School of Business and Industry*, 24.
[22] Jackson and Neyland, *The Florida A&M University School of Business and Industry*, 24–25.
[23] Jackson and Neyland, *The Florida A&M University School of Business and Industry*, 25–26.
[24] Jackson and Neyland, *The Florida A&M University School of Business and Industry*, 20.

Chapter 10

[1] Dale L. Flesher, "*The History of AACSB International,*" AACSB International, (2007), 9.
[2] "In Memory of Dr. Milton Wilson," Government Congressional Record Online, October 2, 2003, H9190–H9191, https://www.congress.gov/crec/2003/10/02/CREC-2003-10-02-pt1-PgH9190-4.pdf
[3] Theresa A. Hammond, *A White-Collar Profession: African American Certified Public Accountants Since 1921* (The University of North Carolina Press, 2022), 100.
[4] Hammond, *A White-Collar Profession*, 100–01.
[5] Hammond, *A White-Collar Profession*, 101.
[6] Hammond, *A White-Collar Profession*, 100–01.
[7] Hammond, *A White-Collar Profession*, 176.
[8] "Texas Southern University," Jesse H. Jones School of Business, accessed April 2021, https://digitalscholarship.tsu.edu/jhjco/.
[9] "The Ford Foundation Annual Report 1965," The Ford Foundation, 1965, 29.
[10] John S. Lash, Hortense W. Dixon, and Thomas F. Freeman, *Texas Southern University: From Separation to Special Designation* (John Hay Whitney Foundation, 1975), 100.
[11] "The Ford Foundation Annual Report 1965," The Ford Foundation, 1965, 29.
[12] Staff writers, "Bus. School Established," *The Hilltop*, October 2, 1970.

[13] Kelley School, "Creating a legacy with The Consortium for Graduate Study in Management," Indiana University Kelley School of Business, accessed February 28, 2020, https://blog.kelley.iu.edu/2020/02/28/creating-a-legacy-with-the-consortium-for-graduate-study-in-management/.

[14] Kelley School, "Creating a legacy with The Consortium for Graduate Study in Management."

[15] Kelley School, "Creating a legacy with The Consortium for Graduate Study in Management."

[16] Kelley School, "Creating a legacy with The Consortium for Graduate Study in Management."

[17] "Who We Are," The Consortium, https://cgsm.org/who-we-are/.

[18] "Ruth Coles Harris," Changemakers, accessed February 2024, https://edu.lva.virginia.gov/changemakers/items/show/170.

[19] Hammond, *A White-Collar Profession*, 176.

[20] "William Louis Campfield," American Accounting Association, https://aaahq.org/Accounting-Hall-of-Fame/Members/2019/William-Louis-Campfield.

[21] Hammond, *A White-Collar Profession*, 108.

[22] Hammond, *A White-Collar Profession*, 105.

[23] Linda Segall, "Larzette Hale, CPA," *Journal of Accountancy*, August 1, 2009, https://www.journalofaccountancy.com/issues/2009/aug/20091763.html.

[24] Hammond, *A White-Collar Profession*, 109.

Chapter 11

[1] Jim Schlosser, "Late A&T chancellor praised for diplomacy," *Greensboro News and Record*, December 19, 2000.

[2] Jim Schlosser, "Late A&T chancellor praised for diplomacy."

[3] "Lewis C. Dowdy," North Carolina Agricultural & Technical University, accessed June 2021, https://www.ncat.edu/academics/honors/dowdy-scholars-program/dowdy-bio.php.

[4] Jim Schlosser, "Late A&T chancellor praised for diplomacy."

[5] Dr. Alvin Blount, Jr., interview, *The HistoryMakers*, May 5, 2013, https://www.thehistorymakers.org/biography/dr-alvin-blount-jr.

[6] David B. Smith, "Forgotten Heroes: Remembering Dr. Alvin Blount, Who Helped Integrate America's Hospitals," *Health Affairs Forefront*, September 1, 2017, https://www.healthaffairs.org/content/forefront/forgotten-heroes-remembering-dr-alvin-blount-helped-integrate-america-s-hospitals.

[7] J.R. Gamble, "Iconic North Carolina A&T Aggies Coach Cal Irvin Passes Away," *The Shadow League*, November 26, 2017, https://theshadowleague.com/iconic-north-carolina-a-t-coach-cal-irvin-passes-away/.

[8] Dr. Lewis C. Dowdy, *An Epoch of Excellence 1964-1979: The Chancellor's Report, N.C. A&T State University* (North Carolina Agricultural & Technical State University, 1979), 2.
[9] Dowdy, *An Epoch of Excellence 1964-1979*, 2.
[10] Dowdy, *An Epoch of Excellence 1964-1979*, 2.
[11] Dr. Lewis C. Dowdy, *New Opportunities for Service* (North Carolina A&T State University, 1973).
[12] *Self-Study, Division of Business Administration* (North Carolina Agricultural and Technical State University, 1969), i–iii.
[13] *Self-Study* 1969, 6.
[14] *Self-Study* 1969, 26–27.
[15] *Self-Study*, 1969, 8.
[16] *Statistical Abstract of Higher Education in North Carolina, 1968-69*, (North Carolina Board of Higher Education, Raleigh, 1968), 369.
[17] Barbara Solow, *Reorganizing Higher Education in North Carolina: What History Tells Us About Our Future* (The North Carolina Center for Public Policy Research, 1999), 11.
[18] Solow, *Reorganizing Higher Education in North Carolina*, 48.
[19] David W. Bishop, "The Consent Decree Between the University of North Carolina System and the U.S. Department of Education, 1981-1982," *The Journal of Negro Education* 52, no. 3 (1983): 354–55.
[20] Bishop, "The Consent Decree," 354–55.
[21] Laurence Marcus, "The Adams Case: A Hollow Victory?," *Peabody Journal of Education* 59, no. 1 (1981): 37.
[22] Marcus, "The Adams Case: A Hollow Victory?," 37.
[23] Bishop, "The Consent Decree," 354–55.
[24] Solow, *Reorganizing Higher Education in North Carolina*, 28.
[25] Bishop, "The Consent Decree," 350.
[26] Schlosser, "Late A&T chancellor praised for diplomacy."

Chapter 12

[1] Tanya Mitchell, Author Analysis of NC A&T State University Annual School Bulletins from 1890 to 1926.
[2] Tanya Mitchell, Author Analysis of NC A&T State University Annual School Bulletins from 1890 to 1926.
[3] Tanya Mitchell, Author Analysis of NC A&T State University Annual School Bulletins from 1890 to 1926.
[4] Steven A. Sass, "Getting Down to Business: The Development of the Commercial Curriculum at the Wharton School in 1910," *Business and Economic History* 10,

Papers presented at the twenty-seventh annual meeting of the Business History Conference (1981): 71.

5 Rakesh Khurana, *From Higher Aims to Hired Hands: The Social Transformation of American Business Schools and the Unfilled Promise of Management as a Profession* (Princeton University Press, 2007), 137.

6 Joseph A. Pierce, *Negro Business and Business Education: Their Present and Prospective Development* (HarperCollins Publishers, 1947), ix.

7 V.V. Oak, "Our Aimless Business Education," *The Crisis* 44, (September 1937): 264.

8 Pierce, *Negro Business and Business Education*, ix.

9 Pierce, *Negro Business and Business Education*, ix.

10 Juliet E. K. Walker, "Racism, Slavery, and Free Enterprise: Black Entrepreneurship in the United States before the Civil War," *The Business History Review* 60, no. 3 (1986): 370–71.

11 North Carolina Agricultural and Technical State University, "Business School Shows Gains," NCAT Student Newspapers. 97., *The Register*, August 4, 1945, 5.

12 North Carolina Agricultural and Technical State University, "College Business Club Visits Atlanta's Negro Business Enterprises," NCAT Student Newspapers. 98., *The Register*, May 1947, 1.

13 North Carolina Agricultural and Technical State University, "Kennedy Speaks At Vocational Opportunity Week," NCAT Student Newspapers. 126., *The Register*, April 1953, 3.

14 Charlie Knight, "Harvey R. Alexander, Tuskegee Airman," North Carolina Museum of History, accessed February 2022, https://www.ncmuseumofhistory.org/blog/tuskegee-airman-harvey-alexander.

15 Tanya Mitchell, Author Analysis of NC A&T State University Annual School Bulletins from 1890 to 1926.

16 Knight, "Harvey R. Alexander, Tuskegee Airman."

17 Knight, "Harvey R. Alexander, Tuskegee Airman."

18 The 55th Annual Commencement of the Agricultural and Technical College (North Carolina Agricultural and Technical College, 1953), 6, https://digital.library.ncat.edu/atcommencement/1

19 Tanya Mitchell, Author Analysis of NC A&T State University Annual School Bulletins from 1890 to 1926.

20 *The Bulletin* (The Agricultural and Technical College of North Carolina), 1953-54), 14.

21 North Carolina Agricultural and Technical State University, "Pi Omega Pi Installed at A. and T.," NCAT Student Newspapers. 134., *The Register*, April 1954, 3.

22 North Carolina Agricultural and Technical State University, "Alexander, Gray Named To Top Post By Board," NCAT Student Newspapers. 175., *The Register*, February 10, 1961, 4.

[23] Tanya Mitchell, Author Analysis of NC A&T State University Annual School Bulletins from 1890 to 1926.
[24] Tanya Mitchell, Author Analysis of NC A&T State University Annual School Bulletins from 1890 to 1926.
[25] Tanya Mitchell, Author Analysis of NC A&T State University Annual School Bulletins from 1890 to 1926.
[26] Tanya Mitchell, Author Analysis of NC A&T State University Annual School Bulletins from 1890 to 1926.
[27] Tanya Mitchell, Author Analysis of NC A&T State University Annual School Bulletins from 1890 to 1926.
[28] North Carolina Agricultural and Technical State University, "Business Society Instituted on Campus," NCAT Student Newspapers. 238., *The Register*, September 25, 1964.
[29] North Carolina Agricultural and Technical State University, "Business Students Make Corp. Management Div," NCAT Student Newspapers. 381., *The Register*, March 6, 1970.
[30] North Carolina Agricultural and Technical State University, "Thirteen Business Majors Begin Local Internships," NCAT Student Newspapers. 184., *The Register*, November 17, 1961, 2.
[31] Jim Schlosser, "Late A&T chancellor praised for diplomacy," *Greensboro News and Record*, December 19, 2000, A10.
[32] Jannette Suggs, "Interview with Jannette Suggs," interview by Tanya Mitchell September 9, 2022.
[33] Akilah Thompson, *Personal letter of gratitude to Dr. Q*, October 2015.
[34] *Self-Study, Division of Business Administration* (North Carolina Agricultural and Technical State University, 1969), 17–18.
[35] *Self-Study*, 1969, 17–18.
[36] "Thirteen Business Majors Begin Local Internships," NCAT Student Newspapers. 235., 2.

Chapter 13

[1] *The Bulletin* (North Carolina A&T State University, 1971–1972), 211.
[2] *Self-Study, Division of Business Administration* (North Carolina Agricultural and Technical State University, 1969), 7.
[3] Tanya Mitchell, Author Analysis of NC A&T State University Annual School Bulletins from 1890 to 1926.
[4] Kenan Heise, "Albert Smart, Author, NIU Business Prof," *Chicago Tribune*, December 16, 1989, https://www.chicagotribune.com/news/ct-xpm-1989-12-16-8903180557-story.html.
[5] *The Bulletin* (North Carolina A&T State University, 1971–1972).

[6] *The Bulletin* (North Carolina A&T State University, 1971–1972).

[7] Cynthia McMurray Washington, *Personal letter of gratitude to Dr. Q*, October 2016.

[8] *The Bulletin* (North Carolina A&T State University, 1976), 369.

[9] *The Undergraduate Catalogue* (North Carolina A&T State University, 1977).

[10] Alice Kidder, "Interview with Alice Kidder," interview by Tanya Mitchell, January 22, 2023.

[11] Kidder, "Interview."

[12] *The Bulletin* (North Carolina A&T State University, 1971–1972), 199–204.

[13] *The Undergraduate Catalogue* (North Carolina A&T State University, 1977), 193.

[14] *The Undergraduate Catalogue* (North Carolina A&T State University, 1977), 533.

[15] *The Undergraduate Catalogue* (North Carolina A&T State University, 1977), 424.

[16] Willie A. Deese *Personal letter of gratitude to Dr. Q*, October 2015.

[17] Deese, *Personal letter.*

[18] Deese, *Personal letter.*

[19] Deese, *Personal letter.*

[20] Deese, *Personal letter.*

[21] Deese, *Personal letter.*

[22] Deese, *Personal letter.*

[23] Deese, *Personal letter.*

[24] North Carolina Agricultural and Technical State University, "Firms Agree on Joint Effort To Assist A&T State University," NCAT Student Newspapers. 354., *The Register*, February 7, 1969.

[25] Dr. Michael Simmons, "Interview with Dr. Michael Simmons," interview by Tanya Mitchell, March 27, 2024.

[26] Gwendolyn Highsmith-Quick, "Interview with Gwendolyn Highsmith-Quick," interview by Tanya Mitchell, April 18, 2023.

[27] Highsmith-Quick, "Interview."

[28] Highsmith-Quick, "Interview."

[29] Highsmith-Quick, "Interview."

[30] Kecia Williams Smith, *Personal letter of gratitude to Dr. Q*, October 2016.

[31] North Carolina Agricultural and Technical State University, "A&T Gets Grant; Kellogg Foundation Gives $195,000," NCAT Student Newspapers. 508., *The Register*, February 22, 1974.

[32] Dr. Lewis C. Dowdy, *Annual Report of the President* (North Carolina A&T State University, 1971), 25.

[33] Kenneth Burton, *Personal letter of gratitude to Dr. Q*, October 2015.

[34] North Carolina Agricultural and Technical State University, "A&T Collects $4 Million in Grants," NCAT Student Newspapers. 442., *The Register*, August 25, 1972, 1.

[35] "A&T Collects $4 Million in Grants," NCAT Student Newspapers. 442., 1.

Chapter 14

[1] North Carolina Agricultural and Technical State University, "A&T Launches Program to Produce Black CPAs," NCAT Student Newspapers. 391., *The Register*, October 9, 1970.

[2] "A&T Launches Program to Produce Black CPAs," NCAT Student Newspapers. 391.

[3] "A&T Launches Program to Produce Black CPAs," NCAT Student Newspapers. 391.

[4] *The Bulletin* (North Carolina A&T State University, 1971–1972), 212–14.

[5] North Carolina Agricultural and Technical State University, "189 March for B.S. Degrees Sunday," NCAT Student Newspapers. 312., *The Register*, June 1, 1967.

[6] *The Bulletin* (North Carolina A&T State University, 1976).

[7] Dr. Sharon Gary Finney, *Personal letter of gratitude to Dr. Q*, October 2016.

[8] Mitchell Martin, *Personal letter of gratitude to Dr. Q*, October 2016.

[9] *The Undergraduate Catalogue* (North Carolina A&T State University, 1977), 424.

[10] *The Bulletin* (North Carolina A&T State University, 1976), 410.

[11] "About Bill Grubbs," Lambers, accessed February 22, 2023, https://www.lamberseducation.com/teachers/bill-grubbs/.

[12] Dan Moore, *Personal letter of gratitude to Dr. Q*, October 2016.

[13] Theresa A. Hammond, *A White-Collar Profession: African American Certified Public Accountants Since 1921* (The University of North Carolina Press, 2022), 148.

[14] Hammond, *A White-Collar Profession*, 148.

[15] *Bulletin of A. & T. College* (The Agricultural & Mechanical College of North Carolina, 1950–1951), 17.

[16] Gwendolyn Highsmith-Quick, "Interview with Gwendolyn Highsmith-Quick," interview by Tanya Mitchell, April 18, 2023.

[17] Highsmith-Quick, "Interview."

[18] James Clausell, *Personal letter of gratitude to Dr. Q*, October 2016.

[19] Bonnie Renee Miley-Simms, *Personal letter of gratitude to Dr. Q*, October 2016.

[20] Francine Mitchell Verdine, *Personal letter of gratitude to Dr. Q*, October 2016.

[21] Tanya Mitchell, Author Analysis of NC A&T State University Annual School Bulletins from 1890 to 1926.

[22] *The Undergraduate Catalogue* (North Carolina A&T State University, 1977), 79–81.

[23] Terry Keith, *Personal letter of gratitude to Dr. Q*, October 2016.

Chapter 15

[1] *Self-Study, Division of Business Administration* (North Carolina Agricultural and Technical State University, 1969), 15.

[2] *Self-Study* 1969, 7.

[3] *Self-Study* 1969, 15.

[4] *Self-Study* 1969, 24.

[5] *Self-Study* 1969, 15.

[6] Terry Williams, *Personal letter of gratitude to Dr. Q*, October 2016.

[7] *Undergraduate Bulletin of North Carolina Agricultural and Technical State University* (North Carolina A&T State University, 1980), 79–81.

[8] East Carolina University, "COB Timeline," accessed February 2023, https://business.ecu.edu/timeline/.

[9] "1979-1988: Steady State, and Then Some," Vanderbilt University Owen Graduate School of Management, accessed February 2023, https://business.vanderbilt.edu/news/2019/09/05/steady-state-and-then-some/.

[10] "1979-1988: Steady State, and Then Some," Vanderbilt University.

[11] "The Mission & History of Beta Gamma Sigma," Beta Gamma Sigma; The International Business Honor Society, accessed March 2023, https://www.betagammasigma.org/about/mission-history.

[12] North Carolina Agricultural and Technical State University, "Honor Chapter Begins At A&T," NCAT Student Newspapers. 859., *The Register*, May 2, 1980.

[13] Willie A. Deese College of Business and Economics, "Inaugural Inductees of A&T SoBE's Chapter of Beta Gamma Sigma," March 2025.

[14] "Bronze Key Statue," Beta Gamma Sigma; The International Business Honor Society, accessed March 2023, https://www.betagammasigma.org/collegiate-chapters/bronze-key-info.

[15] "About Beta Alpha Psi," Beta Alpha Psi, accessed March 2023, https://www.bap.org/about.

[16] Margaret Florentino, *Personal letter of gratitude to Dr. Q*, October 2016.

[17] North Carolina Agricultural and Technical State University, "Accounting Club Organized with New Functions - Goals," NCAT Student Newspapers. 397., *The Register*, November 20, 1970.

[18] Ruth Thaler-Carter, "NABA Founders Look Back, Celebrate Success, Commit to Future," *Spectrum Magazine* (Spring 2019). https://pubhtml5.com/piey/sowf/basic/.

[19] "Announcing the Induction of Members into The Accounting Hall of Fame," American Accounting Association, accessed March 2024, https://aaahq.org/Accounting-Hall-of-Fame.

[20] Sarah Branch Cooper, *Personal letter of gratitude to Dr. Q*, October 2016.

[21] Jim Schlosser, "Late A&T chancellor praised for diplomacy," *Greensboro News and Record*, December 19, 2000.

Chapter 16

[1] Joseph Boyd, "Interview with Joseph Boyd," interview by Tanya Mitchell, March 15, 2024.
[2] Dr. Mark Kiel, "Interview with Dr. Mark Kiel," interview by Tanya Mitchell, January 5, 2024.
[3] Dr. Mark Kiel, *Personal letter of gratitude to Dr. Q*, October 2016.
[4] Kiel, *Personal letter.*
[5] Kiel, *Personal letter.*
[6] Kiel, *Personal letter.*
[7] North Carolina Agricultural and Technical State University, "We Will Survive," NCAT Student Newspapers, *The Register*, October 3, 1980.
[8] North Carolina Agricultural and Technical State University, "Edward B. Fort," Aggie Hub, accessed June 2023, https://hub.ncat.edu/administration/research/about/edward-fort.php.
[9] Dr. Mark Kiel, "Accounting Accreditation Discussion," interview by Tanya Mitchell, April 23, 2022.
[10] Dr. Quiester Craig, *1985-86 Annual Report of the School of Business and Economics*, (The School of Business and Economics, North Carolina Agricultural and Technical University, 1986), 12.
[11] Dr. Michael Simmons, "Interview with Dr. Michael Simmons," interview by Tanya Mitchell, March 27, 2024.
[12] Jack Scism, "Business School Prospers but Nursing is Not Well," *Greensboro Daily News*, June 15, 1981, p. A9.
[13] Jack Scism, "Profile Priorities: Quiester Craig Has Kept His in Order," *Greensboro News & Record*, May 19, 1986.
[14] Theresa A. Hammond, *A White-Collar Profession: African American Certified Public Accountants Since 1921* (The University of North Carolina Press, 2022), 113.
[15] Christine Griffin Howard, "Interview with Christine Griffin Howard, CPA," interview by Tanya Mitchell, April 3, 2024.
[16] Howard, "Interview."

Chapter 17

[1] "About Us," American Accounting Association, 2024, https://aaahq.org/About.
[2] "Accounting Hall of Fame," American Accounting Association, 2024, https://aaahq.org/Accounting-Hall-of-Fame.
[3] "Announcing the Induction of Members into The Accounting Hall of Fame," American Accounting Association, 2025, https://aaahq.org/Accounting-Hall-of-Fame.

4 "Members," American Accounting Hall of Fame, 2024, https://aaahq.org/Accounting-Hall-of-Fame/Members.

5 Dean Quiester Craig Collection, Folder 1, University Archives and Special Collections, F.D. Bluford Library, North Carolina Agricultural and Technical State University, Greensboro, North Carolina.

6 Ned Steele, *Paying It Forward; The PhD Project: Creating Tomorrow's Leaders in Business Through Academe* (The PhD Project, 2014), 19.

7 Bernard Milano, *Personal letter of gratitude to Dr. Q*, October 2016.

8 Jerry Trapnell, "Relationship and Impressions of Dean Craig," interview by Tanya Mitchell, November 23, 2021.

9 Steele, *Paying It Forward*, 20.

10 Steele, *Paying It Forward*, 21.

11 Steele, *Paying It Forward*, 25.

12 Steele, *Paying It Forward*, 21.

13 Steele, *Paying It Forward*, 25.

14 "The American Economy in the 1990s," American History: From Revolution to Reconstruction and Beyond, University of Groningen, https://www.let.rug.nl/usa/outlines/history-2005/bridge-to-the-21st-century/the-american-economy-in-the-1990s.php.

15 University of North Texas Libraries Government Documents Department, "The Changing Demographic Profile of the United States," EveryCRSReport.com, accessed March 2024, https://www.everycrsreport.com/reports/RL32701.html.

16 Steele, *Paying It Forward*, 26.

17 Steele, *Paying It Forward*, 17–18.

18 Steele, *Paying It Forward*, 18.

19 Steele, *Paying It Forward*, 18–19.

20 Steele, *Paying It Forward*, 19–20.

21 Steele, *Paying It Forward*, 20.

22 Steele, *Paying It Forward*, 25.

23 Steele, *Paying It Forward*, 17.

24 Steele, *Paying It Forward*, 20–21.

25 Steele, *Paying It Forward*, 19–21.

26 "Melvin Stith," College of Business, Florida State University, https://business.fsu.edu/feature/melvin-stith.

27 Steele, *Paying It Forward*, 21–22.

28 Steele, *Paying It Forward*, 22–23.

29 Steele, *Paying It Forward*, 23–24.

30 Steele, *Paying It Forward*, 28.

31 Steele, *Paying It Forward*, 27–28.

32 Steele, *Paying It Forward*, 28.

[33] Steele, *Paying It Forward*, 28.
[34] Steele, *Paying It Forward*, 29.
[35] "About Us," The PhD Project, https://phdproject.org/about-us/.
[36] Steele, *Paying It Forward*, 2.
[37] Steele, *Paying It Forward*, 29.
[38] Steele, *Paying It Forward*, 29–30.
[39] Steele, *Paying It Forward*, 32–33.
[40] Steele, *Paying It Forward*, 33.
[41] Steele, *Paying It Forward*, 39–41.
[42] Steele, *Paying It Forward*, 42.
[43] Steele, *Paying It Forward*, 59.
[44] Steele, *Paying It Forward*, 60.
[45] Steele, *Paying It Forward*, 71.
[46] Steele, *Paying It Forward*, 67.
[47] Steele, *Paying It Forward*, 23.
[48] Carolyn Callahan, *Personal letter of gratitude to Dr. Q*, October 2016.

Chapter 18

[1] Beta Gamma Sigma, Note from "Dean Quiester Craig: First HBCU Representative Elected to Two-Year Term as President," 2000, BGS The International Exchange, Copyright 2000 by Beta Gamma Sigma. Reprinted with permission.
[2] Beta Gamma Sigma, "Dean Quiester Craig: First HBCU Representative Elected to Two-Year Term as President."
[3] David Hoard, "A&T Receives $250,000 from Wachovia Corporation," Press Release and Letter of Invitation, June 11, 2003.
[4] *Self-Study, Division of Business Administration* (North Carolina Agricultural and Technical State University, 1969), 38.
[5] Faye Mitchell Moore, *Personal letter of gratitude to Dr. Q*, October 2016.
[6] Jerry Trapnell, "Relationship and Impressions of Dean Craig," interview by Tanya Mitchell, November 23, 2021.
[7] Jennifer Merrit. "Big Strides at Black B-Schools." *BusinessWeek Magazine*, June 18, 2001, 36.

Chapter 19

[1] Terry Worrell Glover, *Personal letter of gratitude to Dr. Q*, October 2016.
[2] Job McCoy, *Personal letter of gratitude to Dr. Q*, October 2016.
[3] McCoy, *Personal letter*.

4 North Carolina Agricultural and Technical State University, "The 77th Annual Commencement of North Carolina Agricultural and Technical State University," *North Carolina Agricultural and Technical State University*, June 2, 1968.

5 North Carolina Agricultural and Technical State University, "The 88th Annual Commencement of North Carolina Agricultural and Technical State University," *North Carolina Agricultural and Technical State University*, May 6, 1979.

6 Tamara Harrison Long, *Personal letter of gratitude to Dr. Q*, October 2016.

7 Long, *Personal letter*.

8 North Carolina Agricultural and Technical State University, "Accounting Grads Excel," NCAT Student Newspapers. 954., *The Register*, November 9, 1982, 3.

9 Joseph Wilson, *Personal letter of gratitude to Dr. Q*, October 2016.

10 Wilson, *Personal letter*.

11 Wilson, *Personal letter*.

12 Wilson, *Personal letter*.

13 Willie A. Deese, *Personal letter of gratitude to Dr. Q*, October 2016.

14 Cain, *Personal letter*.

15 Dawn Stroud, *Personal letter of gratitude to Dr. Q*, October 2016.

16 Sylvia Andrews, *Personal letter of gratitude to Dr. Q*, October 2016.

17 Theresa Davis Lassiter, *Personal letter of gratitude to Dr. Q*, October 2016.

18 India Akins Jackson, *Personal letter of gratitude to Dr. Q*, October 2016.

19 Jackson, *Personal letter*.

20 Diane Frost Hill, *Personal letter of gratitude to Dr. Q*, October 2016.

21 Pamela McCorkle Buncum, *Personal letter of gratitude to Dr. Q*, October 2016.

22 Buncum, *Personal letter*.

23 Willie A. Deese, *Personal letter of gratitude to Dr. Q*, October 2016.

24 Deese, *Personal letter*.

25 Mitchell Martin, *Personal letter of gratitude to Dr. Q*, October 2016.

26 Martin, *Personal letter*.

27 Cheryl Duncan-Gill, *Personal letter of gratitude to Dr. Q*, October 2016.

28 Shandi Barksdale, *Personal letter of gratitude to Dr. Q*, October 2016.

29 Barksdale, *Personal letter*.

30 Dmitri Stockton, *Personal letter of gratitude to Dr. Q*, October 2016.

31 Dmitri Stockton, "Interview with Dmitri Stockton," interview by Tanya Mitchell, February 17, 2023

32 Stockton, "Interview."

33 Stockton, "Interview."

34 Stockton, *Personal letter*.

35 "College and Higher Education Pathways," Encyclopedia.com, accessed January 2023, https://www.encyclopedia.com/education/news-wires-white-papers-and-books/james-donna.

[36] Donna Scott James, *Personal letter of gratitude to Dr. Q*, October 2016.

[37] James, *Personal letter.*

[38] Donna Scott James, "Interview with Classmate Donna Scott James," interview by Tanya Mitchell, January 10, 2023.

[39] Cynthia Williams Turner, "Interview with Cynthia Williams Turner," interview by Tanya Mitchell, January 10, 2023.

[40] Lynn Perry Wooten, *Personal letter of gratitude to Dr. Q*, October 2016.

[41] "About the President," Simmons University, https://www.simmons.edu/why-simmons/university-leadership/president/about-president.

[42] Hilda Pinnix-Ragland, "Interview with Hilda Pinnix-Ragland," interview by Tanya Mitchell, March 28, 2024.

[43] Pinnix-Ragland, "Interview."

[44] Melissa M. Oliver, *Personal letter of gratitude to Dr. Q*, October 2016.

[45] Oliver, *Personal letter.*

[46] Oliver, *Personal letter.*

[47] Edwards, Tara, "Leroy Thornton Edwards Jr Inducted into the National Black College Hall of Fame in 2020," Posted June 27, 2020, by Tara Edwards, YouTube, 8:53, https://www.youtube.com/watch?v=QyCoUVaO1B8.

[48] Jerry Trapnell, "Relationship and Impressions of Dean Craig," interview by Tanya Mitchell, November 23, 2021.

[49] Trapnell, "Relationship and Impressions of Dean Craig."

[50] Trapnell, "Relationship and Impressions of Dean Craig."

Epilogue

[1] Academic Affairs, "Business & Economics Dean Beryl McEwen Named Interim Provost at N.C. A&T," North Carolina Agricultural and Technical State University, August 15, 2017, https://www.ncat.edu/news/2017/08/beryl-mcewen-interim-provost.php.

[2] Dr. Beryl McEwen, *Personal Letter of Gratitude to Dr. Q*, October 2016.

[3] Tanya Mitchell, Author Analysis of NC A&T State University Annual School Bulletins from 1890 to 1926.

[4] "2025 Best Business Schools," U.S. News, 2025, https://www.usnews.com/best-graduate-schools/top-business-schools/mba-rankings.

BIBLIOGRAPHY

The 1920s Education: Topics In The News. Progress Through Curriculum Changes. https://www.encyclopedia.com/social-sciences/culture-magazines/1920s-education-topics-news.

Academic Affairs. "Business & Economics Dean Beryl McEwen Named Interim Provost at N.C. A&T." North Carolina Agricultural and Technical State University, August 15, 2017. https://www.ncat.edu/news/2017/08/beryl-mcewen-interim-provost.php.

Alabama Tribune. "Morehouse 5 to Play S.C. State," December 9, 1955.

Alexander, Robert J. "Negro Business in Atlanta." *Southern Economic Journal* 17, no. 4 (1951): 451–64.

American Accounting Association. "About Us." 2024. https://aaahq.org/About.

American Accounting Association. "Accounting Hall of Fame." 2024. https://aaahq.org/Accounting-Hall-of-Fame.

American Accounting Association. "Announcing the Induction of Members into The Accounting Hall of Fame." Accessed March 2024. https://aaahq.org/Accounting-Hall-of-Fame.

American Accounting Hall of Fame. "Members." 2024. https://aaahq.org/Accounting-Hall-of-Fame/Members.

American Accounting Association. "William Louis Campfield." Accessed June 2014. https://aaahq.org/Accounting-Hall-of-Fame/Members/2019/William-Louis-Campfield.

The American Economy in the 1990s. American History: From Revolution to Reconstruction and Beyond, University of Groningen, https://www.let.rug.nl/usa/outlines/history-2005/bridge-to-the-21st-century/the-american-economy-in-the-1990s.php.

Andrews, Sylvia. *Personal letter of gratitude to Dr. Q.* October 2016.

Association for the Study of African American Life and History. "Editor's: Former Students." *Negro History Bulletin* 26, no. 7 (1963).

The Atlanta Journal. "Morehouse, Fisk Tangle Tonight." January 4, 1957, 15.

Atlanta University. *The Atlanta University Bulletin* (The Catalogue) 3, no. 102 (1957–1958).

Barksdale, Shandi. *Personal letter of gratitude to Dr. Q.* October 2016.

Barr-Pulliam, Dereck. "An Assessment of Dr. William L. Campfield's Contributions to Diversifying Accounting Education and Practice." (February 24, 2012). https://papers.ssrn.com/sol3/papers.cfm?abstract_id=1908752.

Beta Alpha Psi. "About Beta Alpha Psi." Accessed March 2023. https://www.bap.org/about.

Beta Gamma Sigma. "Bronze Key Statue." Beta Gamma Sigma; The International Business Honor Society, accessed March 2023. https://www.betagammasigma.org/collegiate-chapters/bronze-key-info.

Beta Gamma Sigma. "The Mission & History of Beta Gamma Sigma." Beta Gamma Sigma; The International Business Honor Society, accessed March 2023. https://www.betagammasigma.org/about/mission-history.

Bishop, David W. "The Consent Decree Between the University of North Carolina System and the U.S. Department of Education, 1981-1982." *Journal of Negro Education* 52, no. 3 (1983): 350–61.

Boyd, Joseph. "Interview with Joseph Boyd." Interview by Tanya Mitchell, March 15, 2024.

Buncum, Pamela McCorkle. *Personal letter of gratitude to Dr. Q.* October 2016.

Burton, Kenneth. *Personal letter of gratitude to Dr. Q*. October 2015.

"Business Administration Largest Dept. At Lincoln U." *Jet Magazine*, December 24, 1970.

"Business Depart. Offers New Majors." *The Lincoln Clarion*, January 16, 1960.

BvB. "Davis v. Prince Edward County." Accessed April 2025. https://brown65.the74million.org/davisvprince.

Cain, Angela. *Personal letter of gratitude to Dr. Q*. October 2016.

Callahan, Carolyn. *Personal letter of gratitude to Dr. Q*. October 2016.

Capparell, Stephanie. "How Pepsi Opened Door to Diversity." *Wall Street Journal*, January 9, 2007. https://www.wsj.com/articles/SB116831396726171042.

The Carolina Times

Carson, Clayborne. "Martin Luther King Jr.: The Morehouse Years." *The Journal of Blacks in Higher Education*, no. 15 (1977): 121–125.

Changemakers. "Ruth Coles Harris." Accessed February 2024. https://edu.lva.virginia.gov/changemakers/items/show/170.

Chapel, Cynthia J. "Shifting history, shifting mission, shifting identity: The search for survival at Lincoln University (Jefferson City, Missouri) 1866-1997." PhD diss Oklahoma State University, 1997.

City of Atlanta, GA. "Graves Hall." Accessed June 26, 2025. https://www.atlantaga.gov/government/departments/city-planning/historic-preservation/property-district-information/graves-hall.

Clark Atlanta University. "The First Phylon Institute and Twenty-Fifth Atlanta University Conference." *Phylon* 2, no. 3 (3rd Qtr., 1941): 275–88.

Clausell, James. *Personal letter of gratitude to Dr. Q*. October 2016.

Colston, Freddie C. *Dr. Benjamin E. Mays Speaks: Representative Speeches of a Great American Orator* (University Press of America, Inc., 2002).

The Consortium. "History: Changing the face of American business since 1966." The Consortium. https://cgsm.org/about-us/history/.

Cooper, Sarah Branch. *Personal letter of gratitude to Dr. Q.* October 2016.

Craig, Dr. Quiester. *1985-86 Annual Report of the School of Business and Economics.* The School of Business and Economics. North Carolina Agricultural and Technical University, 1986.

Cucchiara, Maia. "New Goals, Familiar Challenges?: A Brief History of University-Run Schools." *Perspectives on Urban Education* 7, no. 1 (Summer 2010): 96–108. https://eric.ed.gov/?id=EJ894472.

Davis, Leroy. "John Hope at Brown University: The Black Man Who Refused to Pass for White." *Journal of Blacks in Higher Education*, (1998–1999): 121–26.

Davis, Theresa Lassiter. *Personal letter of gratitude to Dr. Q.* October 2016.

Deese, Willie. *Personal letter of gratitude to Dr. Q.* October 2015.

Dowdy, Jr., Harry Kendall. *Crimson Waterfall.* Dog Ear Publishing, 2016.

Dowdy, Dr. Lewis C. *An Epoch of Excellence 1964-1979: The Chancellor's Report, N.C. A&T State University.* North Carolina Agricultural & Technical State University, 1979.

Dowdy, Dr. Lewis C. *Annual Report of the President.* North Carolina A&T State University, 1971.

Dowdy, Dr. Lewis C. *New Opportunities for Service.* North Carolina A&T State University, 1973.

Du Bois, W.E.B. "The Cultural Missions of Atlanta University." *Phylon* (1940-1956) 3, No. 2 (2nd Qtr., 1942): 105–115.

Duncan-Gill, Cheryl. *Personal letter of gratitude to Dr. Q.* October 2016.

East Carolina University. "COB Timeline." Accessed February 2023. https://business.ecu.edu/timeline/.

"Economic Department Offers Corporation Course." *The Lincoln Clarion.* January 8, 1965, 1.

Edwards, James D. "Public Accounting in the United States, 1896–1913." *Accounting Review,* April 1955: 240–51.

Edwards, Tara. "Leroy Thornton Edwards Jr Inducted into the National Black College Hall of Fame in 2020." Posted June 27, 2020, by Tara Edwards. YouTube, 8:53., https://www.youtube.com/watch?v=QyCoUVaO1B8.

Erickson, Paul, Neal Gray, Bill Wesley, Elizabeth Dunagan. "Why Parents Choose Laboratory Schools for their Children." *NALS Journal* 2, no. 2 (2012): 1–8.

Fields, Kimberly. "Aggies Celebrate Dean Craig's Legacy." *The A&T Register*. April 24, 2013. https://ncatregister.com/3213/uncategorized/aggies-celebrate-dean-craigs-legacy/.

Finney, Dr. Sharon Gary. *Personal letter of gratitude to Dr. Q.* October 2016.

Flesher, Dale L., and Helen G. Gabre. "NABA: Forty Years of Growth." *Journal of Accountancy*, December 1, 2009. https://www.journalofaccountancy.com/issues/2009/dec/20092033.html.

Florentino, Margaret. *Personal letter of gratitude to Dr. Q.* October 2016.

Ford Foundation. "The Ford Foundation Annual Report 1965." 1965.

Fund for Advancement of Education, *They Went to College Early* (April 1957).

Gamble, J.R. "Iconic North Carolina A&T Aggies Coach Cal Irvin Passes Away." *The Shadow League*, November 26, 2017. https://theshadowleague.com/iconic-north-carolina-a-t-coach-cal-irvin-passes-away/.

Glover, Terry Worrell. *Personal letter of gratitude to Dr. Q.* October 2016.

Hammond, Theresa A. *A White-Collar Profession: African American Certified Public Accountants Since 1921.* The University of North Carolina Press, 2022.

Harlem World. "Harlem's Ron Brown and Sylvia Fitt The New Pepsi Cola 1950." May 3, 2015.

Haskins & Sells. "Haskins & Sells, certified public accountants, A History of the origin and growth of the firm, 1895-1935." Haskins and Sells Publications Deloitte Collection. January 1, 1935.

Heise, Kenan. "Albert Smart, Author, NIU Business Prof." *Chicago Tribune*, December 16, 1989. https://www.chicagotribune.com/news/ct-xpm-1989-12-16-8903180557-story.html.

Henderson, Alex Benson. "Heman E. Perry and Black Enterprise in Atlanta, 1908–1925." *President and Fellows of Harvard College* 61, no. 2 (summer, 1987): 216–42.

Highsmith-Quick, Gwendolyn. "Interview with Gwendolyn Highsmith-Quick." Interview by Tanya Mitchell, April 18, 2023.

Hill, Diane Frost. *Personal letter of gratitude to Dr. Q.* October 2016.

Hill, Susan T. "The Traditionally Black Institutions of Higher Education 1860 to 1982." National Center for Education Statistics, 1982.

Hine, William C. "South Carolina State College: A Legacy of Education and Public Service." *1890 Land-Grant Colleges: A Centennial View* 65, no. 2 (Spring 1991): 149–67.

The HistoryMakers. Dr. Alvin Blount, Jr., Interview. May 5, 2013. https://www.thehistorymakers.org/biography/dr-alvin-blount-jr.

Hoard, David. "A&T Receives $250,000 from Wachovia Corporation." Press Release and Letter of Invitation, June 11, 2003.

Howard, Christine Griffin. "Interview with Christine Griffin Howard, CPA." Interview by Tanya Mitchell, April 3, 2024.

Hutchins, Dawn Byron. "Laboring in the Shade." *Connecticut Explored.* February 9, 2021. https://connecticuthistory.org/laboring-in-the-shade/.

"In Memory of Dr. Milton Wilson." Government Congressional Record Online. 2003. H9190–H9191, https://www.congress.gov/crec/2003/10/02/CREC-2003-10-02-pt1-PgH9190-4.pdf

Jackson, Annette Singleton, and Leedell W. Neyland, *The Florida A&M University School of Business and Industry, SBI: The Sybil Collins Mobley Years, A Historical Perspective.* The Florida A&M University Foundation, 2013.

Jackson, India Akins. *Personal letter of gratitude to Dr. Q.* October 2016.

James, Donna A. "College and Higher Education Pathways." Encyclopedia.com, accessed January 2023. https://www.encyclopedia.com/education/news-wires-white-papers-and-books/james-donna.

James, Donna Scott. "Interview with Classmate Donna Scott James." Interviewed by Tanya Mitchell, January 10, 2023.

James, Donna Scott. *Personal letter of gratitude to Dr. Q.* October 2016.

Jesse H. Jones School of Business. "Texas Southern University." Accessed April 2021. https://digitalscholarship.tsu.edu/jhjco/.

Jones, Edward. "Morehouse College in Business Ninety Years—Building Men." *Phylon Quarterly* 18, no. 3 (3rd Qtr., 1957): 231–45.

Keith, Terry. *Personal letter of gratitude to Dr. Q.* October 2016.

Kelley School. "Creating a legacy with The Consortium for Graduate Study in Management." Indiana University Kelley School of Business. Accessed February 28, 2020. https://blog.kelley.iu.edu/2020/02/28/creating-a-legacy-with-the-consortium-for-graduate-study-in-management/.

"Kenneth Wilbur Perry Obituary." *Anderson News*, September 12, 2012. https://www.news-gazette.com/obituaries/kenneth-perry/article_88c9680a-3a58-54b9-b452-fbe82bf009d0.html.

Khurana, Rakesh. *From Higher Aims to Hired Hands: The Social Transformation of American Business Schools and the Unfilled Promise of Management as a Profession.* Princeton University Press, 2007.

Kidder, Alice. "Interview with Alice Kidder." Interview by Tanya Mitchell, January 22, 2023.

Kiel, Dr. Mark. "Accounting Accreditation Discussion." Interview by Tanya Mitchell, April 23, 2022.

Kiel, Dr. Mark. "Interview with Dr. Mark Kiel." Interview by Tanya Mitchell, January 5, 2024.

Kiel, Dr. Mark. *Personal letter of gratitude to Dr. Q.* October 2016.

Knight, Charlie. "Harvey R. Alexander, Tuskegee Airman." North Carolina Museum of History. Accessed February 2022. https://www.ncmuseumofhistory.org/blog/tuskegee-airman-harvey-alexander.

Knowledge at Wharton Staff. "How Corporate America Came to Recognize Diversity, One Pepsi at a Time." Knowledge at Wharton. February 28, 2007. https://knowledge.wharton.upenn.edu/article/how-corporate-america-came-to-recognize-diversity-one-pepsi-at-a-time/.

Lambers. "About Bill Grubbs." Accessed February 22, 2023. https://www.lamberseducation.com/teachers/bill-grubbs/.

Lash, John S., Hortense W. Dixon, and Thomas F. Freeman. *Texas Southern University: From Separation to Special Designation.* John Hay Whitney Foundation, 1975.

Levinson, Arlene. "Historically Black, Now Mostly White At Lincoln University, Social Life Is Segregated Even If Classes Are Not." *Associated Press,* December 16, 1999. https://www.washingtonpost.com/wp-srv/WPcap/1999-12/16/002r-121699-idx.html.

Library of Congress. "The Civil Rights Act of 1964: A Long Struggle for Freedom." Accessed September 2020. https://www.loc.gov/exhibits/civil-rights-act/civil-rights-act-of-1964.html.

Lincoln University. "Department of Economics and Business." *Lincoln University Bulletin 1967-1968*, Fall 1967.

Long, Tamara Harrison. *Personal letter of gratitude to Dr. Q.* October 2016.

Marcus, Laurence. "The Adams Case: A Hollow Victory?" *Peabody Journal of Education* 59, no. 1 (1981): 37–42.

Marshall, Albert P. *Soldiers' dream a centennial history of Lincoln University of Missouri* (Lincoln University, 1966). https://bluetigercommons.lincolnu.edu/lu_history_book/2/.

Martin, Dr. Harold. *Personal letter of gratitude to Dr. Q.* October 2016.

Martin, Mitchell. *Personal letter of gratitude to Dr. Q*, October 2016.

McCoy, Job. *Personal letter of gratitude to Dr. Q*. October 2016.

McEwen, Dr. Beryl. *Personal Letter of Gratitude to Dr. Q*. October 2016.

Milano, Bernard. *Personal letter of gratitude to Dr. Q*. October 2016.

Miley-Simms, Bonnie Renee. *Personal letter of gratitude to Dr. Q*. October 2016.

Missouri Digital Heritage. "Missouri State Archives: Timeline of Missouri's African American History." Accessed January 2024. https://www.sos.mo.gov/mdh/curriculum/africanamerican/timeline/timeline6#:~:text=MISSOURI%20STATE%20ARCHIVES,of%20Missouri%27s%20African%20American%20History&text=Judge%20Sam%20Blair%20of%20the,students%20on%20June%2027%2C%201950.

Mitchell, Tanya. Author Analysis of NC A&T State University Annual School Bulletins from 1890 to 1926.

Moore, Dan. *Personal letter of gratitude to Dr. Q*. October 2016.

Moore, Faye Mitchell. *Personal letter of gratitude to Dr. Q*. October 2016.

Morehouse School of Religion. "A History of Morehouse School of Religion." Accessed June 26, 2025. https://www.themorehouseschoolofreligion.org/history/.

"New Accounting Course." *The Lincoln Clarion*, January 11, 1963.

Newsome, John. "The Business School Is Dean Craig." *Greensboro News & Record*, June 23, 2013. https://greensboro.com/news/local/the-business-school-is-dean-craig/article_8dbbd0de-dacf-11e2-9136-0019bb30f31a.html.

North Carolina Agricultural and Technical State University. The 55th Annual Commencement of the Agricultural and Technical College (North Carolina Agricultural and Technical College, 1953). https://digital.library.ncat.edu/atcommencement/1

North Carolina Agricultural and Technical State University. NCAT Student Newspaper. 132. *The Register*, April 1954.

North Carolina Agricultural and Technical State University. NCAT Student Newspapers. 369. *The Register*, October 3, 1969.

North Carolina Agricultural and Technical State University. "189 March for B.S. Degrees Sunday." NCAT Student Newspapers. 312. *The Register*, June 1, 1967.

North Carolina Agricultural and Technical State University. "The 77th annual Commencement of North Carolina Agricultural and Technical State University." *North Carolina Agricultural and Technical State University*, June 2, 1968.

North Carolina Agricultural and Technical State University. "The 88th annual Commencement of North Carolina Agricultural and Technical State University." *North Carolina Agricultural and Technical State University*, May 6, 1979.

North Carolina Agricultural and Technical State University. "A&T Collects $4 Million in Grants." NCAT Student Newspapers. 442. *The Register*, August 25, 1972.

North Carolina Agricultural and Technical State University. "A&T Gets Grant; Kellogg Foundation Gives $195,000." NCAT Student Newspapers. 508. *The Register*, February 22, 1974.

North Carolina Agricultural and Technical State University. "A&T Launches Program to Produce Black CPAs." NCAT Student Newspapers. 391. *The Register*, October 9, 1970.

North Carolina Agricultural and Technical State University. "Accounting Club Organized with New Functions – Goals." NCAT Student Newspapers. 397. *The Register*, November 20, 1970.

North Carolina Agricultural and Technical State University. "Accounting Grads Excel." NCAT Student Newspapers. 954. *The Register*, November 9, 1982, 3.

North Carolina Agricultural and Technical State University. "Alexander, Gray Named To Top Post By Board." NCAT Student Newspapers. 175. *The Register*, February 10, 1961.

North Carolina Agricultural and Technical State University. *Bulletin of A. & T. College* (The Agricultural & Mechanical College of North Carolina, 1950–1951).

North Carolina Agricultural and Technical State University. *The Bulletin* (North Carolina A&T State University, 1971–1972).

North Carolina Agricultural and Technical State University. *The Bulletin* (North Carolina A&T State University, 1976).

North Carolina Agricultural and Technical State University. "Business School Shows Gains." NCAT Student Newspapers. 97. *The Register*, August 4, 1945.

North Carolina Agricultural and Technical State University. "Business Society Instituted on Campus." NCAT Student Newspapers. 238. *The Register*, September 25, 1964.

North Carolina Agricultural and Technical State University. "Business Students Make Corp. Management Div." NCAT Student Newspapers. 381. *The Register*, March 6, 1970.

North Carolina Agricultural and Technical State University. "College Business Club Visits Atlanta's Negro Business Enterprises." NCAT Student Newspapers. 98. *The Register*, May 1947.

North Carolina Agricultural and Technical State University. "Edward B. Fort." Aggie Hub, accessed June 2023. https://hub.ncat.edu/administration/research/about/edward-fort.php.

North Carolina Agricultural and Technical State University. "Firms Agree on Joint Effort To Assist A&T State University." NCAT Student Newspapers. 354. *The Register*, February 7, 1969.

North Carolina Agricultural and Technical State University. "Honor Chapter Begins At A&T." NCAT Student Newspapers. 859. *The Register*, May 2, 1980.

North Carolina Agricultural & Technical State University. "The House That Dean Craig Built." *The Alumni Times*, April 2023. https://relations.ncat.edu/pubs/alumnitimes/2013/mar14/dean-craig.html.

North Carolina Agricultural and Technical State University. "Kennedy Speaks At Vocational Opportunity Week." NCAT Student Newspapers. 126. *The Register*, April 1953, 3.

North Carolina Agricultural & Technical University. "Lewis C. Dowdy." Accessed June 2021. https://www.ncat.edu/academics/honors/dowdy-scholars-program/dowdy-bio.php.

North Carolina Agricultural & Technical University. *Self-Study, Division of Business Administration* (North Carolina Agricultural and Technical State University, 1969).

North Carolina Agricultural and Technical State University. "Thirteen Business Majors Begin Local Internships." NCAT Student Newspapers. 184. *The Register*, November 17, 1961.

North Carolina Agricultural and Technical State University. *Undergraduate Bulletin of North Carolina Agricultural and Technical State University* (North Carolina A&T State University, 1980).

North Carolina Agricultural and Technical State University. *The Undergraduate Catalogue* (North Carolina A&T State University, 1977).

North Carolina Board of Higher Education. *Statistical Abstract of Higher Education in North Carolina, 1968-69*, (North Carolina Board of Higher Education, Raleigh, 1968).

Oak, V.V. "Our Aimless Business Education," *The Crisis* 44 (September 1937): 264.

Oliver, Melissa M. *Personal letter of gratitude to Dr. Q*. October 2016.

The PhD Project. "About Us." https://phdproject.org/about-us/.

Pierce, Joseph A. *Negro Business and Business Education: Their Present and Prospective Development.* HarperCollins Publishers, 1947.

Pierson, Sharon Gay. *Laboratory of Learning: HBCU Laboratory Schools and Alabama State College Lab High in the Era of Jim Crow.* Peter Lang Publishing, Inc., 2014.

Pinnix-Ragland, Hilda. "Interview with Hilda Pinnix-Ragland." Interview by Tanya Mitchell, March 28, 2024.

Pro Football Hall of Fame. "David (Deacon) Jones." Accessed July 2023. https://www.profootballhof.com/players/david-deacon-jones/.

Rankin, Pettus."School to End Session Friday." Personal scrapbook newspaper clipping. June 1948.

"Recruiter Schedule." *The Lincoln Clarion*. November 10, 1967.

Rhinehart, Charlene. "Meet 'General Lucas': The First Black Person to Become a Certified Public Accountant in New York." *Black Enterprise*, February 21, 2021. https://www.blackenterprise.com/meet-general-lucas-the-first-black-person-to-become-a-certified-public-accountant-in-new-york/.

Robert Russa Moton Museum. "Biography: Barbara Rose Johns Powell, 1935–1991." Accessed April , 2025. https://motonmuseum.org/learn/biography-barbara-rose-johns-powell/.

Sass, Steven A. "Getting Down to Business: The Development of the Commercial Curriculum at the Wharton School in 1910." *Business and Economic History* 10, Papers presented at the twenty-seventh annual meeting of the Business History Conference (1981).

Schlosser, Jim. "Late A&T chancellor praised for diplomacy." *Greensboro News and Record,* December 19, 2000.

Segall, Linda. "Larzette Hale, CPA." *Journal of Accountancy*, (August 1, 2009). https://www.journalofaccountancy.com/issues/2009/aug/20091763.html.

Simmons, Dr. Michael. "Interview with Dr. Michael Simmons." Interview by Tanya Mitchell, March 27, 2024.

Simmons University. "About the President." https://www.simmons.edu/why-simmons/university-leadership/president/about-president.

Smith, David B. "Forgotten Heroes: Remembering Dr. Alvin Blount, Who Helped Integrate America's Hospitals." *Health Affairs Forefront*, September 1, 2017. https://www.healthaffairs.org/content/forefront/forgotten-heroes-remembering-dr-alvin-blount-helped-integrate-america-s-hospitals.

Smith, Kecia Williams. *Personal letter of gratitude to Dr. Q*. October 2016.

Smith, Robert F. "Celebrating the 100th Anniversary of the First African American CPA: John W. Cromwell Jr." Personal Blog. January 20, 2021. Accessed March 2021. https://robertsmith.com/blog/celebrating-the-100th-anniversary-of-the-first-african-american-cpa-john-w-cromwell-jr/.

Smithsonian Museum of American History Behring Center. "Five Communities Change a Nation." Separate Is Not Equal: Brown v. Board of Education. Accessed January 2024. https://americanhistory.si.edu/brown/history/4-five/five-communities.html.

Solow, Barbara. *Reorganizing Higher Education in North Carolina: What History Tells Us About Our Future.* The North Carolina Center for Public Policy Research, 1999.

Spelman College. "Our Stories: Sophia B. Packard and Harriet E. Giles, Founders." Accessed April 2020. https://www.spelman.edu/about-us/news-and-events/our-stories/stories/2020/04/11/sophia-packard-and-harriet-giles.

Staff writers. "Bus. School Established." *The Hilltop*. October 2, 1970.

State University System of Florida. "Statistics of land-grant colleges and universities 1958/1959." HathiTrust, accessed August 2024. https://babel.hathitrust.org/cgi/pt?id=ufl.31262088525224&seq=57&q1=%22South+Carolina+State+College%22.

Steele, Ned. *Paying It Forward; The PhD Project: Creating Tomorrow's Leaders in Business Through Academe.* The PhD Project, 2014.

Stith, Dr. Melvin. College of Business, Florida State University. https://business.fsu.edu/feature/melvin-stith.

Dmitri Stockton. "Interview with Dmitri Stockton." Interview by Tanya Mitchell, February 17, 2023

Stockton, Dmitri. *Personal letter of gratitude to Dr. Q.* October 2016.

Stroud, Dawn. *Personal letter of gratitude to Dr. Q.* October 2016.

Suggs, Jannette. "Interview with Jannette Suggs." Interview by Tanya Mitchell September 9, 2022.

Teel, Leonard Ray. "Benjamin Mays: Teaching by Example, Leading through Will." *Change* 14, no. 7 (1982): 14–22.

Thaler-Carter, Ruth T. "NABA Founders Look Back, Celebrate Success, Commit to Future." *Spectrum Magazine* (Spring 2019). https://pubhtml5.com/piey/sowf/basic/.

Thirteen PBS. "Acts against the education of slaves South Carolina, 1740 and Virginia, 1819." Accessed May 2024. https://www.thirteen.org/wnet/slavery/experience/education/docs1.html.

Thompson, Akilah. *Personal letter of gratitude to Dr. Q.* October 2015.

Trapnell, Jerry. "Relationship and Impressions of Dean Craig." Interview by Tanya Mitchell, November 23, 2021.

Turner, Cynthia Williams. "Interview with Cynthia Williams Turner." Interview by Tanya Mitchell, January 10, 2023.

U.S. News. "2025 Best Business Schools." U.S. News, 2025. https://www.usnews.com/best-graduate-schools/top-business-schools/mba-rankings.

United States Commission on Civil Rights. "Equal Protection of the Laws in Public Higher Education." 1960.

University Archives. University of Missouri. December 2014. https://muarchives.missouri.edu/c-rg8-s8.html.

University of North Texas Libraries Government Documents Department. "The Changing Demographic Profile of the United States." EveryCRSReport, accessed March 2024. https://www.everycrsreport.com/reports/RL32701.html.

Vanderbilt University. "1979-1988: Steady State, and Then Some." Vanderbilt University Owen Graduate School of Management. Accessed February 2023. https://business.vanderbilt.edu/news/2019/09/05/steady-state-and-then-some/.

Verdine, Francine Mitchell. *Personal letter of gratitude to Dr. Q.* October 2016.

Walker, Juliet E. K. "Racism, Slavery, and Free Enterprise: Black Entrepreneurship in the United States before the Civil War." *The Business History Review* 60, no. 3 (1986): 343–82.

Washington, Cynthia McMurray. *Personal letter of gratitude to Dr. Q.* October 2016.

Weissman, Sara. "An HBCU in Predominantly White Surroundings." *Muddy River News.* June 17, 2022. https://muddyrivernews.com/politics/an-hbcu-in-predominantly-white-surroundings/20220617091838/.

Wendling, Lauren A. "Higher Education as a Means of Communal Uplift: The Educational Philosophy of W.E.B. Du Bois." *Journal of Negro Education* 87, no. 3 (2018): 285–93.

Williams, Carole A. *The Black/White Colleges: Dismantling the Dual System of Higher Education.* U.S. Commission On Civil Rights, 1988.

Williams, Terry. *Personal letter of gratitude to Dr. Q.* October 2016.

Wilie A. Deese College of Business and Economics. "Inaugural Inductees of A&T SoBE's Chapter of Beta Gamma Sigma." March 2025.

Wilson, Joseph. *Personal letter of gratitude to Dr. Q.* October 2016.

Wimpee, Rachel. "The Birth of the Modern MBA." *Rockefeller Archive Center.* November 1, 2019. https://resource.rockarch.org/story/the-birth-of-the-modern-mba/.

Wootton, Charles W., and Carel M. Wolk. "Development of the big eight accounting firms in the United States, 1900-1990." *Accounting Historians Journal* 19, no. 1 (1992). https://egrove.olemiss.edu/aah_journal/vol19/iss1/1.

Wooten, Lynn Perry. *Personal letter of gratitude to Dr. Q.* October 2016.

Zeff, Stephen A. "How the U.S. Accounting Profession Got Where It Is Today: Part I." *Accounting Horizons* 17, no. 3 (2003): 198–205.

INDEX

O

U

Y

Z

PHOTO CREDITS

PHOTO INSERT 1
Courtesy of the Author.

PHOTO INSERT 2
Page 1: Courtesy of the Willie A. Deese School of Business and Economics at North Carolina Agricultural and Technical State University.

PHOTO INSERT 3
Page 9: Drawing provided by MINOAFB & Associates, LLC. Produced from an image of the second-grade class picture provided courtesy of Quiester's Lab High classmate, Jessica Pettus Rankin.

PHOTO INSERT 4
Page 65: Courtesy of SC State Historical Collection & Archives, Miller F. Whittaker Library, South Carolina State University.

PHOTO INSERT 5
Page 66: Courtesy of the Archives, Lincoln University, Missouri, Inman E. Page Library.

PHOTO INSERT 6
Page 125: Courtesy of the University Archives and Special Collections at Bluford Library, North Carolina Agricultural and Technical State University.

PHOTO INSERT 7

Page 126: Courtesy of the University Archives and Special Collections at Bluford Library, North Carolina Agricultural and Technical State University.

PHOTO INSERT 8

Page 191, Courtesy of the University Archives and Special Collections at Bluford Library, North Carolina Agricultural and Technical State University.

PHOTO INSERT 9

Page 192: top: Courtesy of the University Archives and Special Collections at Bluford Library, North Carolina Agricultural and Technical State University.

PHOTO INSERT 10

Page 192, bottom: Courtesy of the University Archives and Special Collections at Bluford Library, North Carolina Agricultural and Technical State University.

Thank you for reading *More Than a Dean.*

If you enjoyed this book, please help to spread the word by leaving an online review.

KEEP IN TOUCH WITH TANYA Y. MITCHELL

Website: www.morethanadean.com
Speaking Engagements: info@morethanadean.com

www.ingramcontent.com/pod-product-compliance
Ingram Content Group UK Ltd.
Pitfield, Milton Keynes, MK11 3LW, UK
UKHW022028190726
13853UKWH00005B/2167